P9-DGN-859

think

think

Straight Talk for Women to Stay Smart in a Dumbed-Down World

LISA BLOOM

Published by Vanguard Press,
A Member of the Perseus Books Group

Books published by Vanguard Press are available at special discounts for bulk purchases in the United States by corporations, institutions, and other organizations. For more information, please contact the Special Markets Department at the Perseus Books Group, 2300 Chestnut Street, Suite 200, Philadelphia, PA 19103, or call (800) 810-4145, extension 5000, or e-mail special.markets@perseusbooks.com.

Editorial production by the Book Factory.
Design by Jane Raese
Text set in 11.5-point Electra

Cataloging-in-Publication Data is available from the Library of Congress.
ISBN 978-1-59315-659-6

10 9 8 7 6 5 4 3 2 1

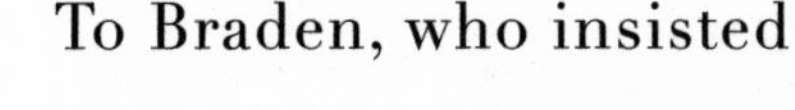

To Braden, who insisted

contents

introduction

TWENTY-FIVE PERCENT of young American women would rather win *America's Next Top Model* than the Nobel Peace Prize.

Twenty-three percent would rather lose their ability to read than their figures.

Argh!

When I read that Oxygen Media survey—that a quarter of us would rather win a contest for looking bootylicious in a thong than for, say, ending genocide—I *tried* to go to my happy place. But I couldn't get there. Because I know we have a problem, one that I don't hear anyone else talking about. The problem is not just about that 25 percent of young women who would rather be hot than smart; rather, it's about a culture that actually makes that a rational choice: rewarding girls for looks over brains. And it's about *all* of us, intelligent American females, ranging from girlhood to old age, who are dazzlingly ignorant about some critically important things.

An aggravating thing happened in the last generation. As girls started seriously kicking ass at every level of education (girls now outperform boys in elementary, middle, and high schools; we graduate from college, professional, and graduate schools in greater numbers than males—go team!), our brains became devalued.

This is part of what I call the Dumb American Syndrome. The majority of American men *and* women can't name a single branch of government, for crying out loud. Europeans and Asians consistently slaughter our high school boys *and* girls in academic competitions. But this book is about some of the fluffy-headed turns our American females in particular have made and how we can find our way again, because girls and women are *my people*. I was born a baby feminist and I've been a women's rights advocate, lawyer, and rabble-rouser for twenty-five years. Sure, it's a shame when men lose their way, too, and someone ought to write a book getting *them* back on course. But *this* book is a manifesto for my team about how we've lost our female minds on matters as big as neglecting our brutally oppressed third world sisters and as small as the fact that we still do *way* too much housework.

All of these symptoms are related. I'll explain.

Our blind spots are galling because damn, we have come so far in just my lifetime. Until the 1963 Equal Pay Act, it was perfectly legal, and common, for employers to pay women less than men for doing the same job. Now young, urban, childless women out-earn their male counterparts, mainly because they're better educated. Until the 1980 enforcement of Title IX began, schools could and did underfund girls' sports. Today no one thinks all the money should go to the boys' teams, and you'd be shamed out of the PTA for trying to keep your daughter away from soccer, which at the high school level is now 47 percent female. The U.S. Supreme Court did not recognize sexual harassment in the workplace as actionable until 1986. Virtually all employers now have written policies, trainings, and investigations to deter and monitor fair treatment of female workers.

We've achieved this historic sea change in laws and values, where nondiscrimination is now the expectation. Wonderful. Long overdue. Thanks Mom and your generation of fearless fighters for devoting your lives to bringing the norm of equality to us. So what exactly are we doing with it? I can remember when people levied serious opposition to Sandra Day O'Connor's 1981 Supreme Court nomination on the grounds that there was no ladies' room on the floor of the justices' chambers. But three more female Supreme Court justices and hundreds of thousands more women lawyers and judges later, more than two-thirds of us don't know what *Roe v. Wade* is.

The situation gets worse. Grown-up women giggle into TV cameras that they don't know how many sides a triangle has, nor can they venture a guess as to what country Mexico City might be in. I don't know which is worse: that we are *playing* dumb or that we *really are* that clueless.

Girls and young women earnestly analyze whether Angelina Jolie has another baby bump but know nothing about her life's work: bringing aid to millions of innocent refugees, people for whom our attention means the difference between life and death, hope or despair. Many of us spend more time looking in the mirror than looking out at our planet, and the thing is that doing so is *rational* because there can be a bigger payoff for being sexy than brainy. Young women have little motivation to think because the rewards for being hot are so powerful. Then, in our middle years a new wave of nonthinking sets in. Married women and working moms spin ourselves ragged in the work-kids-housework-repeat-repeat-repeat cycle. At this stage, who has *time* to think? And after age fifty-five we just want to rest, so we zone out in front of the TV significantly more than any other age group, relinquishing a full 25 percent of our golden years to Cialis ads and *Cougar Town*; as a result, seniors are the most overweight and obese age group.

Excuses, excuses. This has got to stop.

At all ages, we've become seduced by our shallow, self-absorbed celebutainment culture. You know: the one that breaks into regular network programming with Tiger Woods's apology for extramarital schtupping. The one that treats Anna Nicole Smith's or Michael Jackson's prescription drug OD with the kind of breathless coverage once reserved for the assassinations of heads of state. We watch, dazzled and dazed by the shiny, shocking stories, while a little voice stirring within us peeps that somewhere, somehow, there must be more important issues. But who can remember what they are? Who can find substance when we are fed an increasingly bloated, empty diet of reality shows, "news" segments on wrinkle fillers, and updates on drunken starlets? Network execs tell me they have to run these segments, as it's the only way to capture the female audience.

Dear Lord. Let's turn that ship around.

In our personal lives, our mental flaccidity means we outsource most of what our mothers and grandmothers did themselves. They relied upon their wits to pull themselves up out of life's challenges. We, however, have lost confidence in our ability to think for ourselves, so we give our lives over to "experts": therapists, life coaches, self-help gurus, talk radio blowhards. *Whatever. Jersey Shore is on!*

I want to jolt you into reclaiming your brain. You can still watch *Real Housewives* and read an issue of *Us Weekly* every once in a while, but not every day—because I have bigger plans for you.

We've got to use our brains for more than filler in the space beneath our smooth, Botoxed foreheads. The generation before us fought like hell and won for us equality in education and employment. Let's use that for a higher purpose than sending pictures of kittens on Facebook.

Warning: If you're easily upset, this is not the book for you. These issues are urgent and important and I don't sugarcoat the facts about how self-absorbed we've become or the costs of our distraction, like women who have actually died from plastic surgery or the millions of girls enslaved in the worldwide sex trade while we go shoe shopping. I don't like it when people beat around the bush when they have something to say, so I just come right out with it here. That's my style. And you can blast me back at www.Think.tv, where this conversation continues ardently, passionately, blazingly—because that's how thinkers roll.

I'm not going to rant without offering very specific solutions. That would be just taking cheap shots. After I smack you upside the head with the hideous problem we've created for ourselves, how we veered off track into a culture of empty-headed narcissism, I'm going to lay out what each of us can do to reclaim our brains, to take care of business in our own lives, and to become real, true-blue contributors to the world—so we can make our mamas and our nagging little voices proud.

Good news! This isn't even hard once you start pushing back at some of the insulting nonsense our culture is offering up to us. For one thing, you're going to find more time in your life, and you'll learn some underreported fun facts about sex.

Bottom line: your critical thinking skills are desperately needed right now for your own good as well as for the sake of your community, your country, and your planet.

That nagging little voice? It's your brain, and it's telling you that it wants back in the game.

Let's get started.

1

I Came by It Honestly

Think.

That was IBM's corporate logo when I was growing up in the 1970s, and at the time it was the most famous motto in the world. "Dink," "tenk," "pensez"—the company hung those signs in the local language in its offices around the world. My favorite childhood magazine, *Mad*, parodied the slogan with their own sarcastic "THIMK," which I tore out and taped up on my wall next to young Paul McCartney's dreamy puppy dog eyes on my "Let It Be" poster. I giggled whenever I saw it: an exhortation to be intelligent and funny, all in one goofy five-letter package. For a nerdy girl who loved words, it didn't get better than that.

"Think" may as well have been emblazoned over the front door to my home. I was blessed with two parents who were independent thinkers, who got giddy from the thrills of facts and books and ideas. Sure, they sometimes veered off into blazing eccentricity—don't most brainiacs? That was all part of the fun.

You might know my mother, feminist attorney Gloria Allred, who's spent her high-profile life successfully fighting misogynists, sexual harassers, racists, rapists, murderers, Holocaust deniers, O. J. Simpson, Scott Peterson, dry cleaners who overcharged women, Aaron Spelling when he fired a pregnant actress, and airport security who wanted a passenger to remove her nipple ring. I learned at an early age: Don't mess with my mama.

Because he lived an isolated, ascetic life, you don't know my dad. My parents divorced when I was a baby. My father was a true '60s hippie whose hair fell to the middle of his back, even when it all turned silver in his later years. He wore Levis every day of his life. His faded, folded blue bandana in his back pocket served as a hankie for my sniffles, headband for his stray locks, or potholder when camping. At night, if I were lucky, he'd bring out his guitar or Dobro and, between hits of his medical marijuana, softly play Woody Guthrie, explaining to me that "This Land Is Your Land" was a radical, anti-rich-people song. This land isn't *their* land—the land of corporate greed—but *ours*. See, Lisa?

Really? I only knew the first verse, taught to us in school as a patriotic song, like "America the Beautiful" or "The Star Spangled Banner."

> This land is your land, this land is my land
> From California, to the New York Island
> From the redwood forest, to the Gulf Stream waters
> This land was made for you and me.

It always seemed so tame. No, my dad said, look closely at the last two verses, which most people don't know.

> As I was walkin'—I saw a sign there
> And that sign said—no trespassin'
> But on the other side . . . it didn't say nothin!
> Now that side was made for you and me!

> In the squares of the city—In the shadow of the steeple
> Near the relief office—I see my people
> And some are grumblin' and some are wonderin'
> If this land's still made for you and me.

Until my father got me to see whole story, the full lyrics, I didn't get it. Old Woody's anthem embraces people on welfare, folks on the wrong side of "keep out" signs. The song's not just about simple patriotism; it's about class struggle. I'd never thought of it that way. Yeah! The Man can't keep us out! We the people are taking our country *back*! My dad hated the corporate takeover of America—and he had the fine print of a song all schoolchildren learned on his side.

I'd never thought of it that way—the mantra of my childhood.

With my counterculture daddy, there was always some lesson he taught me that I would never have gotten in school, something that seemed subversive and improbable but that he proved with facts or whatever he had available. "Honkies stole rock and roll from black folks," he advised in 1972, when no one else was saying such a thing. He played Chuck Berry and then the Beatles to drive home his point, and damn if they weren't a blatant rip-off. Distrustful of cops due to police brutality against his people, African Americans, he subtly raised a Black Panther fist and crossed the street to avoid them when they approached and then sent me articles from *The Nation* or *Mother Jones* with all the statistics and anecdotes to back up his point.[1]

Oh, the African American thing? He was actually a lily-white descendent of two signers of the Declaration of Independence, but he self-identified otherwise. Both my parents firmly believed that biology was not destiny. For my mom, that meant women should not be limited to certain paths because of our gender. For my dad, it meant that family pictures of jazz greats John Coltrane, Miles Davis, and Louis Armstrong hung on the walls of his apartment next to pictures of my brother and me. If I pointed out that these guys weren't *actually* members of our family, he gave me a withering look. "Failure of imagination, Linseed," he suggested. (Wordplay with my name also produced nicknames like Lysine, Lizzy Borden, and, for some reason, JoJo the Dog-Faced Girl, which I swear was said, and received, with love.)

Neither of my parents believed in dumbing anything down for children. For my birthday my dad gave me Algerian anarchist Franz Fanon's *The Wretched of the Earth*, an anticolonist screed that examines the effects of imperialism on the psyche of colonized African nations. "Dear Lisa, smash the state!" he inscribed. I was twelve.

My father loathed Republicans but equally hated Democrats who were in bed with lobbyists, which he believed was most of them. He believed that every cent he spent was a vote cast for one thing or another, so he put a lot of thought into how he spent his meager Social Security checks. César Chávez's grape boycott, which he enthusiastically supported, warmed him up for so many other corporate boycotts that he actually subscribed to a boycott newsletter, listing which large corporations had polluted the rivers, lost a class-action sexual harassment case, or perpetrated consumer fraud. He took the antishopping list to the market with him and followed it closely. Did Coors really notice he wasn't buying their beer due to their antigay policies of the time? No matter. Though he detested the beer anyway, he boycotted it on principle.

One day, well into my adulthood, I told my dad I was looking forward to hearing the Dalai Lama speak in my town. I knew he'd be proud of me for exposing myself to this great modern progressive thinker.

"The Dalai Lama. *Terrific*," he said sarcastically, turning the page of his book, volume three of *The Rise and Fall of the Roman Empire*.

The Dalai Lama—the nonviolent, contemplative man of peace, exiled as a child by evil China? Followed by millions worldwide, preaching love and kindness? The man who uttered two of my favorite quotes: "Be kind whenever possible. It is always possible," and "If you want others to be happy, practice compassion. If you want to be happy, practice compassion"? My dad has a bone to pick with *him*?

"What's wrong with the Dalai Lama?" I asked.

"Lisa, theocracy is theocracy, whether it's the Taliban or the Dalai Lama."

That stopped me in my tracks. Every other hippie progressive liberal type I knew revered the Dalai Lama. But not my dad. "Beware of anyone who advocates a state religion," he said. "Avoid them like the plague."

"Our system, separation of church and state, is a beautiful system, and it is the *only* acceptable form of government, Lisa. Look up what Thomas Jefferson had to say about it."

So I did. Thomas Jefferson said, "In every country and in every age, the priest has been hostile to liberty. He is always in alliance with the despot, abetting his abuses in return for protection to his own." So much for the Founders setting up a Christian nation, as I, and so many Americans, had believed. Secularization—keeping religion, even a benign religion, entirely out of politics—was a bedrock American principle according to my dad and, well, Thomas Jefferson.

"But, but . . . the Dalai Lama . . ." I sputtered. I'd never thought of him as a theocrat. But it's undeniable. Different incarnations of the Dalai Lama headed Tibet, and from 1720 until China's invasion in 1950, this figure was to Tibetan Buddhism what the Pope is to Catholicism. However benevolent, even saintly, the current Dalai Lama appears to me, he's run the "Tibetan government in exile" since 1959 as a *religious* leader.[2]

Thus I lost another argument before it even began and was forced to think differently about what I'd thought was a settled subject. My dad's constant underlying message to me was: It doesn't matter what everyone else says, even everyone else of your political persuasion. Mull it over *yourself*—deeply. Go to your core principles. Examine the facts: What's really going on? *Think*, Lisa.

I'd never thought of it that way before.

My dad wanted radical hippie change in our country, especially for the poor, but he hauled out and properly hung his American flag on the Fourth of July, Memorial Day, and Veteran's Day and quoted the founders when he needed to. He was proud of our Constitution, our liberty, and our music (well, American music up to 1975), and that warranted flag waving. But he also saw dangerous trends beginning. He presaged the almost complete annihilation of our right to privacy when video cameras began appearing everywhere in the 1980s. "They promised us that social security numbers would never become a state ID number," he said. "But that's what they've become. The state will soon have total access to every bit of information about you. Don't give out your social security number." I thought he was a paranoid curmudgeon. Years later, after everyone else got on the social security number privacy bandwagon, it was too late: I'd been the victim of identity theft three times.

That my dad was so often ahead of his time wasn't an accident. He read almost nonstop every waking hour. As a young man, he was diagnosed with a severe mental illness, then called manic depression and later termed bipolar disorder. He suffered from sometimes weeks-long debilitating bouts of bleak depression and was unable to work. But most of the time that wasn't him. He could function and take care of himself, and during that time, he read. He read the entire local newspaper daily, every word of the Sunday *New York Times*, various esoteric journals like the *James Joyce Quarterly*, and enormous multivolume series on Ancient Greek, Roman, or Chinese history, one after the next. When he found an author he liked, say James Joyce or William Faulkner or Thomas Pynchon or John Updike, he read their work straight through, followed by thick books of annotations and commentaries. Waking daily at 4 a.m. and most days turning the pages until 9 p.m., he reluctantly allowed interruptions only for life-essential activities like grocery store runs, phone calls with me, or rooting for the Steelers.

With an unnerving ability to retain nearly all of what he read, my dad knew everything about everything and had a long, historical perspective when he held forth. He knew his stuff. You know how you grow up and have that moment of awakening when you realize Dad doesn't know everything? Yeah, that never happened to me.

My dad died a few years ago, and his legacy to me is my conscience's nagging reminder to learn more than anyone else about my topic and to assess every issue on its own without preconceived ideas of what I "should" think. In fact, when I'm "supposed to" think one way, a hard-wired streak in me draws me to the other side. My fervent desire in my TV appearances, public speaking, and writing is to provoke my audience into realizing, "I never thought about it that way." There I was on CNN, for instance, lifelong vegetarian and fired-up animal rights girl though I am, defending convicted dog torturer Michael Vick's right to get back in the NFL. I did this because re-employment for released inmates is important to me, and the man did his time (and because real justice—releasing him to a pack of hungry pit bulls—is unattainable).

WHILE MY DAD SAT HOME, using what he learned in his library books to challenge my assumptions about the world, my mother took her independent reasoning out into the light of day, challenging the status quo when it flew in the face of what she knew was right and fair.

I was in middle school when my mother began to practice law. Her first prominent case was on behalf of women prisoners who were shackled when they gave birth in the prison hospital. That struck her as just plain wrong. Were they going to trot off just as their baby's head was crowning? Wouldn't locking the door be a little more reasonable and humane?

She won, quickly, and got the county to change its policy. Mom 1, shackles 0.

Everywhere she looked, something rankled her sense of justice and, with her newly issued law degree in hand, she did something about it. She sued Sav-On Drug Stores, at my instigation, for having an aisle marked "Girls' Toys" (dolls, dress-up clothes, toy vacuum cleaners) and "Boys' Toys" (play guns, soldiers, cars).

Guess which side had all the play money?

In response, the company maintained that this is how toys had always been organized. (Cue the *Fiddler on the Roof* orchestra: traditioooon! TRADITION!) My mom brushed off that feeble argument. Imposing rigid gender roles on little kids was contrary to everything she believed in. The company caved, and now the aisles are simply marked "Toys." (And folks, you are suffering your own failure of imagination if you're giving your daughters, or sons, a play *vacuum cleaner*. Pul-eeze.)

At Back to School Night, other parents admired the kids' artwork on the walls and listened politely to the teachers' presentations. My mother leafed through our history books and asked why they contained nothing about women's history. In English, she wanted to know why we weren't reading any literature by African American authors. Sure, *now* that's all part of the curriculum, but in those days, the curriculum was George Washington, Abe Lincoln, Shakespeare, and Moby Dick—full stop. Boys took wood shop and girls took home economics.

Along came my mom, who enjoyed having me be The First Girl To. . . . See, in those heady days of 1970s feminism, you could be the first girl to do something every day before breakfast, with plenty more to conquer, because there were so many ridiculous boys-only activities and the barriers were dropping fast. I was The First Girl to Take Wood Shop ever at my middle school. Sawing through two-by-fours and working with that big ol' T-square was mad fun and an easy A. (Hey, I wondered, were all the boys-only classes easy A's?) But so were the fresh-baked cupcakes before lunch in eighth grade cooking class, so I took Foods too, alongside the first boys allowed to take that class. We fielded the First Co-ed Softball Team to play against the faculty in what had previously been a boys-only game. I was The First Girl Allowed to Wear Pants to a Square Dance in the fourth grade. And on it went: proud victories for truth, justice, and the American girl.

In college I joined the debate team. After three intensive years of around-the-clock researching, writing our "cases," preparing to attack the opposition, and arguing our little hearts out at universities all over the United States every weekend, we won the national championship, the biggest thrill of my life up to that point. I was featured in the local paper: "Top Female Debater Wins Honors," with a nice grainy picture of me in my peasant skirt and Farrah hair clutching my trophy.

I was pretty psyched. I showed my mom.

"Top *female* debater?" my mom pointed out. "What does *female* have to do with it? You are the top debater, period!"

I'd never thought of it that way. I did not debate the point with her.

OVERWHELMINGLY, my mother's cases have been David-and-Goliath battles, pitting her client, a powerless nobody (a secretary, waitress, security guard, prisoner), against a rich, intimidating behemoth (a Fortune 500 company, the U.S. government, the Catholic Church). Helping ordinary people get the justice they deserve has been my mother's life's work for over three decades. And she wins by outsmarting and outlasting her opponents—simple as that. She will fight for decades up through the court system, then in the legislature, then in the media, and then back to the courts—whatever it takes. She taught me through her example many things: Be skeptical of what the crowd is doing, be even more skeptical of what powerful people tell us, dig up all the facts and appraise them objectively, and, then and only then, reach my conclusion. Because things aren't always what they first appear to be.

And so she stopped me cold one day with this doozy. For my birthday a few years ago I had asked my friends to give to a national relief charity. She was against it. I did a double take. How could anyone be opposed to giving to help the needy—much less my mother, champion of the downtrodden?

"Lisa, don't give to charity."

Say what? There must be interference on the line, I thought. Then I realized I was talking to her face to face.

"Think about it. I get invited to a celebrity fundraiser in Beverly Hills for a hospital for the poor. It makes everyone feel great to support the inner-city hospital. But what about all the other poor people who don't have a celebrity connection to raise funds for them? What about all the other Americans who can't get to *this* hospital, and who die from lack of health insurance and lack of access to health care?"

True enough, I say, but isn't it better to help a few than to do nothing? I lob back one of my favorite quotes, from Edward Everett Hale: "I am only one, but still I am one. I cannot do everything, but still I can do something. And because I cannot do everything, I will not fail to do the something that I can do."

"I'm not advocating doing nothing," my mom says. "Please. *Don't give to charity. Give to change.* Take the money you would give to the hospital and give it to an advocacy group working to change the system so *everyone* can have access to health care. Give to a candidate who will fight for universal coverage. It's less glamorous than going to a fundraiser. But in the long run, political change is what we need. The forces of the status quo are always well funded. So we have to fund our side too."

"Give to change?" Had *you* ever thought of it that way? She didn't entirely persuade me—I still asked for, and received, charitable donations that birthday and all the birthdays since—but she did make me *think*. When I give to charity, am I just putting a Band-Aid on the problem? What can I do to address the root problem itself? My mother's life has been devoted to changing minds, setting precedent, and changing laws to improve the lives of millions of people.

Some people think my mom is a knee-jerk liberal, but actually her knees don't jerk. They don't even twitch. It's her mind that's always ticking away, reasoning through each issue on its own. Unlike me, my mom supports the death penalty. She thinks it's justice for the "worst of the worst" murderers; I think our system is too riddled with human error to execute prisoners. She called for the impeachment of Bill Clinton—whom she'd supported and donated money to—when he lied to us about Monica Lewinsky. My mother does not brook liars.

Just because she was a women's rights lawyer didn't mean she wouldn't represent men . . . against women—against feminist women, even. (What? This one made my head hurt.) She represented a man who wanted to be on the Santa Monica Commission on the Status of Women, a government committee charged with eliminating gender discrimination in the city. Why shouldn't a man be on the committee, she asked. Gender discrimination is wrong when used against men too, and men can be feminists, she liked to say. A feminist is simply someone who believes that women should have equal rights with men. And don't we need as many men as possible on our side?

Uh . . . *I never thought of it that way.*

We have a close relationship because my mom is much more of a hoot than you might imagine after watching her doing her tough lawyer routine on TV. You haven't lived until you've seen her leaping on the back of a "Dykes on Bikes" Harley at the gay pride parade in her St. John suit or mwa-ha-ha-ing over her latest scheme to bring down some bigot.

We do have our differences, however. I'm vegan; she's nice when I ask the waiter to leave the feta out of my salad, but I know she thinks it's a little batty. She didn't understand why I would climb Mount Kilimanjaro when there is a perfectly nice beach resort a few hours down the coast of California where they accept our currency and speak our language (if our language consists overwhelmingly of the word "dude"). Mom practically believes in an attorney-negotiated, arms-length prenup before the first date. I'm a little looser about romance.

Yet I respect her for thinking things through with her own gray matter and for zealously fighting injustice like no one else on God's green earth. Like my dad, my mom taught me to use my noggin, figure things out, reason my way out of problems, and get deeply into the issues by learning more about them than anyone else. My parents led by example, each following the facts to their own conclusions and encouraging me to challenge their positions with a better argument, if I had one.

Knowledge is power. My parents gave me a great gift: the lesson that power comes with owning my own brain, that it's up to me to use it, and that I'd be a fool not to; that recognizing what's truly going on in my world and then acting to improve it has to start with open eyes and an open mind; that getting the right answer every time is supremely important, and there's only one route to the right answer—get the facts. I've had a successful career as a television talk show host and commentator, I had some great results for my clients as a civil rights lawyer, and I raised two smart, kind kids mostly as a single mom. Every fearsome challenge in my life has taken me to the library (and, later, to the Internet) to research it, learn about it, and then to devise strategies to overcome it. It ain't easy, but it's the only way I know.

Think.

USING YOUR BRAIN to figure out your world, your life, and your stuff seemed to me a pretty noncontroversial idea, like using a can opener to open a can. I didn't really think there was much debate about it until I began to notice a certain lack of interest in thinking in the media, where I work some of the time. In television journalism, for example, the misdeeds of drunken starlets have taken over what we used to call "news," and hardly anyone questions this. Normal, intelligent grownups pore over gossip rags as though they'll be tested on them, spiking the sales of titillating tabloids while dozens of real newspapers that inform us about corruption, politics, education, and world affairs are dead or dying.

For a decade I've been a television legal analyst, hosting my own daily Court TV show from 2001–2009, and covering all the big crime and justice stories regularly on CNN, HLN, ABC, CBS, and other television and radio networks and shows during that time and to date. My passion is international war crimes tribunals, and I was proud to cover Saddam Hussein's trial on Court TV for several months during 2005 and 2006. This was truly the trial of the century, as thousands of American and Iraqi lives were lost due to our invasion of Iraq and our commitment to bring Saddam Hussein to justice. Was the evidence against him there? It was. Would a panel of Iraqi judges give him the death penalty? They did. Would this tribunal serve as a deterrent to future despots? That remains to be seen. But televising and analyzing that trial was as worthy a story as I could dream of covering.

Early on, my networks assigned me election fraud cases, civil rights trials, Supreme Court rulings, violent crimes, and, sure, for a little zazz, the occasional celebrity story. That worked for me. Focus on what matters, and throw in a little color now and then. Sure. Fine.

But as the years went by, the priorities flipped. I noticed that my networks asked me to talk more and more about legal stories that really were inconsequential to the rest of us: Paris Hilton's drug bust, Tiger Wood's divorce, or Lindsay Lohan's revolving-door jail terms. I literally made dozens of national television appearances on each of these stories in 2010 while real stories of significance got crowded out. By 2011 I estimate that around 95 percent of the television appearances I'm asked to do involve reality stars, sex tapes, celebrity drug busts, or famous rich people's divorces. There isn't a network in America that would devote months of airtime to Saddam Hussein's trial now—or weeks, or days . . . or even hours.

Keep in mind: I'm a *legal analyst*, not an entertainment reporter. But whether we like it or not, all of us in the media seem to be entertainment reporters now.

I don't get to choose my assignments. The suits pick the stories. Still, I try. How about the war crimes tribunal currently prosecuting genocidal Khmer Rouge leaders in Cambodia? No. The California same-sex marriage federal trial that recognized for the first time equal rights under the U.S. Constitution for gay Americans? No. Voting rights litigation? No.

No, because the viewers won't watch. No, I'm told, because they want Paris and Tiger and Lindsay.

I find it astounding that thought-provoking journalism seems to matter so little to programmers and to all of us who read, watch, or listen to the news.

I have a tendency to get riled up. Maybe I was making too much of this? A few years ago, when it was all starting to get to me, I decided to take a break to clear my mind. I went grocery shopping. (Food is one of my happy places.) There at the supermarket, I saw *two* major magazines with the blaring headlines: Did Fergie's Husband Cheat on Her with a Stripper?

Oy! The manager chooses to give us *this* in the store's prime real estate, eye level at checkout?! In my dream world, customers would be screaming to high heavens about this insult to our intelligence. Instead, the shoppers just shoved their food onto the belt, and most of the women picked up and read the tabloids as they waited, without a hint of embarrassment.

I remembered the first time my mother was in the *National Enquirer*, decades ago. She wanted to see what the piece said about her but was too embarrassed to be seen buying it. Would I pick it up for her? "*What?!*" I replied. "*Are you crazy?* Don't make me do your dirty work!" What would my friends think? People used to buy tabloids furtively, stuffing them into the bottoms of paper bags, hoping their neighbors weren't watching.

I dream of a world in which, if we have to have celebrity magazines at all, they'd have blaring yellow headlines about stuff that matters, like,

> Sting and Wife Trudy Styler Bring Fresh Drinking Water to Ecuadoran Villagers Allegedly Cancer-Stricken from Chevron's Oil Spills, and Help Fund Groundbreaking Lawsuit Against the Oil Company

Because they did. Bravo for them. You'd know only that if you watched an obscure little documentary about the lawsuit against Chevron, called *Crude*. Spoiler alert: There are no strippers or sex triangles in the film.

The tabloid media makes us dumb, and watching an endless loop of stories about celebrity stupidity slashes our IQs. If we cared about our brains, we'd look away. And yet we're not; instead, we're flocking to celebrity websites, TV shows, and gossip rags.

Danger! Danger!

Then I noticed something else. Call it obsession with our appearance.

My childhood book heroines were the scrappy plain girls like Harriet the Spy or Nancy Drew who solved mysteries behind thick glasses and showed those vain pretty rich girls what was what! Hah! I loved 'em. Now the paradigm seems to have reversed, and in adolescent literature the vain, pretty rich girls, like Gossip Girls, rule the day. I meet young women who are quite open about the fact that their driving mission in life is to save up enough money from their starter jobs to get breast implants and mothers whose high school graduation gift to their daughters is their first round of plastic surgery. Ten million of us a year now have cosmetic procedures, a 162 percent increase since 1997, according to the American Society for Aesthetic Plastic Surgery. The problem isn't the nips and tucks per se; rather, it's people's endless attention inward to our image in the mirror, wondering, "should I get my eyes done?" or "is that a pimple/wrinkle/varicose vein?" that diverts our attention from looking *outward* at the world. Many of us know considerably more about waxing and Botox than the issues in our local election.

Danger! Danger!

All this matters profoundly. Without thinking clearly, without meaningful information, we suffer tragic outcomes. For example, as a television legal analyst, I often debate hot-button issues like rape and child molestation. As an attorney who has represented many sexual assault victims, getting the story right is important to me, and this means research, research, research. Yet on air, I'm told that many women believe that pop singer Rihanna *had* to be responsible for her boyfriend Chris Brown's violent attacks on her (blaming a domestic violence victim for getting herself punched in the face? Are we going *backward*?); that rape victims "often" lie (no, statistically false rape reports range from 3–8 percent[3]); that kids who commit crimes should be locked up for life because there's a "juvenile crime wave" (uh, no, juvenile crime has sharply declined, and we may be the only country on earth so brutal that we lock up our kids for life). Ignorant of atrocities committed against girls and women abroad, "friends" blast me on my Facebook page for supporting girls' schools in Asia and Africa: "Why aren't you helping people in the United States?" they demand, angrily. "Charity begins at home!" (Uh, okay, *maybe*, but does it have to end there?)

These folks are not encumbered by the facts when they're railing about this or that. Their mind-opening can opener is rusting in the drawer from inactivity. And how can they be mentally stimulated when their only reading materials are magazine pieces like Ten Sex Secrets Men Don't Want You to Know!* Or Stars' Skin Secrets!† Because they only read the dumb stuff, and so the media cranks out more dumb

*Believe me, it's not a secret: If you get naked with them, they are happy. The end.

†Their secret is not eight glasses of water a day. Stop it. It's plastic surgery, every time. You know it and I know it.

stuff, and the consequences are that rape victims are not believed, we cruelly lock up our children for the stiffest prison terms in the world, and we ignore the suffering of God's children abroad who are literally withering away from our inattention. And that's just the beginning.

That's why I can't let it go: because our choice not to know, not to think, has dire consequences, and those consequences are upon us now. And that's why we have to reprioritize, now, and stop allowing trivial nonsense to distract us, now, and refocus on what we all know is meaningful, now. Our country, still the world's only superpower, has the power to bomb or to heal. Which would you prefer? Will you participate in that decision? And politics aside, each of us is an individual superpower, blessed as we are with a first world education, the ability to pick up a book and read it, the freedom to click around for real news online, the means to write a $20 check that will send an Ethiopian girl to school for a year.

Or we can fantasize about getting a knockoff of Paris Hilton's purse. It all depends on what we choose to focus on.

Because the more that I considered what's happened to us, the more I saw that this wasn't my overheated imagination. When it comes to thinking, we've taken a very wrong turn down a very dark alley.

PART ONE

the problem

2

What a Waste It's Been to Lose Our Minds

Nothing in the world is more dangerous than a sincere ignorance and conscientious stupidity. —Martin Luther King Jr.

Great minds think alike? No. Great minds think for themselves! —Sarah Bloom (my daughter), age ten.*

WHEN DID NOT-THINKING become not-embarrassing? I'm unscientifically pegging it to 1991.

The United Negro College Fund is an old-school, highly respected charity founded in 1944 that funds scholarships to send African American kids to college. As of 2005 UNCF has supported approximately sixty-five thousand students at over nine hundred colleges and universities with approximately $113 million in grants and scholarships. About 60 percent of these students are the first in their families to attend

*I know. My kids are blazingly brilliant.

college, and 62 percent of them come from families with annual incomes of less than $25,000.[1]

Cool, right? So prestigious and well respected is UNCF that when President John F. Kennedy won the Nobel Prize for Literature in 1959 for his book *Profiles in Courage*, he donated all the prize money to the fund.

When I was growing up, UNCF's gripping commercials featured a baritone voiceover, soberly intoning over a picture of a cute little pigtailed girl growing up in the ghetto:

> The United Negro College Fund. Because a mind is a terrible thing to waste.

Oh! It made me want to dash off a check to them right away because I really wanted that little girl to go to college. I couldn't bear for her mind to go to waste. I didn't have a checking account at age eleven, but I donated all my Hanukkah money one year to the UNCF.

I didn't know at the time that "a mind is a terrible thing to waste" was considered one of the most-recognized slogans of the day and that it had won a bunch of big advertising industry awards. I only knew that those eight little words stuck in my head and packed a punch.

Fast forward to 1991, when Vice President Dan Quayle addressed the United Negro College Fund—a Republican who addressed an African American organization! Crazy, right? But it happened, and that's not the most stupefying part.

There was Vice President Quayle addressing this august group, and he told them he admired their motto:

> "What a waste it is to lose one's mind."

Yeah, he did.

But let's be fair to the fair-haired vice president. His entire quote was:

> "What a waste it is to lose one's mind. Or to not have a mind is being very wasteful. How true that is."[2]

Ah, how true that is!

This wasn't a unique gaffe for Quayle. Throughout his vice presidency, Quayle's blathering was reliably empty-headed, as though he'd just smoked a bowl of strong ganja:

> "The Holocaust was an obscene period in our nation's history. . . . No, not our nation's, but in World War II. I mean, we all lived in this century. I didn't live in this century, but in this century's history."

Wouldn't you just expect a long string of giggles from him here, and maybe a "duuuude?"

Quayle was the kind of VP from whom we expected very little. He was pretty, he wasn't required to do much, and he could be counted upon to say things now and then that made even my dog cock her head in confusion.

> "Mars is essentially in the same orbit [as Earth]. . . . Mars is somewhat the same distance from the Sun, which is very important. We have seen pictures where there are canals, we believe, and water. If there is water, that means there is oxygen. If oxygen, that means we can breathe."

> "I have made good judgments in the past. I have made good judgments in the future."

I am not making these up. When all was said and done, though, I had to hand it to the former senator from the Hoosier state. Finally, at least, Quayle manned up and showed some class, with

> "I stand by all the misstatements that I've made."

Of course, Quayle isn't the first or the last to make political gaffes. Plenty of politicians before and after him showed a demonstrable lack of intellect. Historically speaking, Quayle came just after President Ronald Reagan, who insisted "trees cause more pollution than automobiles do" and, regarding whether California's majestic old-growth redwoods should be spared from logging, "a tree is a tree, how many more do you need to look at?" What's more, Reagan's USDA attempted to classify ketchup as a vegetable for the purpose of school lunch programs[3] (my son Sammy would have loved that). Perhaps Reagan, who Americans loved despite his clueless comments, set the tone and laid the groundwork for Quayle, who said,

> "I love California. I practically grew up in Phoenix."

Or maybe Quayle was eerily self-aware, an idiot savant, with his

> "People that are really very weird can get into sensitive positions and have an enormous impact on history."

Quayle was VP during some of my formative years, and the general reaction to him was chuckles at his dunderheaded gaffes. The hits just kept on coming, and we kept on smiling. Few were genuinely concerned that at the time of the first Gulf War, our second-in-command didn't, as my dad used to say, know his ass from his elbow.

I'm not saying Quayle started it—sure, we had ignoramuses in power before and after him—but I am suggesting that maybe he set a tone for my generation. That his smiling presence on the national stage as our second-in-command, notwithstanding his stunning inability to form a coherent thought, ended any shame associated with not doing one's homework. As long as you look nice and have high-powered friends, who needs knowledge, right? What I do know is that now our blithe cluelessness is broad and deep, and the rest of the world is not chuckling along with us. They're laughing at us—and not just because we can't fit through doors.

The Quaylification of America

One in five Americans now thinks the sun revolves around the earth,[4] an idea Galileo disproved in 1632. Sixty-eight percent of Republicans don't believe in evolution, a scientific principle widely proven since the nineteenth century and replicated daily in the plant and animal kingdom.[5] Nearly one-fifth of us believe President Obama is Muslim, even though he's attended Christian church for decades and encountered significant headaches from his longtime pastor, Jeremiah Wright, during his presidential campaign.[6] One-quarter of Americans believe in their horoscopes, though astronomers have long known that all of the zodiac positions that form the foundation for astrology are wrong.[7]

An Australian interviewer, Julian Morrow, caught regular, non-frothing-at-the-mouth Americans on camera saying they didn't know how many sides a triangle has, where the Berlin Wall is located, or what the national religion of Israel is. None of the good citizens of the United States he approached could name a country that starts with a "U," though some tried valiantly:

"Yugoslavia?"

"Utopia?"

"Utah?"[8]

Our stupidity is so bad that the satirical Australian television show CNNNN made the "Stupid Americans" segment a recurring gag, as the correspondent easily convinced gullible Americans that the Leaning Tower of Pisa, the Eiffel Tower, the Taj Mahal, and the Great Wall of China are all located in Australia. To the question, "*Star Wars* is based on a true story. True or false?" Americans answered: "True!"[9]

But that's little different from the fun late night host Jay Leno has on American television, with his "Jaywalking" segment, posing impossibly easy "who's buried in Grant's tomb?" questions to amiable adults—people who seem to be in possession of all their faculties.

"Marxism is an economic theory based on the work of Karl ____," asks Leno. His guest giggles nervously, jiggling in her pink tank top with her red bra straps exposed. "I don't know," she finally concedes. "Can you think of anybody named Karl?" he asks. She tries: "Carl's Junior?"

"When did Christopher Columbus discover America?" A professional-looking brunette who could be a lawyer or banker in her silk bow tie blouse says, "1942!" When everyone laughs, she realizes her error: "Oh, 1842! 1842!"

Shown a picture of FDR riding in a car, a contestant guesses it's Thomas Jefferson.

In a car.

When was the Declaration of Independence signed? "1907?" She's told the correct answer, 1776. "Wow, that was a long time ago," the contestant muses.

The questions were drawn from a fourth-grade civics book.

Cue audience laughter.

Oh yes, everyone's laughing and having a grand time at this game of How Stupid Are We? We are not ashamed to be ignorant. We think it's a riot! Not to be outdone by the Australians, we have our very own TV game show devoted to showcasing dumb Americans: Are You Smarter than a Fifth Grader? Regular folks go on the show and let all the world see that they can't, as my dad used to say, find their ass with both hands and a map. Even celebrities, who presumably care about their public reputations, have no problem appearing on the show and demonstrating to everyone that they have the IQ of a turnip.

For instance, country music singer Kellie Pickler went on the program and was asked, "Budapest is the capital of what European country?" "I thought Europe *was* a country," she laments. "Boo-da-pest," she says tentatively, sounding it out, as if that might reveal the answer. "I've never even *heard* of that. I know they speak French there. Is France a country?" Okay, she's young. Maybe she's never heard of Budapest . . . or Hungary. She could have simply said, "I don't know." But she felt no shame in letting us know that she thought Europe was a country and France probably was not, that they speak French in Budapest, and that she'd never heard of the city at all. Hee hee hee![10]

The lack of embarrassment stuns me. American celebrities—even politicians—don't mind broadcasting to the world that they don't know what they don't know.

During the 2008 Presidential campaign, we had to wonder whether Republican vice presidential candidate Sarah Palin was smarter than a third grader named Brendan, who asked her, "What does the vice president do?" "That's a great question, Brendan," Palin began, perhaps stalling for time, perhaps just sucking up. "They're in charge of the United States Senate, so if they want to, they can get in there with the senators and make a lot of good policy changes that can make life better for Brendan and his family and his classroom. It's a great job and I look forward to having that job!"[11]

Although the vice president formally "presides" over the Senate, he or she is not "in charge" of it and votes only in the rare case when there is a tie. They don't "get in there" nor do they "make a lot of good policy changes." Article I of the Constitution says so. It's the kind of document we might have once expected someone running for vice president to read and understand.

Have we gotten used to our leaders saying dumb things? Even though President George W. Bush said, "I know how hard it is for you to put food on your family" early on in his political career, overall, Americans loved him as the kind of guy we'd like to have a beer with. Many found a modicum of beery charm in a guy who said of his critics, "They misunderestimated me." Back in the innocent pre-9/11 days, maybe we could cotton to this: "I do know I'm ready for the job," he said, "and if not, that's just the way it goes," or "Families is where our nation finds hope, where wings take dream." More brewskis![12]

There's boneheaded thinking on the left as well. Democratic vice presidential candidate Joe Biden said in 2008 that President Franklin D. Roosevelt went on television in 1929 to talk about the stock market crash. Two tiny details: FDR wasn't president in 1929, nor was there television then. Biden is known for his gaffes, like saying that Barack Obama was the first African American candidate who was "articulate and bright and clean." A year later Biden was Obama's pick for vice president.[13]

However, I've noticed that for Democratic male politicians, the whoppers usually stem from thinking with the little head, no matter how smart the big head might be. Former president Bill Clinton wagged his finger into the camera and told us that he "did not have sex with that woman," though Monica Lewinsky had a DNA-soaked blue dress proving otherwise, and then actually thought he'd outsmarted us all by squirming around sworn deposition testimony with, "that depends on what the definition of 'is' is."

But surely the grand dunce cap should be awarded to former Democratic senator and presidential hopeful John Edwards, who believed that he could (1) have an affair with a campaign staffer during the 2008 campaign and not get busted (the staffer was a *videographer, hello*); (2) be forgiven by the public when the story leaked in 2009 by offering up the least sympathetic excuse for philandering *ever*: his wife Elizabeth's cancer may have been "in remission" at the time; (3) lie to the public about his love child from that affair, saying on camera that the timing made it *impossible* that Quinn was his daughter (could he not subtract nine months?); and (4) get another married staffer to claim paternity of the child (ever hear of a DNA test, John? They hand 'em out like Chiclets on *Maury*).

And these are our *leaders*, often being shamelessly stupid in word and deed. They set a negative example for the rest of us.

IN POLL AFTER POLL, we Americans know little of the basic facts of our world. Who is Tony Blair? "Linda Blair's brother?"[14]

That was a real on-camera answer from an American man to interviewer Julian Morrow. No, the former prime minister of Britain is not related to the child star of *The Exorcist*. But we are, typically, better versed in pop culture than we are in facts about our world. We're more likely to know the name of an actress in a thirty-year-old movie than the recent leader of our closest ally. And so we can't answer simple questions about, as Morrow puts it, the very world our country runs.

The majority of Americans cannot name a single branch of government. That one especially galls me because our tripartite system, with its limits on government power, makes me proud to be an American. It's one of our shining features. (We also have Jonathan Franzen and Oprah.) We are hopelessly confused about religion in schools: A 2010 Pew Forum study found that fewer than one in four Americans knew that a public school teacher is permitted "to read from the Bible as an example of literature." And only about one-third knew that a public school teacher is permitted to offer a class comparing the world's religions.[15]

More than two-thirds of Americans don't know what *Roe v. Wade* is about, though more than one-third of American women of childbearing age will have an abortion by age forty-five. My feisty New York City gynecologist included on her intake evaluations—along with questions about prior medical history, diet, and nutrition—"Are you registered to vote?" When women answered no, she assigned them Jeffrey Toobin's Supreme Court book, *The Nine*, to wake them up about how precariously close we are to losing our reproductive rights.

When they returned for their next visit, she nagged them: "Did you read the book? Did you register to vote?" I teased her that she was the only doctor I knew who required women to study for their Pap test. She didn't crack a smile: "I had a young woman in this morning. I told her, 'You've had two abortions and you don't VOTE? ARE YOU CRAZY?!'"

Nearly all Americans, though, could tell you the name of the pretty blond *Friends* star Brad Pitt dumped for Angelina Jolie or how many kids Jon and Kate have.

How much of our federal budget is spent on foreign aid? The average American voter thinks it's 24 percent.[16] Not even close: It's less than 1 percent. However, military spending is 20 percent of our federal budget. But as a direct result of this wild overestimation of foreign aid, 71 percent of the American public wants to cut the amount of money we give to needy people abroad.[17] Economic aid pays for schoolteacher training and girls' schools in Afghanistan, irrigation projects in Iraq, and anti-AIDS programs in Kenya. Cuts in these programs and failing to fund similar projects mean that girls remain ignorant, children suffer, and parents die.

What's more, 89 percent of Americans have never heard of the Millennium Development Goals, to which the world's nations agreed in 2000. The concrete targets are designed to halve the grinding, extreme poverty that a billion people in the third world suffer. As UN Secretary General Ban Ki-Moon describes them, "The Millennium Development

Goals set time bound targets, by which progress in reducing income poverty, hunger, disease, lack of adequate shelter and exclusion—while promoting gender equality, health, education and environmental sustainability—can be measured. They also embody basic human rights—the rights of each person on the planet to health, education, shelter, and security. The Goals are ambitious but feasible."[18]

But they're not even on our radar. Says economist Jeffrey Sachs, frustration dripping from his words, "In the U.S., it's not as if people are debating whether we are going to meet the promises or not, there is simply no debate happening at all."[19]

See, this is when we cross over from being lovable airheads to flat-out dangerous, like three-year-olds with loaded machine guns. Our legislative, executive, and judicial branches will keep on ticking whether our citizenry can name them or not. But when the world's only superpower is a democracy run by people unmoored from knowledge, unencumbered by the faintest interest in critical thinking, we make devastatingly bad choices that hurt real people both around the world and here at home.

We're Number . . . Thirty-one! . . . or Thirty-seven! . . . or Sixty-eight!

One wrong answer I hear over and over again is the widespread American belief that we are number one in the world in nearly everything that's important. Does this stem from high school football? I used to go to my school's games, sit in the bleachers, and follow along when our team's cheerleaders whipped up the crowd during the call-and-response:

"Who's number one?"

"WE'RE NUMBER ONE!"

"Who's number one?"

"WE'RE NUMBER ONE!"

"I CAN'T HEAR YOU!"

"WE'RE NUMBER ONE!
"WE'RE NUMBER ONE!"
"WE'RE NUMBER ONE!"

Except . . . we weren't. And, just as on cable news, yelling it louder didn't make it so. We fielded a middling football team. In the rare year we made it to league playoffs, we lost in early rounds. Nevertheless, our cheerleaders were bubbly and cute. Furthermore, our high school had a dedicated, inspiring English teacher (Ms. Osterman, I've never forgotten you), and our drama department churned out professional-quality plays year after year. I guess we were like most high schools of the time; we had our strengths and weaknesses. One of our coaches was perpetually drunk and hit on the girls who developed early, but our speech teacher got us to the final round in a big statewide speech competition.

Still, we insisted with everything we had, as a matter of school spirit—school *pride*—that we were *number one*! We yelled it to our just average football team, even though we did no spirited bragging for the classes and activities in which we really *did* excel.

I had always hoped that high school would be different from real life, but to me, our nation is still yelling "we're number one" about all the wrong things.

For example, most Americans believe we have the best health care system in the world. That's a platitude we heard a lot on cable news when health care reform was batted around. "We have the greatest health care system in the world!" said U.S. senator Orrin Hatch on CNN, as did pundits during nearly every health care debate. The implication being: Why would we want to mess with it? *Yeah! We're number one! We're number one!*

Some of my audience actually gets angry and considers me unpatriotic when I point out any area in which we are not, in fact, number one. But I don't know what patriotism has to do with fact-checking. I'm sticking with former U.S. senator Daniel Patrick Moynihan: "You're entitled to your own opinion, but you're not entitled to your own facts."[20]

According to the World Health Organization, we're not even in the top ten health care systems in the world—or top twenty or thirty. When it comes to health care, we're number . . . thirty-seven! On the plus side, we did edge out Slovenia, number thirty-eight. (Their average annual income, in U.S. dollars, is $19,000. Ours is double that. So they do nearly as well in delivering health care to their citizens as we do, but on half the budget.) But we got our asses kicked by war-torn Columbia (twenty-two) and Cyprus (twenty-four). Ouch. Tiny countries most Americans have never heard of—San Marino, Andorra, and Malta—slaughtered us, coming in at numbers three, four, and five, respectively. The itty-bitty Caribbean island of Dominica (thirty-five) edged us out. We have a maternal mortality rate eleven times higher than Ireland. Do you think women dying in childbirth is largely a nineteenth-century phenomenon? In Ireland it is. In the United States, however, it's still happening—and at an alarming rate. The United States has a higher ratio of maternal deaths than at least forty other countries, even though we spend more money per capita for maternity care than any other country.[21] Amnesty International's 2010 Report, "Deadly Delivery: The Maternal Health Care Crisis in America," reports that two to three women die in childbirth *every day* in the United States.[22]

Yet 38 percent of Americans believe that our health care system is "above average" or "the best in the world."[23]

This "we're number one!" chant is the kind of statement that's easy to fact-check if you have an Internet connection, opposable thumbs, and twelve seconds. Nonetheless, talking heads simply repeat it, knowing no one will fact check them—and hardly anyone does.

The faux patriotism riles me. When Hillary Clinton was running for president, I'd often hear people say, "only in America!" They were so proud that we had a serious female contender in the race. Hah! We are modern and egalitarian, not like those murky, backward places overseas, where all the women walk ten steps behind their men with bushels of wheat on their heads. We are far ahead of the rest of the world and those other sexist countries, aren't we? *We're number one! We're number one!*

Nope. The World Economic Forum's 2009 Global Gender Gap Report gives the gold medal to Iceland, which ranks number one in the world for gender equality according to four measures: economic opportunity and participation, health, education, and political representation. We are number thirty-one because of American women's "stagnation in the political empowerment index." Translation: We have a pitifully small number of women holding elected political office in this country. *Eighty* nations surpass the United States in the percentage of women holding elective office. In many parts of the United States, there are fewer women in elective office now than there were twenty years ago.

Hillary Clinton was the exception, not the rule. And, by the way—not to put too fine a point on it—she lost.

Women have been winning elections to become heads of state abroad for decades. If Hillary Clinton had won, she'd have served alongside Tarja Halonen, currently (as we go to press) the president of Finland; Cristina Fernández de Kirchner, currently the president of Argentina; Dalia Grybauskaité, currently the president of Lithuania; Gloria Macapagal-Arroyo, the president of the Philippines until June 2010; and Michelle Bachelet, until March 2010 the president of Chile. And in the first years of her presidency, she'd have been joined by Roza Otunbayeva, elected president of Kyrgyzstan in April 2010; Laura Chinchilla, elected president of Costa Rica in May 2010; and Dilma Rousseff, elected president of Brazil in January 2011.

I know Clinton would have been especially delighted to serve alongside Ellen Johnson-Sirleaf, currently the president of Liberia, who was elected after the peasant women of her country staged insistent nonviolent demonstrations that ultimately brought to an end the brutal civil war that devastated the country. This brave struggle is beautifully documented in the film *Pray the Devil Back to Hell.*

Only in Monrovia!

Oh yes, and then there is Pratibha Patil, the current female president of India, who heads a country of one billion people.

Only in New Delhi!

And I'm just getting warmed up. Worldwide, heads of state not only come in two genders but also in several titles. Current female presidents are just the beginning. Switzerland is run by a seven-member Swiss Federal Council. Five of those heads of state are now women. Angela Merkel is the current chancellor of Germany. Luisa Diogo was the prime minister of Mozambique until early 2010. Hasina Wazed is Bangladesh's current prime minister. Jadranka Kosor, Iveta Radičová, Mari Kiviniemi, and Kamla Persad-Bissessar are the current female prime ministers of Croatia, Slovakia, Finland, and Trinidad-Tobago, respectively. Ukraine's female prime minister until her 2010 resignation, Yulia Tymoshenko, one of my faves, rocked her traditional Ukrainian blonde braid up and over her head while negotiating multi-billion-dollar deals with the International Monetary Fund.

Only in Kiev!

In 1960 Sri Lanka had the world's first female prime minister, Sirimavo Bandaranaike. She received her third government mandate in 1994 from her own daughter, Chandrika Kumaratunga, who was elected president then. This was the first time in history that a woman succeeded another woman as head of state.

You tell me what is cooler than that! Go ahead, tell me. Because I don't think anything is. I want to be president and swear in my mother as prime minister. That would make my day.

But Iceland, to me, takes the cake. Iceland had the world's first elected female president, Vigdis Finnbogadottir, in 1980. She was a divorced, single mother with an adopted daughter, and as far as I can tell, Icelanders couldn't have given a rat's ass about that.

Jóhanna Sigurðardóttir is the current prime minister of Iceland. She is an out lesbian. Big deal. Ho hum. They don't care.

By the way, do you notice something both Iceland presidents have in common? Take a close look at their names. I know, those are some weird-ass names to our Western eyes.

They both end in "dóttir," Icelandic for "daughter." In Iceland, women's last names consist of their father's first names, followed by "dóttir." (Men's surnames are their father's first names followed by "son".)

So Johanna's father's name was Sigurðar, and Vidgis's was Finnboga. I realize this is still a patrilineal naming system, but I'd rather be a dóttir than a son, personally. And women in Iceland don't change their names when they marry because why would they?

Bottom line: Depending on whether you count positions like member of the Federal Council of Switzerland or captain regent of San Marino, *several dozen* countries have elected women as heads of state by now, several multiple times. In some places, it's hardly even noteworthy anymore. Ireland's had presidents named Mary for the last twenty years (Mary Robinson, then Mary McAleese).

What about women in legislative bodies? We had House Speaker Nancy Pelosi, didn't we? Take *that*, Scandinavia! Does that make us number one in, say, women in legislative power? Far from it. The U.S. Senate and House of Representatives is only 17 percent women, ranking us number sixty-eight in the world for female legislators. You'll never guess what country is number one, eking out Sweden in 2007, for having the largest proportion of female legislators in power. I wouldn't even have guessed the right continent.

It's Rwanda. Since September 2008 this East African nation has had a majority of female legislators. In 1994, 800,000 Rwandans were killed in one hundred days of brutal genocide, a story documented in the heartbreaking film *Hotel Rwanda* and the searing book *We Wish to Inform You That Tomorrow We Will Be Killed with Our Families*. In the aftermath of the genocide, perpetrated overwhelmingly by men, the country felt that they needed radical change and that electing women would be more likely to bring peace. Fifty-five percent of Rwanda's lower house is now composed of women. Now, according to Nicholas Kristof, Pulitzer Prize–winning *New York Times* correspondent, "Rwanda is one of the least corrupt, fastest-growing, and best-governed countries in Africa."

Well, naturally.

We have to stop confusing home team pride with the facts. Our natural warm stirrings for our homeland does not mean we're number one at everything or that cool things like female leaders occur "only in America."

However, we do have many real reasons for patriotism. We have free and fair elections. We value freedom and equality. We have the most diverse physical beauty of any country I've seen, from the dramatic cliffs of Big Sur, California ("the world's greatest meeting of land and sea"[24]), to the Grand Canyon, the Rocky Mountains, the oceanic majesty of the Great Lakes, the Florida Everglades, the White Mountains of New Hampshire, the rolling green hills of the Long Trail of Vermont, our Atlantic, Pacific, and Caribbean beaches, Death Valley deserts, and the red rocks of Sedona. . . . I mean, come on, God did shed His grace on us.

In what other areas do we truly rule the world? U2's Bono says that we have the most creative economy in the world, and he points to the fact that our music, film, television, and video game industries comprise nearly 4 percent of our gross domestic product. I can't say that we are more or less creative than, say, India, with its rich culture of music, dance, art, and Bollywood. But I do know that wherever I go in the world—to the windswept Serengeti of Tanzania, the Atacama Desert of Chile, or along the Mekong River in Laos—the radios play American music and the vendors sell bootleg American DVDs (always for "one dolla, one dolla!"). In the remote High Atlas Mountains of Morocco, the locals passionately mourned Michael Jackson's passing, and our Berber guide's favorite television show, hands down, was *Dr. Phil*. No question: We are number one for world domination by music, television, film, and video games.

We have much to be patriotic about. On a recent trip to China, frustrated by our guides' poignant inability to tell us the truth about their own recent history ("Tiananmen Square? I really can't say what happened because our government doesn't tell us," one said, smiling), we burst into the USA pavilion at the Shanghai Expo shouting "USA! USA! USA!" In my mind, we were chanting, "We can say! We can say!"

I passionately love our First Amendment, with its ironclad guarantees of freedom of speech, freedom of religion, freedom of assembly, and freedom of the press. We can criticize our government before and after breakfast, lunch, and dinner every day of our lives if we so choose and no jack-booted thug will come pounding on our door. We're so wild about complete and utter freedom of the press that we exceed even liberal Europe in some ways. During the 2005 Michael Jackson child sexual abuse trial, I often appeared on CNN International. The charming European anchors would ask me politely, "Sorry"—Brits always preface questions with "sorry"—"but how is it that you are permitted to report on this trial while it is still ongoing?" They generally can't cover trials or comment on the evidence until the trial is done. Answer: because we have the First Amendment, folks, and that protects any of us who want to comment on any branch of our government—executive, legislative, or judicial. Transparency, baby. "But doesn't that create a circus in the courtroom, as it did in the O. J. Simpson trial?" Absolutely not. The cameras didn't *create* a circus in that courtroom; rather, the cameras *exposed* the circus that was taking place there. That's the great gift of freedom of the press.

We know about our Tiananmen Squares. We know when our government opens fire on our own citizens, whether it occurs at Kent State, Ohio, in 1970; on the MOVE organization in Philadelphia in 1985; or Waco, Texas, in 1993. There are investigations and recriminations and allegations, and we hear all sides—fully aired. Government here—government everywhere—makes mistakes. But here, those mistakes are in the media glare.

I also wave my stars and stripes proudly every Fourth of July, glowing about the fact that our republic does not have, and never has had, *royalty*, thank you very much. I know I must be respectful to our allies, but wow, it is hard for me to take seriously countries where inbred family members, supported entirely by taxpayer money, still mince around with jewel-encrusted scepters and ermine stoles and have even theoretical political power. Britain's elected prime minister has to go bow and scrape before the queen before he can roll up his sleeves and get to work. Please! A British friend told me, "Oh, it's just for tourism." Sure! No tourist has ever been to France since its eighteenth-century democratic revolution, right? No! Paris is a ghost town!

The British have the royalty because they like their royalty. A portion of their House of Lords, their "upper," largest legislative house, is still hereditary: Noblemen—and I do mean *men*—are born into it. Normally that man is the first-born male from a legitimate marriage between a "peer" and someone else, which also means, despite Britain's growing racial diversity, that those are overwhelmingly white folks. British kids learn this kind of thing in school: The ranks of the peerage are, in descending order of rank, duke, marquis, earl, viscount, and baron; the female equivalents are duchess, marchioness, countess, viscountess, and baroness, respectively. I'm so glad American kids learn that one isn't born into Congress, and they don't memorize anachronistic peerage rankings. You gotta earn it here.

We elect our officials, and we can't imagine doing it any other way. Nobody gets to rule over us because of an accident of birth. What's more, our press is free to go after corruption. We preach and, for the most part, practice religious tolerance, gender and racial equality, and the idea that any kid can grow up to be anything he or she wants to be. These are our strong suits, national values to be celebrated, though many other countries share these values with us. The bravest, most enterprising, hardworking people—immigrants—come here, to America, to make a better life for their kids, thereby enriching us with their diversity. Most Americans I know have at least a couple people who don't look like them around their Thanksgiving table. Raise a glass to that.

But we are also, sadly, number one in some chilling areas. We imprison far more of our population than any other country in the world, something I often railed about on my Court TV show. We incarcerate more of our own population, in raw numbers, than China, a notoriously punitive country with more than four times our population. We are also, appallingly, number one in the world, by far, in punitive sentences for our own children who commit crimes.

A few years ago Amnesty International, the respected monitoring organization that often brings to our attention human rights abuses across the world, completed a comprehensive report on American inmates who have been sentenced to life without the possibility of parole for juvenile crimes.

The number of prisoners that are currently serving life without parole for juvenile crimes in the United States is 2,225.

The number of prisoners that are currently serving life without parole for juvenile crimes in the entire rest of the world is 12.

This "we're number one" story received next to no media coverage here nor any particular public concern.

How Did This Happen to a People as Nice as Us?

How'd we get this way? How do so many misperceptions float blissfully along in American culture, buoyed aloft by our ignorance? How can so many Americans really think that the sun revolves around the earth or that we lead the world in areas in which our showings are dismal?

It's no secret that our schools are in decline. For all our talk about "education presidents" and all the politicians who run on mom-and-apple-pie platforms of improving schools, we don't have a strong enough political will to bolster our schools in the way that we do to, say, lock up criminals. In my home state of California, for example, in the 1980s, 17 percent of the state budget went to higher education and 3 percent went to prisons. Today, those priorities have radically changed. We now spend more on prisons (10 percent) than on what used to be our fine public colleges and universities (9 percent).

I am a graduate of one of those fine public universities, the University of California at Los Angeles. My college education was just over $200 per quarter, and I studied alongside California's best and brightest (we had to be in the top 12 percent of high school grads to be accepted), regardless of income. I didn't know and didn't care about my classmates' financial backgrounds. Some students had modest living-expense loans to pay off after graduation, loans that they could repay entirely within a few years. This was exactly as it should be. Kids should have to be smart and hardworking to attend college—not smart, hardworking, and rich.

Today, tuition at the UC schools exceeds $10,000 per year—and recently just experienced a 32 percent jump in just one year. As this book wen to press, another big hike to $12,150 was in the works.

Although that's a bargain compared to the elite private colleges like my kids' schools, the University of Pennsylvania ($49,080 annually for tuition, room, and board, *ouch*) and George Washington University ($51,730 a year, *ouch, make it stop*), high fees at state universities swiftly cull working-class kids from the ranks. California state universities have turned away forty-five thousand eligible students (top third of their graduating classes) due to funding issues. Those who do attend these schools—if they can get into their desired classes at all—are squeezed into larger classes or sit on the floor of their overcrowded classrooms. Young people now graduate hundreds of thousands of dollars in debt simply because they chose a university education.

Priorities have shifted: We will pay more for prisons, but not for education.

And that's a shame because American kids start strong. We have the brain potential, but we squander it. ABC's John Stossel gave identical tests to high school students in New Jersey and Belgium. His summation: The "Belgian kids cleaned the American kids' clocks. The Belgian kids called the American students 'stupid.'" The Americans were shocked at how poorly they did in comparison to their far more advanced European counterparts.[25]

In fairness, someone should have warned the New Jersey kids that we nearly always fare poorly when tested against Europeans and Asians. Weak American schools consistently produce uncompetitive American students. Early on, at age ten, our kids score well above average. But by age fifteen our kids are twenty-fifth out of forty first-world countries. The longer kids stay in American schools, the less competitive they are, even against countries that spend less on education than we do.[26]

What are our academic priorities? In 2010 Utah state senator Chris Buttars proposed eliminating the twelfth grade statewide to save about $60 million. The same state legislature, during the same month, proposed a new law to criminalize "reckless" conduct by pregnant girls or women that could lead to a miscarriage: driving without a seatbelt, say, or drinking or smoking.[27] Outlawing a new class of behavior, of course, comes with its own significant costs for investigations, prosecutions, and incarcerations—money the state would come up with, somehow, for this new priority. The inevitable constitutional challenges alone would mire the state in significant legal expenses.

No matter. For that, the money would be found. But to some, the twelfth grade was disposable. Why? Buttars argued that senior year is "nothing but playing around."[28] Senioritis does set in for many kids. I observed my kids' and their friends' senior year, frittering their time away with a lot of "independent projects" (read: writing an occasional poem after late-night parties) and study hall periods (spent IMing friends and watching YouTube and Hulu) because once they've been accepted to college—or decided they're not going—motivation goes down the drain. One Illinois high school student said of the proposal: "Your last year is your slack-off year and if we get rid of (senior year), junior year will be a slack-off year."[29] That logic hits home to many. Kids have *earned* the right to a slacker year, students and parents seem to believe, and the school system, for the most part, plays along, asking next to nothing of them in their final year of high school. Even the executive director of the American Association of School Administrators acknowledges, "For many youngsters, it's a waste of time."[30] Given this, hey, why not eliminate twelfth grade entirely?

Because there's a better alternative, which is viewing education as not something to be sloughed off, not something odious that kids "deserve a break" from but rather something to be *cherished*. If senior year needs to be revamped, let's revamp it. Bored teenagers are disasters waiting to happen. Even the good ones, given too much time on their hands, will sample exciting new activities like shoplifting and apple bongs.[31] Let's challenge them: Create stimulating curricula and get their minds moving forward. But releasing them early onto the streets, with their educations incomplete? Are we nuts? Education is a reward, not a punishment.

Utah is not the only state proposing to slash funding for education. Hawaii, faced with its state budget shortfall, cut seventeen days from its public school year in 2009—10 percent of the total school days. My hometown, Los Angeles, cut five days from its 2010–2011 school year and will cut seven the following year. The debate over fewer school days centered on preserving teacher jobs and avoiding teacher layoffs; next to no voices complained that our kids were being shortchanged. My eleven-year-old foster son, a Los Angeles Unified School District middle school student, wondered why the school district did not even bother to assign him a book to read during that extra September week of summer vacation. After all, that wouldn't cost a thing. There's only one answer to this question: because the loss to children's education was not a concern.

Thirty-five states permit early graduation, as if high school is something from which kids should be released early for good behavior.[32] As Americans, these kids already have one of the shortest school years in the world. Our kids average thirty-two hours of school weekly, compared to thirty-seven hours in Luxembourg, forty-four in Belgium, fifty-three in Denmark, and sixty in Sweden. And after school, our kids average one hour of homework daily, whereas Japanese and Chinese students do considerably more, then consistently wipe the floor with us on international academic tests.[33]

Because of our three-month-long summer vacation—baffling to the rest of the world—American kids already, before all these cuts, have one of the shortest school years anywhere, a mere 180 days compared with an average of 195 for European countries and more than 200 for East Asian countries. Over a span of twelve years, that fifteen-day difference means American children lose an *entire year* of school compared to their European competitors.

Study after study tells us that our long summer vacations cause our kids to forget much of what they'd learned the previous years. During those long summers, a throwback to the era when kids were needed on our farms during growing and harvest season, our kids forget an average of one month's instruction in many subjects and three months' worth in math.[34] Fewer than 2 percent of American families work on farms today, and of course, child labor has long been illegal in the United States. And long summer vacations hurt the kids at the bottom rung of the economic ladder the worst. We've got to let go of our Huckleberry Finn fantasies that kids are enjoying carefree rural summer days, whiling away the hours in canoes and catching fireflies. Poor kids aren't building tree forts at the family vacation home, and actually, few rich kids are either. Children from affluent homes go to camp, computer classes, and other enrichment activities during our long, American, school-free summers, both to keep them educated and because both parents work during the day. Poor kids spend June, July, and August playing video games, staring at TV screens, or languishing on street corners. And this three-month-long lack of intellectual stimulation for underprivileged youth is the single biggest contributor to the educational achievement gap between rich and poor kids.[35]

And when did colleges sneak in so much time off? I've been dumbfounded at my kids' six-week-long college *winter* breaks and, of course, those galling three or four months of summer vacation in addition to various "reading periods," spring break, and periodic long holiday weekends. It all adds up to a total university school year of just seven months. Those five months off are broken up into odd chunks that make getting jobs difficult, so there's a lot of thumb-twiddling and, of course, Facebooking and sleeping until noon. Seriously, can't we better use the time of our best and brightest?

OUR SCHOOL DAYS ARE TOO SHORT, our hacked-up school years seem designed to make retaining knowledge as challenging as possible, and I haven't even addressed the sorry state of American education during those infrequent hours kids are actually in class (only one-third of our high school seniors read proficiently). The point is that we don't value education. We see it as something to be cut during budget crises, something to let kids escape from whenever possible, an evil that perhaps isn't even necessary. We teach our kids to rejoice when school's out and to dread going back to school when it resumes. Learning is perceived as somewhere between a tedious obligation and an outright pain in the ass. As a result, our teenagers graduate without knowing the basic facts about the world we run.

But we can't sit back and simply blame schools for our ignorance. The fact that we undervalue education runs through our entire lives. Our kids are blessed with free public education—books and computers and science labs and playing fields that, sure, could all use improvement, but would be viewed as gifts from heaven above to third world children, especially girls, some of whom are not even allowed to go to school.

All those years of celebrating no-school days and grumbling about classes and tests and assignments set the foundation for a life of intellectual flaccidity. I say this because those of us who are out of school are not off the hook. Once we graduate, our ignorance is our own damn fault. Just as you can't continue to blame Mommy for your emotional immaturity after about age thirty, we can't lay all the blame for our fuzzy thinking as grownups on our lackluster schools.

According to the National Endowment for the Arts in its comprehensive 2004 survey, To Read or Not to Read, one-third of high school graduates never read another book for the rest of their lives. Eighty percent of American families did not buy or read a book last year. Seventy percent of U.S. adults have not even set foot in a bookstore in the last five years. Reading proficiency rates are stagnant or declining in adults of both genders and across all education levels. Nearly half of all Americans ages eighteen to twenty-four read no books for pleasure.[36]

You can't blame that on short school days or your mean eighth-grade history teacher. It's as though we learned just enough to get through school and then, phew! Thank God *that* chore is over. We passed the tests, and now we want nothing more than to switch off our brains and beat a hasty retreat from books and knowledge and learning.

We *can* read, of course. We just so rarely use that power wisely. What could drive my point home better than the *Complete Idiot's Guide* Series? Or the "for Dummies" books? How low have we sunk in taking pride in ignorance when we buy books that right there on the cover proclaim they are for ignoramuses? The *Complete Idiot's Guide* books are among the most successful ever in American publishing: twenty million readers since 1993, 450 titles, translated into twenty-six languages. The thing is, they're not really for idiots. They are useful, straightforward how-to books. But they are marketed, right there on the covers, to idiots. Nobody ever went broke underestimating the intelligence of the American public, as H. L. Mencken said. But this really takes Mencken one step further, doesn't it? Weren't marketers of old supposed to pretend they didn't think the consumers were a bunch of damn fools? Now, however, we find new gold to be had by flat-out appealing to consumers as dumb asses.

Am I the only one who doesn't want to tote around a book announcing to the entire world that I am a Dummy or a Complete Idiot? Am I the only one discomfited by titles like, "The Koran for Dummies"?

Tabloid Media Is Making Us Stupid, Narcissistic, and Self-Loathing

You know the phrase "garbage in, garbage out"? Computer programmers initially coined it to explain that a computer's output is only as good as the information the computer is given. GIGO is a principle digital recorders use, meaning that an audio or video file, digitized, is only as good as its analog counterpart. Likewise, in organic chemistry, if the materials used in the organic synthesis are impure, the resulting mixture will be of low quality.

Or how about this one: "We are what we eat"? Sure, our health depends on the right input of nutrients. And so it is for the mind. We are what we read—and what we view on all those television and computer monitors in our lives. The information we take in daily shapes our outlook, our context, and our view of what's important.

Most of us read ingredient warnings and consider what we're putting into our mouths. But how many of us consider the quality of what we're feeding our minds on a regular basis?

For women, what we read, increasingly and sometimes exclusively, is celebrity rags and blogs: *People*, *U.S. Weekly*, *In Touch*, *OK*, *Star*, *National Enquirer*, *TMZ.com*, *PerezHilton.com*, *Radar Online*.

TMZ.com has ten million unique visitors each month, and Yahoo's celebrity gossip page, "OMG!" has twenty million. These skew overwhelmingly female. Young women especially pore over the tabloids like they'll be tested on them.[37]

In 2003 *U.S. Weekly* had a modest eight hundred thousand subscribers per week. That number more than doubled to a circulation of nearly two million weekly by 2010.[38] An editor there tells me they count at least ten readers per subscriber, as the glossies are popular in doctor's offices and nail salons; I see them in waiting rooms everywhere.

Janice Min, the glossy's outgoing editor-in-chief, says her core market is the thirteen million American women who are "avidly involved" in pop culture. This would presumably include the ten million people who tuned in to the 2009 season premiere of *Jon and Kate Plus Eight* after *U.S. Weekly* "broke the news" of their separation and featured cover stories on Jon and Kate six weeks in a row in the summer of 2009.

Garbage in, garbage out. Read glossy rags about the personal lives of celebrities and then turn on the show to watch them sit on the couch and whine and fester. Then buy next week's magazine to read up on the new hairstyle or mistress. This process is a complete ecosystem, except that as in organic chemistry, the impurities you're pumping into your brain are lowering your IQ, convincing you that this crap cosmically matters, and damaging your mental health.

Seriously, that's what's happening. Dr. Drew Pinksy (syndicated radio host of *Loveline* for over twenty-five years and host of *Celebrity Rehab*) argues in his book *The Mirror Effect: How Celebrity Narcissism Is Seducing America* that our current fame obsession is a public health issue, and I am with him on this. He subjected two hundred celebs to a standard psychological test, the Narcissism Personality Inventory, and found that they were 17 percent more narcissistic than the average person. Reality TV stars were the absolute worst of all.[39]

Dr. Drew explains that, from a psychological standpoint, "narcissism" doesn't mean that stars are in love with themselves but rather that the celebrity behaviors so many seek to emulate grow out of genuine personality disorders rooted in "unbearable feelings of internal emptiness. When the image in the looking glass disappoints them, or fails in some way, they turn to other solutions. These other solutions—addiction, extreme vanity, sexual drama, and dysfunctional relationships, exploitativeness, and outrageous entitlement—have come to dominate celebrity culture." In his view, "the mirror effect" is the result: We, the viewers, become as narcissistic as the celebrities, adopting all their arrogance, lack of empathy, and sense of entitlement.

"Whenever you choose the entertainment media's offer of escapism cloaked as 'news,' you do so at the expense of a real connection with humankind. You're anaesthetizing yourself, while reinforcing and amplifying your latent narcissistic traits. You're abdicating your interest in the world and surrendering to the false image of the world as you wish it to be," he says.

In other words, we become almost as bad as the egomaniacs, drunken starlets, and arrogant attention-seekers we read about. We become desensitized to the lying philanderers. We start to believe that their squabbles and fashion don'ts and DUIs mean something. We lose touch with what matters.

And, weirdly, even as tabloid media makes us more narcissistic, it also makes us hate what we see in the mirror.

We've long known that the more girls and young women read celeb mags or watch music videos and TV, the more they hate their bodies. The comparisons with the perfectly sculpted (and now always, always Photoshopped) forms of celebs is just demoralizing. In one study of nearly 550 working-class adolescent girls, the majority were dissatisfied with their weight and shape. Almost 70 percent of the sample stated that pictures in magazines influence their conception of the "perfect" body shape. Further, adolescent girls who were more frequent readers of women's magazines were more likely to report being influenced to think about the perfect body, to be dissatisfied with their own body, to want to lose weight, and to diet.[40]

Overall, young people who watch TV and soaps and read tabloid magazines have more body dissatisfaction. Furthermore, the more girls identify with television stars or models, the more they experience body dissatisfaction.

Singer Jessica Simpson has said that when she looks at herself, airbrushed and retouched on magazine covers, she wishes *she* looked like that—because she knows that's not her. Hell, my cover photo on this book is, of course, professionally retouched. All of us in the media know that the stylists, hairdressers, makeup artists, and lighting crew work hard to make us look much better than we actually appear off-camera.

Tabloid media's evil twin is reality TV, which women, especially young women, watch compulsively. A typical example of this popular genre is *The Hills*, the most successful show in the history of MTV. (I wistfully remember when there was actually music on Music Television.) During its time on air, it received two to four million viewers, overwhelmingly teenage girls and young women. As far as I can tell from watching most of one episode on Hulu.com until I went numb from boredom, this "loosely scripted" reality show (huh?) follows around the three most self-absorbed young women on the planet. They shop and they fret about romance. They talk endlessly about why they broke up with this boyfriend or may reunite with that one. They look off longingly into the distance while doleful music plays. They have lunch in Beverly Hills and talk about who they should invite to their beach party. There is a beautiful Malibu beach house, but no one is the least bit grateful for the use of the place, much less the open-ended wardrobe budget. We have to wonder if these women have ever had a thought in their pretty, empty heads about anyone other than themselves.

One of these breathtakingly self-obsessed young women, Heidi Montag, attempted to launch a singing career with songs like "Superficial," with the lyric, "I don't care what they say / It isn't fair / That I wear diamonds for breakfast," and "Girls say that I'm conceited 'cause they really wanna be me."

That's her argument that she's not superficial?

Like other celeb wannabes who clawed their way up from obscurity to fame without any discernable talent, Heidi has no shame about her self-obsession. Apparently she spends nearly all of her free time looking in the mirror, considering expensive medical options to improve her appearance. She readily gave magazine interviews about her "addiction" to plastic surgery. As the *Chicago Sun-Times* reported in January 2010,

> Reality TV star Heidi Montag confesses in a new interview that, despite her good looks, she is so obsessed with plastic surgery that she recently had 10 procedures—in one day.
>
> "For the past three years, I've thought about what to have done," Montag says in the January 25 issue of *People*. "I'm beyond obsessed."
>
> Montag, twenty-three, who had breast augmentation and a nose job in 2007, says she "shopped around" for body parts in the pages of *Playboy* magazine before she appeared on its cover in September. "When I was shopping for my boobs, I wanted the best," she says. "So I sat down and flipped through a bunch of Playboys."
>
> She told *People* in August that more surgeries were ahead: "I plan to get a few more upgrades. . . . I'm sure as I get older I'll need some touch-ups. I think I want to go bigger on my boobs for [husband Spencer]."

Montag's procedures included:

- Buttocks augmentation
- Boob job touch-up
- Nose job touch-up
- Chin reduction
- Liposuction in her neck
- Liposuction in her waist and thighs
- Mini brow lift
- Botox in the forehead
- Fat injections in her cheeks and lips
- Pinning back her ears

For her brazen "look at me now" attitude about plastic surgery, Montag landed the coveted cover of *People* magazine, America's number one celeb weekly. She posed for photographers in Las Vegas later that year with her new G-cup breasts barely contained by her bikini.

I shudder to think how many young women and adolescent girls will follow her lead. Apparently that's of no concern to Heidi, or at least she hasn't publicly expressed any concern about that. Instead, she's spent years staring in the mirror—"beyond obsessed" in her words—rather than looking outward at what her contribution to the world might be. In return, we glorify and reward her self-absorption with major magazine covers and hit television shows, encouraging girls to be like her.

And every time we watch *The Hills* or *Real Housewives* or *Keeping Up with the Kardashians*, a clump of our brain cells resign in defeat.

So, how did this happen to a people as nice as us? Incrementally, step by step, each day of school lost to budget cuts, each time we choose to pass up the book store for the shoe store, each time we click on Perez Hilton or "Teen Mom," each time we participate in glamorizing empty shells of women who define themselves by their resemblance to Barbie rather than by their ideas and accomplishments.

And what a shame, because we've come so far, so quickly. Luckily, we still have time to get back on course.

In Just One Generation, Women Got Smarter—and, I'm Sorry to Say, Dumber.

As we journey through the troubling lack of thinking in our country today, did you notice that it was my gender that gave a lot of the dimwitted answers to Jay Leno and the Australian "Stupid Americans" interviewer? I looked for general examples of dumb Americans, and to my chagrin, many of them ended up being women.

Say it ain't so!

This happened despite the fact that I always root for my home team, we of the XX chromosome. One of my greatest regrets in life is that my friend Eric Cotsen trademarked the phrase "girls rule" and, therefore, I cannot. Eric, how could you? Girls* rule! Girls rule! Girls rule! (Go ahead, Eric, sue me. Make my day.)

Yes, we do. That's my view and I'm sticking to it. But what about all those giggly silly girls I kept finding, the ones who were easily persuaded that the Eiffel Tower was in Australia, who weren't sure if we were even *in* the Vietnam War. They worry me. How could they be so unabashedly ditzy when girls, in measurable educational achievements, actually do rule?

And we do. We rule big time. Check this out: Girls now outperform boys at every level of education. We now score higher overall on achievement tests in elementary school, middle school, and high schools. In every state, at each of three levels tested, girls read more proficiently than boys. Compared to 65 percent of boys, 72 percent of girls graduate from high school, and that gap is even wider for teens of color. The National Honor Society says that 64 percent of its honorees are girls.[41] That stands to reason because the average high school grade point average is 3.09 for girls and only 2.86 for boys.[42] Women outnumber men in colleges and universities, graduate and professional schools. Women receive 58 percent of the bachelor's degrees in this country (time to rename them "bachelorette's degrees"?) and half of the professional degrees. Female college students significantly outnumber male college students in *Iran*, for crying out loud, a country where education is viewed as a luxury for rural girls, who are married off as

*Already my mother is plotzing. She, like many rabble-rousing women of her generation, hates the word "girl" as applied to anyone over the age of eighteen. "Would you want a 'girl' to run your Fortune 500 company?" she would say. "Girls are children. Grownups are women." I know. I get it. But my generation uses "girl" in a friendly, go-girl way, as in Girls' Night Out, or as the beginning of a raucous lovefest when I unexpectedly bump into my friend Lauren Lake in the CNN green room. "GIRRRRRL!" we both shriek, recently to the amiable consternation of Republican strategist Ed Rollins who was waiting for his pundit turn and was subjected to our manic screaming. "Why don't *men* do that when they run into each other?" he mused. Because they don't have the same capacity for heartfelt love and enthusiasm for their girlfriends, I suggested, reasonably. Because, as always, *girls rule*.

young as twelve and then expected to stay home to run the household.[43] Back home in the United States, some college admissions officers have openly acknowledged that they practice affirmative action for males because if they simply admitted students based on merit, the schools would tip at least two-thirds female. And we can't have *that*, for some reason.

We are leaving the boys in the dust. They are scrambling to keep up with us in schools. There's an entire cottage industry of books like *The Trouble with Boys*, *Why Boys Fail*, and *Boys Adrift* written about "the boy crisis" and how we may need to masculinize the curriculum to motivate all those underperforming guys: Do they need more running-around time? More sports references in the reading material? Insert racecars in the math problems? Some lobby for special boys' schools to help them out because it's just *not fair* that they have to compete straight-on with girls.

Oh, boo hoo.

How things have changed in only one generation. My kids' generation does not expect a PhD to be male or the president to be white. In fact, a few years ago my then five-year-old son Sammy, whose mother and grandmother are lawyers, was astonished to learn that *men* could be lawyers at all. We had to set him straight. Yes, dear boy, males can have professional careers, if and only if they can keep up with the high-achieving women.

If you're under thirty, all this female educational achievement news may be a big yawn. You're used to girls being the straight-A, hands-up-in-the-front-row ace students. But when I went to Yale Law School in the early 1980s, women were one-third of the class, and this was considered a shockingly *big* number—so big that we women had to fight constantly against the assumption that we were there because of affirmative action. When I was a second-year associate attorney at a major New York City law firm in the late 1980s, I sat in a conference room conferring with an important client. A senior partner walked into the mahogany paneled chamber and said to the client, right in front of me, "Would you prefer a male lawyer?" When I shot him the stinkiest stink eye I had, the partner said, "What? He's the client!" (Bless the client for telling that old dinosaur he was perfectly happy with me, thanks very much.)

Apart from college degrees and outperforming the boys on report cards, aren't women just plain smarter than men? Seriously. I always thought so. A man can't even look at a girl in a bikini and tell you his mom's maiden name. (There are actual studies about how the male IQ drops right into the toilet when they look at hot babes.[44]) A woman can drive a car full of screaming toddlers, close a multimillion-dollar business deal, figure out a nutritious dinner based on her mental inventory of the sad little ingredients left in her fridge, and recalculate her adjustable mortgage all at the same time. We rule. We know we do.

And yet we clearly are not applying our brains across the board. And I say this because a funny thing happened in the last generation. Girls got smarter, but female brains became devalued. I marvel at this. How did it happen?

When Girls Got Smart, Did Smart Go Out of Style?

Can we take a quick walk down memory lane? In 1960 women were only 39 percent of college undergraduates, often assumed to be there only for their "Mrs." degree.[45] A generation ago, males out-tested females (especially in math and science) to such an extent that social scientists wrung their hands over the problem. Was it women's smaller brain size? Were girls biologically stuck with inferior intellects? If so, was admitting them to colleges, graduate, and professional schools a colossal waste, taking seats away from good men who would go out and conquer the world with their degrees?[46]

This was the sociological debate in the 1960s and 1970s. Nonetheless, women plugged away in that world of astonishing sexism. Just as on the unnerving hit television show *Mad Men*, male bosses smacked secretaries on their rear ends and told them that typewriters were "easy enough for a woman to use!" In the classroom, overt sexism was rampant. Most of us who remember that era recall being called on less, challenged less, and openly told certain school activities were off limits for us. I remember my eighth-grade journalism teacher laughing loudly at the idea that a girl could cover sports. Another teacher constantly admonished us girls to smile "because girls who smile are pretty, and girls who don't smile aren't pretty." That was in history class, when we were studying the American civil war, which I didn't exactly consider a happy-face era.

In a 1992 *Glamour* magazine survey, 74 percent of the female respondents remembered having a teacher who was biased against girls or who paid more attention to boys. Ask a high-achieving woman born before 1970 about her experiences with gender bias in the classroom and you'll likely get a story like this one:

> In my AP physics class in high school in 1984 there were only three girls and twenty-seven boys. The three girls, myself included, consistently scored at the top end of the scale. On one test I earned a 98. The next closest boy earned an 88. The teacher handed the tests back saying, "Boys, you are failing. These three pretty cookies are outscoring you guys on every test." He told the boys it was embarrassing for them to be beaten by a girl. He always referred to us (the girls) as "Cookie" or made our names sound very cutesy![47]

When my mother went to the University of Pennsylvania in the early 1960s, female students—the university had only just begun integrating them—did not have full access to student life. I guess the school felt it had to ease into the female student thing slooowly. Girls were not permitted to write for the school paper, for instance.* And my favorite: They were not allowed to be *cheerleaders*. Yup. That was a prestigious little extracurricular activity, and girls weren't thought to have the fortitude for it.†

---

*Can you freaking *imagine*!?

†Can we bring back just this one little bit of sexism?

When my mother went to Loyola Law School in the 1970s, women composed 5 percent of the class. Female law students were like circus freaks, except they were groped more.

When I was in high school in the 1970s, girls' sports got roughly the same funding as the leaky water fountain by the janitor's closet. Jumping for baskets or running goals could, we were told ominously, irreparably damage our lady equipment.

Those arguments are now as anachronistic as IBM Selectric typewriters and Earth shoes. Thanks to gender pioneers like my mother and millions like her, we no longer hear pundits puzzling about women's delicate constitutions or itty-bitty brains.*

I heard conservative radio talk show host Larry Elder once argue that feminists should *declare victory*. The women's movement has made sweeping gains, he said. Nearly all Americans now believe that women are equal to men and support women's rights to any education they want, any job they merit. The movement has won! Why not declare it?

I'm always a little fidgety when I find myself agreeing with an extremist.† However, every now and then they do say something that's true. (Mathematically speaking, left long enough at a typewriter, a parrot will eventually peck out the complete works of Shakespeare.) Was this one of them?

As every law school professor I ever had would say, yes and no.

I'm with Gloria Steinem: "In my heart, I think a woman has two choices: either she's a feminist or a masochist." Either you believe that women and men should have equal rights to everything they damn

---

*Except former Harvard University president Lawrence Summers, who infamously mused in 2005 that women were underrepresented in the highest ranks of science and engineering because we lack "intrinsic aptitude." He apologized, but some believe that that boneheaded remark cost him the job of Treasury Secretary in the Obama administration. If so, that works for me. (He currently serves as director of the White House National Economic Council.) In 2009 two of the three winners of the Nobel Prize for Medicine were women.

†I love you, Larry, because you're a fearless independent thinker. But when you're opposed to public education, you're an extremist.

well please, or you should go live in a cave, perhaps alongside Osama bin Laden, your ideological comrade.

Oh, and we have won big in many areas: Most Americans whose ancestors have walked on their hind legs for two generations now believe that women should have equal rights and funding in education and sports (witness the explosion of girls' soccer) and that women should be considered for any job for which we're qualified. And we are rocking the house in education.

And yet we can't do a complete victory lap yet.

As I mentioned at the beginning of this book, 25 percent of American women aged eighteen to thirty-four would rather win *America's Next Top Model* than the Nobel Peace Prize, and 22 percent would rather lose the ability to read than their figures.

They'd rather lose their ability to READ?!

Al Gore, Mahatma Gandhi, and the Dalai Lama have won the Nobel Peace Prize for alerting the planet about the dangers of climate change, advocating nonviolence, and saving thousands of lives. One in four of my young American sisters would rather win some ninny reality show for teetering down the runway in six-inch heels than join the ranks of the world's leading thinkers? What kind of women would seriously answer the poll that way?

The same women who would trade literacy for a hot bod. Wow.

The younger the sample, the worse things get. A Pew Research Center poll found that 51 percent of eighteen- to twenty-five-year-olds said that *becoming famous* was their most important or second most important life goal. Half of young women would rather get hit by a truck than get fat.[48]* But it's bad news for us across the board, at all ages. One-third of women in a representative survey consider their ap-

---

*In fact, Heidi Montag, mummified head-to-toe in bandages after her plastic surgeries, the pain so severe "I thought I was going to die," likened her experience to having been hit by a truck. For thinner thighs, bigger breasts, and tighter skin, women now choose the searing pain, black and blue bodies, swelling, and nausea previously experienced only from traumatic accidents.

pearance their most important quality, more important than job performance or—*sigh*—intelligence.[49]

When I simmered down, I realized, grudgingly and painfully, that those twenty-five percenters, in their own twisted way, admitted something that is true for nearly all of us modern girls. Maybe you can confidently say you'd take the trip to Stockholm for the Nobel over Tyra Banks calling you "fierce" on the catwalk, but how about this: The vast majority of young American women value their hairstylist over their accountant, according to the same Oxygen Media survey. Can you honestly say you don't fall into that category? Or this: Young American women who consider themselves attractive spend more time grooming themselves than watching or reading the news. Lots of us—dare I say, *most* of us—spend more time wielding a blow-dryer than a newspaper.*

This is what we've become, despite our educational achievements, despite our brainpower.

I once knew an overweight female judge who'd spent a lifetime trying, unsuccessfully, to lose weight. She told me she'd do anything, even *give up the bench*, if she could just be thin.

Breathe in, breathe out. Regain composure.

Here's the nagging problem. Perhaps it's not individual vanity and shallow-mindedness that led to those answers. Because I believe that these statistics are a reaction to something much bigger. What if they are rational responses to a culture that values a specific, high-maintenance feminine beauty ideal over female brains? Because we now require more—much more—tweezing and hot waxing and highlighting and contouring and Botoxing and body sculpting of our female bodies than we did a generation ago. And most of us do most of it most of the time because if we don't, we don't get the cultural goodies: the boyfriend, the job, the social status. Even though we have breathtaking equality compared to our mother's generation, we now jam our toes

*Howzabout listening to the news *while* grooming ourselves? In my family, the sounds of women getting ready always include audibly arguing with cable news.

into sky-high platforms our mothers would never have worn and, to our mothers' horror, submit our bodies to plastic surgeons because the hot girl *gets rewarded*. The 25 percent of young American women who'd rather keep their figures and win a modeling contest know something; they know there's a big brass ring for them merely for looking good, and brains—well, maybe there's a payoff there, and maybe not. But the hot girl generally gets what she wants. That's the promise our culture makes to girls: Be *hot* and you will *get*. In film, television, magazines, and online, there's one constant question to our girls: Are you hot or not? So it should not be surprising that when given a choice, they choose *hot*—because we still don't offer a big enough payoff for choosing brains.

How My Moroccan Muslim "Mama" Made Me Rethink My World

I am a travel junkie. If I don't leave the country at least a couple times a year, I get itchy. I travel when my otherwise frugal, responsible self can't afford it. I travel off the grid even though being unreachable by Blackberry threatens my career. I travel though my mother begs me not to go *there*. I travel alone when no one wants to go with me. I drag my bewildered boyfriend to the other side of the globe to join me, sleeping on the floor of mud huts and squatting over smelly holes in the floor.

I have to. Because when I leave the country and go to places where they don't speak my language, practice my religion, or eat my food; where their history leads them to an entirely different way of life, I return home like a space invader, looking at everything we do with fresh eyes. Before I traveled extensively, I assumed naively that how we do things is preordained, inexorable. The funny thing is that that's how everyone sees their culture's ways. Thus, a busload of Turkish villagers once pulled over so that the passengers could all get out and snap pictures of *me*, wildly, improbably, fantastically (to them) dressed in my faraway country's native garb of jeans, a T-shirt, and sneakers, and no head scarf. There I was, odd woman out, the locals looking at my uncovered head squeamishly, just as I gazed upon their different female attire, thinking, wondering, processing what it all means—especially those veils.

I've always been uncomfortable looking at veiled women. When I traveled to the Middle East, especially the rural areas, I saw many women wearing burkas that covered not only every strand of their hair but also every pore of their faces, save a tiny slit for their eyes. Even then, sometimes a screen covers the eyes.

I tried not to stare at these women with my unscreened eyes. Sometimes I'd take a mental snapshot, look away, and then mull it over. What must it be like to be draped in fabric all of one's life whenever outdoors? What did the world look like through the slits, the screens, the pinpoint holes in mesh fabric? Was it like walking around virtually blindfolded? Were they off-kilter from perpetual lack of peripheral vision? What facial expressions—disgust, resentment, acceptance, contentment—were hidden from view?

I've read Geraldine Brooks's *Nine Parts of Desire*, which lays out the fundamentalist Muslim thinking that women carry around all responsibility for human sexuality, that male sexuality is uncontrollable and impulsive, that males might fly into a sexual fury and rape a woman if he chances upon a glimpse of too much skin or tempting female hair. Thus, these men require total cover for postpubescent girls and women in fundamentalist areas. I've read *Infidel*, in which the brave Ayaan Hirsi Ali describes being taught this heavy responsibility for keeping violent male sexuality in check as a little girl, being compelled to wear the veil and the burka to preserve the family honor. I've read *The Trouble with Islam Today*, Irshad Manji's flames thrown at the heart of Islam's misogyny, which that veil, of course, symbolizes.[50]

Some Muslim women, I know, see the veil as *liberating* because it frees them from being sex objects. Men do not stare lasciviously at them on the streets as Western men do, they argue. They feel it brings them respect. And I have observed in Muslim countries that at least out on the public streets, the men harass only immodestly dressed Western women, not covered locals. But that still puts all the burden of sexual responsibility on women and blames the victims, women in immodest clothing, for sexual harassment or assault. I don't see liberation in draping myself in ten yards of fabric to hide myself from hungry wolves. Liberation is taming the wolves and holding men legally accountable for harassment and sexual assault. Full stop.

So when I traveled to Morocco, a secular Muslim country, in 2009, I knew I was going to struggle to come to terms with covered women. Unlike, say, residents of Iran or Saudi Arabia, Moroccan women are not legally required to cover. Yet most do. And I was there in July, where the temperature sizzles like the surface of Mercury. The men wore western clothing: knee length shorts or light cotton pants, T-shirts. But for women, the *de rigueur* outfit nearly all wore was a nightgown-like, long-sleeved, loose-fitting jelaba covering cotton pants, topped with a head scarf.

Few Moroccan women wear black burkas, and their faces are not concealed. Still, to my Western eyes, all this covering was a sign of women's oppression. They can tell me that they all want women to have equal rights in this country, that the king is a feminist, and that 10 percent of Morocco's Parliament is set aside for female representation.[51] All true and good. But as long as their culture dresses them in all this fabric and those head scarves, I wasn't buying it.

We left the explosive, teeming, wild ride of Marrakech and ascended the High Atlas Mountains to villages so remote that children stopped dead in their tracks to gawk at my uncovered blonde hair. Here we go again. I may as well have been an albino gorilla strolling down their main dirt road. We spent the night with a Berber farming family in a simple mud hut, folks who were generous enough to share their bowl of couscous and vegetables with us—utensils not an option.

After dinner it was time for entertainment. But as it turned out, *I* was the entertainment. The mother of the family asked with a twinkle in her eye if I would like to be dressed in their traditional garb.

Sure, I said. I'm up for anything, especially when I'm traveling.

My temporary Moroccan Mama soberly flattened my unruly hair (gone *au naturale* while traveling without hair appliances) back behind my ears and popped the scarf on me. Her practiced hands swiftly got every lock of hair into place. She tied it at the nape of my neck.

Next, she handed me the jelaba. I put it on.

Mama smiled mischievously. "Kohl?" she said, pulling out a worn little nub of an eye pencil.

As a television talk show host, I'd been under the tight control of a lovely makeup artist, Vincenza Carovillano, who, for years advised me—okay, ordered me—to use or not use certain face washes, moisturizers, and serums, and, above all, not to share unclean makeup with others. (I've had two eyelid surgeries to remove lumps from makeup infections—occupational hazard of wearing thick TV paint every day.)

I imagined Vincenza having heart palpitations at the thought of that kohl pencil rubbing on my eyelids.

But how could I say no to Moroccan Mama, who had welcomed us into her home, made us dinner, and was now grinning and giddy from dolling me up in her treasured garments? I could not.

Mama jabbed me, making a saw-tooth pattern in black above and below my eyes. I think it was supposed to be a straight line, but maybe her eyes weren't very good or her hands weren't, or something.

"Ha ha!" she said, clapping her hands, handing me a mirror.

Staring back at me was a moon-faced girl with zigzag eyeliner, a black-scarved flat head, and a billowy maxi dress.

"No one looks good in those outfits," my boyfriend, Braden, sympathized.

I sat down on the bed. The boyfriend and I hung out. We planned our hike for the next day. I forgot about what I was wearing. I flopped over sideways and propped myself on an elbow as we continued talking. I lazed, and our conversation meandered.

An hour later, it hit me: I was awfully *comfortable* in the jelaba and head scarf. Because my hair was neatly wrapped, my face was unencumbered by the wild mass my hair morphs into on vacation. It reminded me of the '70s, when I used to wear a red or blue bandana with my faded

Levis, my hair wild behind me, pulled smoothly off my face. It felt *nice*, like when I pull all my hair back into a ponytail so I can run or think.

The world's most comfortable hairdo took her all of about twenty seconds to complete: over the hair, soft cotton tied neatly behind the neck, bam! That's all there was to it. I felt *clean*. With my hair out of the way, my face could get down to business, in this case, reading the guidebook and maps.

And from the neck down, nothing was *poking* me, digging into my flesh or girl parts. I had no desire, as I normally do at the end of a day, to climb out of my clothes and into my pajamas. My jelaba was soft and loose and thin, less constricting even than my Western pajamas, which my culture allows me to wear only at night.

Then I thought about morning rituals. To get ready, it appears that Berber women brush their teeth, throw on the Moroccan bandana and nightgown, skip the makeup (maybe a swipe-swipe of the kohl, that's it, and if Mama's skills were typical, they'd do better skipping that step altogether), flat shoes, and presto! They are good to go.

What do we Western women do? The blow-dry, in my case, is a tedious half hour of time I'm never getting back, followed by curling iron or flat iron or both depending on the humidity, and then there are time-consuming skin toners, serums, astringents, moisturizers, SPFs, and makeup (foundation, concealer, blush, eye shadow, liner, mascara, brow pencil, lip pencil, lip gloss) all to achieve that natural look, right?

Stilettos, tight jeans, thong underwear, underwire push-up bras, constricting skirts, Spanx, shaving our legs and armpits, bikini waxes, eyelash curlers—all Western conceits it appears Berber women cheerfully live without.

Who is oppressed in this picture and who is liberated?

The politics and symbolism of the headscarf blinded me so much that I failed to see the easy breezy comfort of flowing soft cotton, unpainted faces, and no bad hair days. These women may not have the equal rights we do, despite sweeping 2004 reforms,[52] but when it comes to the daily drudgery of making our female selves presentable, damn, maybe they are onto something.

Their culture defines beauty differently, in a way that requires next to no wasted time or money, or pain or discomfort for women. And my Muslim Mama's husband looked at her with great love and affection, and judging by their large family, they had an exuberant sex life. He didn't seem to find her less attractive for the normal droops and wrinkles of middle age.

Okay, you're not going to see me sporting a black head wrap and caftan on my next *CBS News* appearance. As I perform my daily television rounds, I can't escape the TV makeup and hair coiffing. But off camera, I often wistfully invoke my Moroccan sisters in the High Atlas Mountains, draped and relaxed and never having to suck in their stomachs, with their fresh, naked faces turned toward the warm air.

From my Moroccan Mama, I learned that a headscarf is not a burka, that a makeup-free life can be liberating (I'm just going to forget about the kohl pencil), and that I participate in a cultural norm that is—let me say it here—ridiculous. We don't have to fall prey to what the fashion industry, cosmetic companies, and plastic surgeons sell us. There are whole countries and cultures where women do not do as we do, and their men, their friends, and their children think they are beautiful and love them just as they are. We could likewise choose not to participate in all the nonsense. Before we ridicule faraway cultures for wearing "oppressive" attire, let's walk a day in their women's soft, flat shoes. Let's consider *us* from *their* point of view: all that crap we do to ourselves daily? Entertaining, laughable, even, and, most important, *optional*.

The Tyranny of Hot

Hoy-day! What a sweep of vanity comes this way!
—William Shakespeare.

If vanity does not overthrow all our virtues, at least she makes them totter. —François de la Rochefoucauld

"Vanity" is an old-fashioned word we don't hear much anymore. I had to go back centuries for these quotes. There was a time when a woman was faulted for paying too much attention to her appearance. After all, her family duties, her town, her books were waiting! Step away from that mirror, you vain girl!

In twenty-first-century America, however, we are bombarded with the opposite message. Head to toe, we are negligent if we don't have coiffed, highlighted, fashionably styled hair, often with extensions; appropriate makeup; this season's clothing and jewelry; manicured fingers and toes; body hair waxed away; and muscles toned. But wait! Don't step away from that mirror yet! Are your brows properly tweezed—not too thin, not too thick? Elbows sloughed? Dry skin exfoliated? Teeth professionally whitened? Is that the right bra for that outfit? Is that a pimple coming? A wrinkle? Look closer. Hmm. Time for an over-the-counter product or a dermatologist appointment?

During the 2008 campaign Sarah Palin's makeup artist was paid more than her foreign policy expert. In fact, in October 2008 Palin's makeup artist was the highest paid person in the McCain-Palin campaign. Palin's hairdresser was number four.[53]

What a sweep of vanity comes this way.

When I mention this ratcheting-up of the female beauty ideal in our time and culture, men tell me that, hey, they too must be groomed adequately, shave, and replace the soup-stained tie when they want to attract a woman. What's good for the goose is good for the gander, right?

Hardly. Everything is different for women. Our bodies bleed and ache during menstruation and then gestate and nurse and bloat and suffer the hormonal changes of our pregnancies and babies and menopause. The current cultural ideal, at least in Southern California, Texas, and Florida, requires us to work those bodies into slender reeds and then surgically adorn them with giant boobs. All this is enough to make you want to yank out your hair.

But don't, because you'll need that hair to be hot—"hot" being an increasingly important and stringent requirement for American women of every age. Being "hot" demands, as Nora Ephron quipped,[54] hair and face freshly washed and pressed. Being "hot" demands a toned, pert body, earned at the gym or purchased at the surgeon's or both. Being "hot" demands time and money devoted to personal appearance on a level few men comprehend.

London Times writer Tad Safran tried to break it down in an article posted online in December 2007:

> An informal poll of my U.S. female friends revealed that they spend roughly $700 a month on what they consider standard obligatory beauty maintenance. That covers haircut, highlights, manicure, pedicure, waxing, tanning, make-up, facials, teeth whitening etc. They will spend a further $1,000 a month on physical conditioning such as military fitness, spinning sessions, Bikram yoga, Pilates, deep-tissue sports massage, personal training etc. On top of that, add the occasional spa day, a weeklong "bikini boot camp" in Mexico at the start of every summer and seasonal splurges on personal shoppers and clothing.[55]

Granted, that was just before the recession, and surely it was a sampling of his well-to-do friends. Still, most of us would not want to add up our beauty spending, honestly. We just don't want to know. And Safran, incidentally, wasn't *mocking* American women for profligate beauty spending or vanity but rather encouraging their British counterparts to follow suit. He did allow, though, that

> Their obsession with their looks, however, can be unattractive and can even turn unpleasant. My American friends wouldn't reveal to me, for example, their annual expenditure on Botox, liposuction, Restylane, tummy tucks, boob jobs, collagen fillers, chemical peels, or any other procedures that involve scalpels, anesthetics, lasers, and needles.
>
> When I asked if they dabbled in such areas, they just shook their wrinkle-free, tight-as-a-drum, shiny, expressionless faces.

That tight-as-a-drum, glowing look is, of course, utterly inconsistent with the life of a young mother who's been up all night (again) because the baby has croup, or the lawyer billing 2,500 hours a year, or the businesswoman taking her umpteenth flight to Dubuque for the sales conference—real women, in other words. And try getting out of a dermatologist's office for less than $1,000. The beauty ideal is untenably *expensive* for most women. And yet so many of us aspire to it, save for plastic surgery, or, hell, just put it on a credit card because looking smooth, polished, and toned is that important to our sense of self-worth and even our careers.

Studies show, and we all know it to be true, that hot women don't get only the *guy*, but they also get the *job*, better raises and promotions, and all kinds of daily cultural goodies. Psychologists call it the "halo effect." We seem to have a hardwired stereotype that beautiful people are *good* people. We desire nice things for them. We have some kind of illogical bias that beauty on the outside reflects beauty on the inside. We *expect* attractive people to succeed. Beautiful people get more positive feedback, spurring them on, and thus those expectations become self-fulfilling prophecies.[56]

I used to ride the subway to my Court TV morning show every day, without makeup, straggly haired, and blissful as my citymates ignored me and I read my newspaper on the 7 train. Around lunchtime, post show, dolled up by my professional TV hairdresser and makeup artist and then nattily dressed by our stylist, I'd go down the block for lunch, and the difference in the reaction was night and day. Suddenly, life was all smiles from the grumpy New Yorkers, with men and women opening doors for me, deli guys offering me freebies, strangers striking up conversations. That's the beauty bias. And surely that's why so many women obsess about looking good—because there is a big fat payoff. Anyone who pretends otherwise has her head in the sand.

So all those young American women who choose beauty over brains may, sadly, be a heck of a lot smarter than we give them credit for. They may be coolly, realistically assessing outcomes, determining that a hot bod will get them further than knowledge, that money is better spent on a boob job than job training. I want to tell them they are wrong—I want them to *be* wrong—but the fact is that ratcheting up their appearance *will* give them a significant boost in reaching their goals, whatever their goals may be. This is because we are deep in a double standard, and we women know in our bones that looking good has assumed such importance that many of us are slaves to it.

But we also have the choice to *think*, to really examine all these choices we are making, and to reject the double standard. We have the choice to lead our daughters and mothers away from the craziness. Because the consequences of the beauty double standard can be appalling.

The Ugly Side of Beauty

The fact is that we've gone significantly *backward* in one generation when it comes to what we are expected to do to our female selves before we go out in public. We could never have predicted a generation ago that American women would make such sweeping advances in education and careers while taking three steps back in our acceptance of our ridiculous new American beauty ideal. Feminists actually thought that *leg shaving* and high heels were oppressive in my lifetime, in the late 1960s. Hah! That ain't nothing compared to what we squeeze our carved-up, spray-tanned bods into now.

Though my mom's generation of feminists was often—and sometimes still is—called bra burners, that was all a bunch of hooey. As the myth-debunking website Snopes.com tells it,

> In the late 1960s, radical feminists began using rhetoric and protest tactics as a way of indelibly imprinting their message on the public. They staged dramatic and at times deliberately provocative demonstrations (which they called "zap actions") to focus attention on women's need for liberation. The first and most famous of these stagings occurred at the 1968 Miss America beauty pageant when a small group of women picketed the pageant with signs proclaiming "Let's Judge Ourselves as People." They crowned a live sheep and then dumped girdles, cosmetics, high-heeled shoes, and bras into a "freedom trash can" while the cameras clicked. There [were] no busty feminists stripping off bras in public to toss them

> onto bonfires, but the image of brassieres going into a trash can was captured in a memorable photo. A flippant print reference to bra-burning then melded itself into memories of this photo to create the false memory now so vivid in recall.[57]

Bra burning *didn't happen*, but the sentiment was there, to cast off those uncomfortable contraptions! (And who could blame them? Picture a '60s itchy, too-tight polyester cover-all bra, four hooks up the back, granny-style. Ugh. Chuck it!)

Suppose "bra burning" masks the real story: the dramatic rise of the cosmetics industry and our culture's requirement (upon pain of job loss, even) that women buy and wear copious amounts of the stuff.

In 1965 U.S. cosmetics retail sales totaled $2.9 billion. That's billion with a B, and in 1965 the average American house cost $14,200 and gas was 32 cents a gallon, so really, that was quite a lot of makeup. Notwithstanding some feminists' zap-actioning their makeup into the garbage and the popular "natural look" of that time, by 1976 Americans were buying nearly $6 billion of cosmetics annually. Some in the cosmetics business thought they might be topping out in the mid-1970s, as women were surely buying all the rouge and lipstick they needed at that point.[58]

The industry needn't have worried. Today American cosmetics companies lead the industry, selling us over $52 billion worth of the stuff annually.[59] That's a lot of concealer.

African American women alone spend $7.5 billion annually on beauty products, shelling out 80 percent more money on cosmetics and twice as much on skin care products than the general market, according to *Essence* magazine.[60] The theory is that women of color have to try more products to get something that works for them. Makeup artists say that darker skins are more complex, as shades can range from lighter to darker dark tones, with complex undertones. In other words, finding the right makeup is a bitch for African American women.*

*Still, they overcome. I can't help but notice that my African American girlfriends, every last one of them, are always done to the nines, crisply eye-lined, lips gleaming, skin glowing warmly. I often feel ratty and sallow in their presence.

In 2007 American women averaged $12,000 per year on cosmetics and salon purchases. (No wonder women have only 35 to 40 percent of men's retirement assets. We've spent it all on lip plumpers.) Stanford Law professor Deborah Rhode says in her book *The Beauty Bias: The Injustice of Appearance in Life and Law* that only 7 percent of our cosmetic dollars spent goes for the actual ingredients in the makeup. The rest is packaging and marketing.[61] Is the industry, behind our backs, laughing at our folly—all the way to the bank?

Yet we continue to spend, recession or not, because without daily makeup, as one study's participants put it, women "do not appear healthy, heterosexual or credible." The vast majority of American women wear makeup daily, nearly all starting as young teenagers. Fifteen to eighteen percent of American girls *under age twelve* now wear mascara, eyeliner, and lipstick regularly. Three-quarters of American girls under seventeen wear foundation. Neither my mother nor I wore any real makeup until well into our thirties. She'd go out fresh faced, pop the car visor down, slide on some lipstick in the little mirror's reflection, and be good to go. However, for most American women those days are gone. Our country buys far more cosmetics per woman than any other: 42 percent of the worldwide total. And of the top one hundred cosmetic companies in the world, thirty-four are American.[62]

The view that we're not really dressed without elaborate cosmetics is not preordained. French women (Juliette Binoche, Catherine Deneuve) are considered among the most beautiful in the world, and they wear significantly less makeup than their American counterparts. In a 2004 poll by the market research group Mintel, 64 percent of American women said they sometimes use foundation, compared with 47 percent of French women; 81 percent of Americans use lipstick compared with 70 percent of French women; and 59 percent of Americans use blusher, compared with 43 percent for the French.[63] Those French women who do wear makeup wear significantly less and more natural colors than Americans. French women want a natural glow. Invisible pores, polished skin—that's their beauty ideal. French women think made-up American women look like streetwalkers. They are shocked at how even young teenage girls here are so heavily painted. Their word for it: *vulgaire*.

Back here in the States, Shenoa Vild was a bleached-blonde twenty-nine-year-old California beach girl living in San Diego, California. She'd waitressed for five years at Trophy's, a sports bar with a surfboard bolted to the wall. She was a popular waitress with a good performance record who was asked to train new employees. The French would love her unpainted clear skin and big, white-toothed natural-girl smile.

One day new management came to the restaurant and decided that all their women employees should wear makeup. Shinoa said, "I always thought I looked silly wearing makeup" and chose to stick to her fresh-faced look. Plus it costs money and takes time, she pointed out. She was promptly sacked.[64] (And the law is on the restaurant's side, creeps though they are, because American employers can fire for any reason they like, absent a contract or discrimination based on race, sex, age, disability or religion. Courts have held that different appearance standards for male and female employees do not constitute sex discrimination. Go figure.)

Requiring women to cover their faces in public, at least with paint, is now an American cultural norm.

I wonder what makeup exactly would have been required for Shenoa to keep that waitress job. Eye primer, or just eye shadow? Lash extenders, or just mascara? Lip pencil plus gloss, lipstick, contouring, bronzer, blush—some or all? Brow highlighter? Because there's no end to it. I know of what I speak here. When a makeup artist arrives to paint me for a TV appearance, and I'm the only person she's doing that day, she wheels in a suitcase the size of a dorm room refrigerator filled with lacquers, paints, and potions. Seeing everything that is required is daunting.

Remember the great film moment when Thelma, or was it Louise, celebrated her exhilarating new lawlessness by tossing her lipstick out of the convertible? Lipstick, hah! That's amateur hour compared to what American women undergo to present a socially acceptable appearance now.

In the twenty-first century, women spend significantly more time and money on their hyper-feminine appearance than they did a generation ago. Fair women get tanned and dark women get their skin bleached—which, if you think about it, is nuts. Plastic surgery is considered basic good grooming in upscale circles. I recently attended an elegant dinner in an upscale Chicago restaurant with a dozen high-powered couples. All of the women (except me) were dripping in diamonds, gold, and platinum. I wondered how our hostess could lift her hand under the tangerine-sized diamond ring she bore. But there was something else. All of the women had smooth, shiny faces, gravity-defying breasts, and small noses. I find this to be universally true in affluent circles. The men age, gray, and soften while the women get taut and frozen. This is in addition to perfectly processed, cut, highlighted, blow-dried, and flat-ironed or curling-ironed hair along with makeup that often includes applying false eyelashes daily, threading their eyebrows, and waxing their bikini lines weekly. The French manicures they all sported look great, sure, but they probably rule out any activities that connect with the human hand, like cooking, arts and crafts with the kids, gardening, playing the guitar, swimming, or hot baths.

We are educated and smart and earn our own way, thank you very much, but many agree with an alpha girl who scored a perfect 2400 on her SAT and yet still thinks "it is more important to be hot than smart." "Effortlessly hot," she added.[65] And, oh, the costs we pay for that look.

From adolescence to the grave, the quest to be hot never ends. Until our last breath, many of us slave away at the time-consuming drudgery of hair and skin maintenance. As Nora Ephron says, "I sometimes think that not having to worry about your hair anymore is the secret upside of death."[66]

As a television personality, I spend a fair amount of time keeping up with all this nonsense, including hair coloring, manicures, dermatologist visits—and I hate it. In my law practice, I generally sport a simple skirt and blouse, five-minute makeup, and a ponytail. But on the air, I can't ignore that I work in a visual medium and that looking even-toned and shiny-haired is a part of it. A big part. And look, I'm not an actress. I am playing myself on TV, though a much more dolled-up, smooth-skinned, blonde-rooted, false-eyelashed, and hair-sprayed version of myself. In makeup rooms at TV studios, female on-air types often bemoan the time we, but not our male counterparts, sit for hair and makeup daily. When I cohosted my Court TV show, I came in *an hour earlier* than my male cohost, every damn day, to sit for hair and makeup. This is typical in my business. Female call times are significantly earlier than male call times. That's hundreds of hours a year we're not getting back, and it doesn't include all the hours of appointments and self-care outside the makeup room.

It's no different for women who make a living off air. How many of us envy our husbands, kicking back and watching the game or reading a magazine as we prep to go out? They hit the snooze button in the morning while we leap out of bed, knowing we need to put in the time in the bathroom once again in order to be socially presentable?

Our culture is saturated with impossible beauty ideals. Popular plastic surgery shows like *The Swan*, *Extreme Makeover*, *Dr. 90210*, and *Nip/Tuck* show tantalizing, seemingly magical transformations. On E!'s *Bridalplasty*, women compete for pre-wedding day nose jobs, breast implants, and liposuction because, according to the show's publicist, "only perfection will do."[67] In an era when tens of millions of Americans struggle for access to basic health care, the fastest growing medical specialty is cosmetic surgery. Nonessential cosmetic procedures are up 400 percent in the last decade. Women who can't afford or opt out of wrinkle fillers like collagen and Restylane, who reject eye lifts or face lifts or chemical peels are increasingly seen as "letting themselves go." Yet women with noticeable plastic surgery, lips swollen from injections or with frozen faces, are ridiculed as "trying too hard."

We rarely hear about the risks. According to the National Clearinghouse of Plastic Surgery Statistics, the most common cosmetic surgery in the United States is breast augmentation, which has gone up 36 percent each year since 2000. However, 40 percent of breast augmentations result in complications within three years.[68] Model Anna Nicole Smith suffered chronic lifelong pain from her breast enlargement surgery and repeated repair surgeries, pain that left her addicted to prescription medications that ultimately claimed her life at age thirty-nine.[69] The Food and Drug Administration warns that most—most!—women with breast implants will experience painful ruptures within a decade, requiring further surgery. Pain, contracture, displaced implants, infection, or suspected ruptures motivate the majority of women who undergo follow-up breast implant surgeries. For example, singer Amy Winehouse had breast augmentation surgery in October 2009. One month later she was hospitalized with complications from the surgery. In April 2010, in "agony" from the extreme breast pain, she was rushed to the hospital again. And she's not a model or an actress. What do breasts have to do with singing?

A year after her headline-grabbing multiple plastic surgeries, Heidi Montag described plastic surgery as "dangerous" and voiced her regrets, including the excruciating postsurgical pain, and the strain on her relationships with her husband and mother, who'd both opposed the surgeries. "I wish I could jump into a time machine and take it all back," she says. She feels "stuck" with her cartoonish breasts but doesn't want to go under the knife again for a breast reduction.[70]

The female breast, in its natural state, has two glorious functions: to deliver sexual pleasure to its owner and nutrition to an infant. Breast implants significantly undercut both of these functions. From 10 to 18 percent of implant patients permanently lose nipple sensation.[71] And women with implants are three times as likely to have an inadequate milk supply, called lactation insufficiency, for their babies.[72] Those babies, in turn, lose all of the myriad benefits of mother's milk.

Mammograms, which screen for cancerous growths, can cause breast implants to rupture, and breast implants make cancer detection more difficult during mammograms, according to the FDA. In one study, 55 percent of breast tumors were missed in women with breast implants, compared to 33 percent of tumors missed in women without implants.[73] Women with breast implants are three times more likely to die from respiratory tract cancer, two to three times more likely to die from brain cancer, and four to five times more likely to die from suicide than the comparison group, according to the National Cancer Institute (part of our government's National Institutes of Health).[74]

Other increasingly common cosmetic surgery procedures cause women's suffering, even death. Best-selling *First Wives Club* author Olivia Goldsmith went into a coma and died during a chin tuck in 2004, as did another woman undergoing a cosmetic facial procedure in the same Manhattan hospital shortly thereafter. Rapper Kanye West's mother died from complications of cosmetic surgery in 2007. In December 2009 a former Miss Argentina, only thirty-seven years old and the mother of seven-year-old twins, died from complications following elective surgery on her buttocks.[75]

In a study reported in *Plastic Reconstructive Surgery* evaluating the safety of office surgical facilities, one death occurred for every 58,810 cosmetic surgical procedures in accredited facilities with board-certified surgeons. And death rates are even higher without those safeguards. One and a half million cosmetic surgical procedures occur annually in the United States, even during the recession. And serious complications, like respiratory and heart problems or internal bleeding, occur in 1 in 299 cases.[76]

Women are literally dying to be beautiful.

Ignoring known skin cancer risks, twenty-eight million Americans, mostly women, annually lie in tanning beds. In 2009 the World Health Organization bluntly pronounced tanning beds "carcinogenic to humans" and placed them in the agency's highest cancer-risk category, which includes radon gas, plutonium, and radium.[77]

Risking neurological damage and cancer, women of color slather on skin bleachers. Side effects include burning, liver damage, and kidney failure. The Pink Cheeks Salon in Los Angeles specializes in—brace yourself—*anal bleaching*, using hydroquinone, a bleaching product banned in Europe as carcinogenic but perfectly legal for use in the United States. Vaginal and nipple bleaching are also gaining traction here.[78]

Women account for 80 percent of all foot surgery, largely because of our culture's insistence that high heels are sexy.[79] High heels almost entirely preclude one of life's greatest pleasures: walking. I am always amazed when my friends, high-powered feminist achievers, can't stroll around the block with me after dinner because they have chosen to be hobbled by designer shoes. In fact, the newest hot trend in foot surgery is removal of part of women's toes so that they can fit into narrow, high-end stilettos.[80]

After all the implants, bleaching, tanning, slicing, and dicing, is our happiness and self-esteem lifted, at least? Because that's the number one reason women give for cosmetic surgery. Sad to say, but there's only a short-term boost, and it evaporates quickly. As Rhode says,

> Investments in appearance often do not yield enduring satisfaction. Once their novelty wears off, or one "problem" seems fixed, new forms of self-expression or self-improvement seem necessary. Social scientists refer to this as a "hedonic treadmill." The more one has, the more one needs to have.[81]

From our Botoxed foreheads to our silicon-crammed breasts to our pinched, sliced-up feet, we are lining up for pain and suffering to a degree that is completely out of whack with our newfound equality in education and employment. Putting on a pretty blouse or some eye shadow as a matter of self-expression or even self-love is one thing; volunteering for increased cancer risks or paying thousands of dollars for, say, breast implants, when the most likely outcome is pain and future repair surgery, with its attendant costs and health dangers, is entirely another.

The time, the money, the serious risks to our health and even our babies' health—we have lost our balance. Without a whimper, we have submitted to rigorous, demeaning cultural demands that insist that we constantly fix nonproblems to line the pockets of enormous cosmetic companies as well as plastic surgeons who opt out of using their medical training to help sick people. To what extent do we even *think* about what we are sacrificing in order to look hot? And as each of us nips, tucks, smoothes, and augments, we create social pressure on our friends to do the same, lest they be accused of—gasp!—"letting themselves go."

I'm not exhorting you to give it *all* up. How can I, when I don't go anywhere important without succumbing to some of these beauty rituals myself? But I am suggesting we *think* about how extreme we've become, how unbalanced.

Think about the huge number of wasted hours we as a group spend staring at ourselves in the mirror when there are so many other worthy issues begging us to look out at them for few minutes.

Think about the cost, when there are so many other worthy places we could send a few dollars—or a few hundred or a few thousand.

Think about how women in other cultures, like France and Morocco, have their own beauty norms that reject our excesses and send their women confidently out into the world feeling vibrant and alive.

Think about *recalibration*, adjusting our time and money to true priorities rather than unthinkingly shuffling along with what the multibillion-dollar makeup and cosmetic surgery industries want from us.

Because as we self-obsess, our communities and our world cry out for our attention.

3

The Fallout

FAILURE TO *think* has consequences big and small. Our inadequate educations, our lack of interest in reading, our distraction by tabloid media, our obsessive attention to high-maintenance beauty regimens, our skewed priorities in where we choose to focus our minds all have profound consequences not only for our own emotional and physical health but literally, for the fate of our families, our towns, our country, and our world. A tuned-out populace means that the most important issues of the day pass us by. While we're reading "Who Wore It Better," trying out new lash extenders, and mopping the kitchen floor yet again, our leaders, unchecked and unwatched by a distracted populace, allow the wrong country to be bombed, the extreme poor of the world to perish, genocides to ravage on, and the planet to face the worst environmental catastrophe in human history.

To consider what we don't know because we choose to look at fluff and nonsense instead of what matters is heartbreaking. To consider what we as global citizens are not doing because we lack even rudimentary awareness of the crises occurring right now, during our lifetimes, is even more disturbing. As a result, those brave few who do devote their lives to combating the world's tragedies go it alone, without the groundswell of focused support we should be giving them.

I grew up a nice Jewish girl—going to temple, learning a little Hebrew, saying a few prayers. I opted out of my bat mitzvah, but in college I fell in with a Hillel group and felt more connected to and inspired by my ancient, wise religion. We had weekly Shabbat dinners, and one of my friends, a rabbi in training, led us in discussions about the great political issues of the day. Pass the challah!

During the somber times, at Passover and during the occasional sermon, we would remember the Holocaust. The sobering bigness of the murder of six million Jews and five million others was impossible to fully grasp. The pure evil of the Nazis forced us to grapple with the depths and horrors that humans are capable of. And these discussions and memories always ended with the simple two-word mantra that Jews worldwide chant:

Never again.

Never again!

Non-Jews say it too at Holocaust remembrances. Frankly, doing so is the only way to function after looking at photos of concentration camp victims. That burning anger has to turn to something productive, and so, going forward, we all vow, *never again*. As concerned citizens of the world, we will never allow another holocaust to take place on earth. We will speak out, rise up, and never allow such a horror again. Not on our watch! Never again!

But we don't really mean it.

Here's a chilling example. Do you know the answers to these questions?

1. How many genocides have happened on our planet since the Holocaust?
    a. one
    b. two
    c. three
    d. five

2. What has our country, the United States, done to stop them?
    a. massive military intervention

b. intensive diplomatic efforts
c. assumed moral leadership, our president speaking out and pressuring for change
d. next to nothing

Journalist Samantha Power spent three years, from 1993 to 1996, covering the grisly massacres in Bosnia and Srebrenica, and she became increasingly frustrated with how little the United States was willing to do to counteract the genocide occurring there. After an extraordinary amount of research spanning the next decade, she discovered a pattern. "The United States had never in its history intervened to stop genocide and had in fact rarely even made a point of condemning it as it occurred," she writes in her compelling, Pulitzer-Prize winning book, *"A Problem from Hell": America and the Age of Genocide.*[1] Power explains that U.S. leaders were aware of the horrors as they were occurring against Armenians, Jews, Cambodians, Iraqi Kurds, Rwandan Tutsis, and Bosnians during the past century, providing detailed evidence to back up her claims.

The correct answer to number 1 is d (five). Since the 1970s innocent people have been slaughtered in genocides in Cambodia, northern Iraq, Rwanda, Bosnia, and Darfur. And as Power painstakingly details, our government knew about each one of these crises and failed to act, other than in Bosnia, when we were part of NATO's military intervention in response to attacks on UN "safe areas." The correct answer to number 2 above is also d. We did next to nothing. We ignored genocide.

Based on declassified information, private papers, and interviews with more than three hundred American policymakers, Power concludes that a lack of political will was the most significant factor for our failure to intervene during the Cambodian genocide as well as the ensuing genocides against Kurds in northern Iraq, against Tutsis in Rwanda, and against Bosnian Muslims. (Her book was written before the twenty-first-century slaughter of ethnic Africans in Darfur, Sudan.) The vast majority of our elected politicians disregarded the issue because we, the people, did too. Power says that "no U.S. president has ever suffered politically for his indifference to its occurrence. It is thus no coincidence that genocide rages on."[2] And some politicians who did try to speak out actually suffered negative repercussions and were voted out of office for focusing on people half a globe away rather than on their own constituencies.

This is the consequence of a populace that's not thinking, that has laserlike focus on the sex lives of celebrities but only the dimmest understanding of the people beyond our borders. We say "never again," but our elected officials know we don't mean it, and thus they fail to take any meaningful actions, even to stop mass killings. For example, our politicians knew there would be no consequences, no outcry from their electorate when they directed UN peacekeepers to leave Rwanda while blood was streaming in the streets or when they refused even to use satellite technology to block Rwandan radio broadcasts inciting and directing mass murder. At the time, President Bill Clinton would not even call the ongoing slaughter of the Tutsi people "genocide," as that would have triggered an obligation to act under international law. Senator Paul Simon said later, "If every member of the House and Senate had received 100 letters from people back home saying we have to do something about Rwanda, when the crisis was first developing, then I think the response would have been different."[3]

One hundred letters.

Later, in 2005 former president Bill Clinton visited a genocide memorial in Rwanda's capital, Kigali. He expressed regret for his "personal failure" to take action to stop the killing in 1994.[4] More than eight hundred thousand men, women, and children were slaughtered.

Most Americans, if asked about Bill Clinton's major shortcoming as president, would probably name the Monica Lewinsky sex scandal that nearly caused his impeachment. Lurid personal failings of our leaders grab and hold our attention, as that one did for over a year of breathless front-page reporting, including a twenty-one-day Senate trial in 1999.

Our leaders' failure to stop the extermination of a people does not grab and hold our attention and is not even considered a scandal. Our leaders have no fear of losing their jobs for failing to act. As murderous despots rage and our officials remain silent, cable news does not buzz with outrage. Citizens do not swarm the capital, demanding swift action. Office workers do not dissect the details at water coolers. Talk shows do not run hand-wringing segments on how to explain ongoing genocide to our children. They don't have to, because there is no risk children will overhear public discussion about it. There is no public discussion.

Though we all agree genocide is the nadir of human evil and though many of us earnestly pledge that we will never again allow it on our planet, we permit ourselves to become distracted, so we ignore it. Thus, we sit back and refuse to use our military, the strongest in the world; our diplomatic corps; our technology; even our influence in the United Nations to make a difference when it is happening. We don't dwell on it or even pay much attention to it. And machetes butcher men, women, and children.

This is the human price of our distraction.

Hot Air

Our indifference to matters of substance is wreaking havoc not only on human inhabitants but also on our planet itself. Nowhere is the cost of our distraction more alarming than in our inattention to climate change, about which there is overwhelming scientific consensus that immediate action must be taken to avert what is shaping up to be the biggest humanitarian and ecological crisis in human history. Nevertheless, low poll numbers show that the majority of Americans haven't looked at the scientific facts, are easily duped, or willingly enter a state of denial to avoid the whole topic.

Only 34 percent of Americans think climate change is a serious enough problem that immediate, drastic action should be taken, according to Gallup pollsters. A full 13 percent think we should just keep on a-doing what we're doing and not make any changes whatsoever to protect our environment. Furthermore, there is a widespread belief in the United States that "global warming" may be junk science or at least that some scientists believe in it and some don't, so we laypeople can't be expected to sort it out.

These beliefs fly in the face of the evidence. Virtually all reputable, mainstream scientific organizations are exhorting us to wake up and get moving against climate change (the preferred term).

First, the official position of the U.S. government, as voiced through its own scientific agencies, is that climate change is real, human caused, and a significant threat to our planet's future. Our own Environmental Protection Agency's official 2010 report, "Climate Change Indicators in the United States," sounds the call:

> Over the last several decades, evidence of human influences on climate change has become increasingly clear and compelling. There is indisputable evidence that human activities such as electricity production and transportation are adding to the concentrations of greenhouse gases that are already naturally present in the atmosphere. These heat-trapping gases are now at record-high levels in the atmosphere compared with the recent and distant past.
>
> Warming of the climate system is well documented, evident from increases in global average air and ocean temperatures, widespread melting of snow and ice, and rising global average sea level. The buildup of greenhouse gases in the atmosphere is very likely the cause of most of the recent observed increase in average temperatures, and contributes to other climate changes.[5]

On the official website of the U.S. National Aeronautic and Space Administration, www.climate.nasa.gov, there are reams of facts, graphs, and charts sounding the alarm about climate change. NASA's graphs document the steep rise in carbon dioxide in our atmosphere since 1950 and the exponential rise in the last ten years. You can look at remarkable, disturbing photos and videos of the actual growing hole in the ozone over Antarctica and the rising sea levels, increasing rapidly since the 1990s. To quiet doubters, NASA has set up, on its official climate change site under "evidence," a web page entitled "Climate Change: How Do We Know?" Here, NASA states, "Scientific evidence for the warming of the climate system is unequivocal" and then meticulously details the rise in sea levels, the rapid rise in temperatures over the last decade, warming oceans, shrinking ice sheets, declining Arctic sea ice, retreats of glaciers, the increase in extreme warm weather events along with the decrease in extreme cold weather events, and an increase in ocean acidification.[6]

Pick a mainstream, reputable scientific organization at random and you'll get the same conclusion. The National Oceanic and Atmospheric Administration (NOAA) says, "Human activity has been increasing the concentration of greenhouse gases in the atmosphere," concluding categorically that "there is no scientific debate on this point."[7] The NOAA's National Climactic Data center documents that 2010 was the hottest year since record keeping began in 1880.

The venerable National Geographic Society, one of the oldest and largest nonprofit scientific and educational institutions in the world, warns on its website that warming has already raised oceans levels four to eight inches, and if Greenland's massive ice sheet were to melt, which is foreseeable if present trends continue unabated, "The consequences would be catastrophic," said Jonathan Overpeck, director of the Institute for the Study of Planet Earth at the University of Arizona in Tucson. "Even with a small sea level rise, *we're going to destroy whole nations and their cultures that have existed for thousands of years*." [8]

National Geographic continues,

> A recent Nature study suggested that Greenland's ice sheet will begin to melt if the temperature there rises by 3 degrees Celsius (5.4 degrees Fahrenheit). That is something many scientists think is likely to happen in another hundred years.
>
> The complete melting of Greenland would raise sea levels by seven meters (twenty-three feet). But even a partial melting would cause a one-meter (three-foot) rise. Such a rise would have a devastating impact on

> low-lying island countries, such as the Indian Ocean's Maldives, which would be entirely submerged.
>
> Densely populated areas like the Nile Delta and parts of Bangladesh would become uninhabitable, potentially driving hundreds of millions of people from their land.
>
> A one-meter sea level rise would wreak particular havoc on the Gulf Coast and eastern seaboard of the United States.[9]

"No one will be free from this," said Overpeck, whose maps show that every U.S. East Coast city from Boston to Miami would be swamped. A one-meter sea rise in New Orleans, Overpeck said, would mean "no more Mardi Gras."

To put it mildly. A one-meter sea rise in New Orleans would make Hurricane Katrina look like a light drizzle.

Low-lying and impoverished Asian coastal cities such as Dhaka, Manila, and Jakarta (which has already experienced massive flooding from climate change) could be wiped out from a rise in sea levels. Tokyo, London, and New York City could be underwater within a century.[10]

Much of the rest of the world understands that climate change is already underway. On a 2009 trip to the Pacific islands of Fiji, I learned that rising sea levels have already caused entire villages to relocate. Under current projections, the sea will swallow whole nearby Tuvulu, consisting of nine low-lying atolls, in less than fifty years. Ben Namakin, an environmentalist and native of nearby Kiribati, says that in his homeland, saltwater intrusion is already ruining taro patches and spoiling well water. Houses are being flooded, coastlines are receding, and a causeway whose beauty he had appreciated since he was a child has collapsed. And as in many such Pacific island nations, there is little higher, habitable land for people to move to.[11]

Their countries are being slowly but surely annihilated. If I were a South Pacific islander encountering vacationing Americans, I'd want to tackle us to the ground and pummel some sense into our thick skulls with coconuts. That's because we are 5 percent of the world's population, yet we emit 20 percent of the world's carbon dioxide emissions, and the world knows it. Instead, these gracious people offered me warm smiles, tropical fruit juice, and garlands of fragrant frangipani everywhere I went. A village chief politely explained that the sea rise threatened the homes of many of the families in his community, as I gazed out at surf crashing a stone's throw from their huts, imagining engulfment. Every last one of these islanders understands that climate change is real and a direct threat to their survival. They may send their children to school in open-air rooms with thatched roofs, but they are all conversant in the earth science that can wipe them out. Ignorance is not an option.

The photos, charts, and graphs on NASA's website back up the islanders' claims. Climate change is already upon us. A recent UNICEF Report warns that climate change is already reducing the quality of the lives of the world's most vulnerable children by reducing access to clean water and food supplies, particularly in Africa and Asia.[12]

Ninety-one-year-old international children's aid organization, Save the Children, reports even more starkly that children are *already dying* from the effects of climate change. Save the Children estimates that a quarter of a million children now die annually due to the effects of climate change, and unless we act swiftly, that number will rise to 400,000 by 2030. By that year, it estimates, 175 million children per year will suffer the consequences of natural disasters such as cyclones, droughts, and floods; 900 million children will be affected by water shortages, and 160 million more will be at risk of malaria, one of the world's biggest killers of children under five. Its report, "Feeling the Heat," bluntly says that climate change is the biggest global health threat to children in the twenty-first century.[13]

Despite the convergence of so many credible scientific, educational, and relief organizations begging us to wake up to the urgent reality of climate change, still there are dissenters. Turn on a cable news discussion about it and you'll find two scientists bickering about whether it's real, whether it's human caused, whether it's worthy of our concern. I believe that is why so many Americans still don't believe—

because it's falsely presented as a topic on which reasonable minds can differ.

So, I have an idea. Let's think. Think big. How about we convene all the world's leading scientists? Get me the hot shots from every relevant discipline and force them to get together, hash it all out, and issue one gigantic report that they all agree on. And if they say climate change is real, how serious is it? We need to know. I want the top scientific minds from all over the world. Ladies and gentlemen, be you earth scientists, oceanographers, biologists, botanists, geophysicists, climatologists, what have you—get in a room, butt heads, review all the scientific papers, work it out, and report back to us.

Pretty great idea, right?

Except that it's already happened. Four times since 1990, actually, most recently in 2007. For two decades the United Nations has convened all the leading international experts—2,500 of them—to study the issue and report back. They reviewed thousands of peer-reviewed studies and articles across every relevant discipline.

They concluded that not only is the warming of our planet clear and unequivocal but also that it is human caused and it is upon us.

The UN Panel, the Intergovernmental Panel on Climate Change, the largest group of scientists of this caliber ever assembled in human history, then went on to win the 2007 Nobel Peace Prize, together with former Vice President Al Gore, whose film, *An Inconvenient Truth*, got out the word that climate change is real and a serious threat to our children and grandchildren.

Over one hundred world governments, including the United States, then endorsed the IPCC's scientific findings, findings no government wants to hear because the only implication is that we have to make swift, radical policy changes, which no elected leader wants to have to make, like capping emissions and investing in alternative energy—changes that evoke a hue and cry from the electorate and from some of the richest industries on earth, such as oil companies. Nevertheless, even Saudi Arabia, the world's largest oil exporter, endorsed the IPCC's findings. So did China and India, which, together with the United

States, are the world's largest emitters of greenhouse gases.[14] In the law we'd call this an "admission against interest," that is, highly credible evidence because the perpetrator is admitting to the crime.

In our country not only did presidential candidates Barack Obama and Hillary Clinton confirm that climate change is scientifically real, that it poses a major threat to our children and grandchildren, and that significant steps, such as reduced emission standards, must be taken, but so did George W. Bush and John McCain. So did every other political leader with a pulse.[15]

There is no respected national or international scientific body that denies the reality of climate change. Instead, the national science academies of eleven countries—including the United States, all the G8 countries, and China, India, and Brazil—jointly declared that "there is now strong evidence that significant global warming is occurring" and that "it is likely that most of the warming in recent decades can be attributed to human activities." The statement urged the G8 countries to "identify cost-effective steps that can be taken now to contribute to substantial and long-term reductions in net global greenhouse gas emissions."[16]

Despite all this, there is a profound disconnect between what Americans believe and what our scientific experts and leaders from both parties, along with the international community, know to be true. Americans do not regard climate change as a top-tier issue, if they believe in it at all. Discouragingly, as the scientific consensus has intensified each year, as prestigious organizations have warned in increasingly dire language of the need for action, Americans have grown *less* interested in the issue. According to Pew, in 2007, the first year it asked Americans whether global warming should be a top domestic priority for the president and Congress, 38 percent agreed. That year, out of a list of twenty possible legislative priorities, such as "dealing with moral breakdown" or "reducing middle class taxes," "dealing with global warming" was ranked third to last. In 2008 the number of Americans who believed climate change should be a top priority dropped to 35 percent; in 2009 just 30 percent of Americans believed climate change should be a top priority. In its 2010 list only 28 percent rated it a top priority. Americans have now ranked climate change *dead last* on the priority list for each of the last three years.[17]

A survey by the Pew Global Attitudes Project showed that the public's relatively low level of concern about global warming sets the United States apart from other countries. That survey found that only 19 percent of Americans who had heard of global warming expressed a great deal of personal concern about the issue. Among the fifteen countries surveyed, only the Chinese expressed a comparably low level of concern, at 20 percent. Nearly half of Americans had "little or no concern," significantly more apathy than any other country.[18]

I am not a scientist, but, like you, I can evaluate facts, read reports, analyze photos and videos, and appreciate which side clearly has the better part of this wholly lopsided "debate." The IPCC, one hundred world governments, the leaders of both our Democratic and Republican parties, the EPA, NASA, and NOAA—come on, folks. I can't think of any other "controversial" issue that has as many of the world's sentient beings on the same side as this one does. I am not predisposed to be an activist on this type of issue. To be honest with you, what I am really passionate about is combating genocide and global poverty, promoting girls' education and women's rights in the third world, and stopping animal cruelty. These are "my" issues. But I realized long ago that if entire coastal cities are annihilated, if our children's generation faces one billion global refugees and frequent extreme weather events and natural disasters around the globe, then all other issues become secondary. If our planet becomes increasingly uninhabitable, we are, literally, cooked. So it's my—our—responsibility to learn about this global threat and, at a minimum, speak out about it and vote for leaders who have the guts to take action on it.

And what is the number one cause of climate change? Again, astonishingly, most of us don't know. In a 2006 report that was met with radio silence from the American media, the UN Food and Agriculture Organization concluded that worldwide livestock farming has that distinction—more than all the cars, trains, planes, and boats in the world.

Former lead environmental adviser to the World Bank Group Robert Goodland thoroughly analyzed all aspects of the raising of cows, pigs, and chickens, and he concluded that animal production causes a whopping 51 percent of global greenhouse gases. This is because, first, animals raised for slaughter take up a lot of space—nearly one-third of the earth's landmass. For example, the FAO estimates that 70 percent of former forest cover in Latin America has been converted for grazing. All those bulldozed rain forests heat the planet because trees absorb carbon dioxide while they're alive. When we cut or burn them down, we decrease this absorption and, therefore, more greenhouse gas is released back into the atmosphere. Second, what comes out of the animals is toxic: the hundreds of billions of cows, pigs, and chickens the world raises for slaughter exhale over eight million tons of carbon dioxide. The manure of the world's 1.5 billion cows releases nitrous oxide, with 296 times the warming effect of carbon dioxide, and methane gas emitted from cows has twenty-three times the warming impact of carbon dioxide. Reducing methane emissions will start to show results in slowing climate change within a decade, not a century, as is the case for carbon dioxide, which lingers in the atmosphere. Thus, the quickest and most effective way to reduce greenhouse gases is to reduce animal consumption, thereby reducing the worldwide livestock count, and then reforest grazing lands. Goodland also reminds us that in doing so we'd also reduce greenhouse gases from carbon-intensive treatment of the millions of zoonotic illnesses, like swine flu, and chronic degenerative illnesses, like heart disease, cancer, diabetes, and hypertension, caused by eating animals. Therefore, animal consumption's contribution to climate change is even higher when we factor in the construction and operation of medical facilities and pharmaceutical companies used to treat these illnesses.[19]

As this book went to print, our leaders, facing an electorate uninterested in this issue, sat on their hands. In the summer of 2010 a comprehensive climate change bill died in the Senate, and President Obama signaled an intent to go after the issue "piecemeal" in 2011. Any American politician who makes climate change a priority seriously jeopardizes his or her reelection prospects.

If we were *thinking*, we would be avidly following the science, listening to the world's climatologists, reading their reports, regularly checking their websites and analyzing the data. While scientists skirmish around the edges—how fast will the ice caps melt, which cities will be struck first, how much will temperatures rise in twenty or thirty years—we wouldn't lose sight of the main point: that climate change is real, urgent, and upon us now. If we were *thinking*, we'd be scrutinizing candidates' positions on this issue, learning which politicians had the guts to take meaningful action to address the root causes of this threat to our climate—and support them. We'd pester our elected officials to get moving and hound them when trivialities distracted them. We'd analyze our own carbon footprint, cut down on habits that increase greenhouse gases, and participate in grassroots efforts for change.

If we were *thinking*, we wouldn't let our media get away with phony debates that imply that there is a genuine scientific disagreement on the basic merits of this issue—because there is not. We'd demand that television, radio, print, and Internet news cover this issue relentlessly and drop this nonsense about Tiger and Paris and Lindsay.

If the news media answered to a thinking audience, climate change would be the top story every day, trumpeted at the start of every newscast, above the fold in every paper, a flashing banner atop every web page:

> ANOTHER DAY PASSES WITHOUT FIRST WORLD COUNTRIES DOING A DAMN THING TO SLOW DOWN THE IMPENDING WORST ENVIRONMENTAL AND HUMANITARIAN CRISIS IN HUMAN HISTORY THEY ARE CAUSING. TICK TOCK, PEOPLE.

Our mainstream media doesn't do this, not by a long shot, though individual reporters and editors and programmers know we should. So I must ask the question: Are we ignorant and apathetic because of our media? Is this all the fault of our news outlets?

The only thing I can do is tackle this issue head on. For me, the media isn't "them" but rather "us." I've been a full-time contributor to the mainstream media for the last decade, reporting and analyzing and anchoring on Court TV, ABC, CBS, CNN, and others daily. I have talked on air about Tiger and Lindsay and Paris more than I care to think about.

It's a fair question. Is an ignorant public our fault? Is it my fault?

Is the Media Making Us Stupid?

On September 11, 2001, I was living in New York City, a new anchorwoman at Court TV. My family and I had moved to Manhattan from Los Angeles a few months beforehand so I could take the job. That day was my kids' first day of school. I walked them to school on that gorgeous, clear, sky-blue morning. At home, I prepared for work with the *Today Show* on.

One plane, then two.

I ran back to my kids' school, about five miles north of the World Trade Center. They are fine, I was told. All the kids are fine. They don't know what happened. We'll keep them here and have a normal school day.

I ran back home. I knew I would be needed to go on the air. Because I lived in Manhattan, I could get to our midtown studios. Other anchors and reporters who lived in the outer boroughs or New Jersey would not be able to get onto the island, as all the bridges and tunnels were immediately closed.

I suspected there would be transportation problems. I wished I had a bike. I looked around my small city apartment. My kids had a couple of those fold-up metal scooters that were popular then. I grabbed one and headed for the door.

I got halfway down the subway steps when hundreds of people came streaming up. The subways were now closed. Half a million people who were down in the New York City subways were released onto the sidewalks, confused and panicked.

A bus approached. I jumped on, but two blocks later the bus driver got word that all bus service was shut down too. Getting out, I hailed the first cab. We went south on Sixth Avenue, the radio blaring about the terrorist attack, with the broadcaster's fear loud in his voice: "One of the World Trade Towers has fallen! It is DOWN! I REPEAT, a tower has FALLEN! We don't know how many people were inside!" I was horrified. Good God, I thought, I don't know what I'm going to do when I go on the air, but it won't be that. I will be calm and factual, I thought. Beyond that, I had no idea what I would be reporting. I'd lived through major earthquakes and riots in Los Angeles, and in a crisis I focus on what has to be done: *Stay cool, help the injured.* My own fear and emotions could come later. For now, my urgent imperative was to get to work where I was needed.

Looking through the taxi's windshield down the wide avenue toward downtown, I saw the second tower fall. It went down in a cloud of fury right before my eyes. I was now living inside a horror film. Dear Lord, thousands of my neighbors were just murdered, I realized with a grip in my chest. At that point, hearts and time and traffic stopped. After a dazed silence, the earth began spinning again, and the crowd, coming back to reality, screamed, volume gaining and echoing through Manhattan's concrete corridors. I paid the driver (I think I did . . . I hope I did), unfolded my kid's scooter, and, heart pounding, rode it the last mile to my studio. My producers and office staff and crew and I did what I'm sure everyone in the New York news business did that day: We hugged each other hard and asked about each other's families. Many of my coworkers could not locate multiple family members or friends, and their eyes were hollowed in fear. Nevertheless, we got to work because covering tragedies and crises is what we did.

The most surreal experience of my life was getting my hair blow-dried and makeup applied in the minutes after thousands had just been murdered. I wanted to scream, *who cares what I look like at a time like this*? What could be more shallow and stupid, even disrespectful to the victims? I'm getting a third coat of mascara as they are trying to extricate themselves from rubble? But then my makeup artist said that if I went right on air, because of the bright studio lighting, I'd look white as a ghost and the viewers would be *more* worried. So I submitted to the makeup chair. Then I went on the air live for three hours, with no breaks, reporting all the facts my producers fed me, questioning our reporters and interviewing witnesses. Were there five planes? Was the fifth still in the air? Where was the president? We didn't know, and we said so. I stayed calm and reported only confirmed facts.

My children's school e-mailed to say that the school had summoned psychologists and that, please, when we picked up our children that afternoon, to do so calmly and quietly out of respect for those children whose parents would not be coming.

I hugged my kids with everything I had that evening. We watched the news loop over and over again. I gave myself a crash course on Afghanistan and Al Qaeda and Osama bin Laden. I knew we would promptly declare war and that the world would be changed forever. The days of peace were over.

After I put the kids to bed, I tidied up. On my kitchen table was that morning's *New York Times*, printed the night before the attacks. On the front page was an article debating the pros and cons of whether teenage girls could wear midriff-baring shirts to school, an article I had read and considered just that morning.

A chill went up my spine. In the course of one day, everything had changed. We would never see fluff pieces like that again, I thought. No one would care about such silly nonsense. We had more important concerns now. We had been attacked. Thousands had been murdered. Perhaps more attacks were imminent. We would immediately plunge into war, with all that entails: savage, needless deaths; young men and women returning home injured physically and mentally; families ripped apart; civilian casualties, the world divided for us and against us. Certainly, I thought, we would turn a new page toward seriousness and away from triviality. We needed to understand the root causes of what happened: What caused such murderous hatred? How much more was out there? What did we need to do, as a nation, to respond to this attack and prevent further terrorism in the future? What would be the right course of action for us as a nation now, in such a perilous world? We had the world's most powerful military, but surely we had to be cautious and justified in its use. And at home, I knew, a new seriousness would descend upon us as we helped one another through this crisis. How could we pull together?

For the next few months a new sober sense of purpose did grip the country. After 9/11, we hung American flags, paid respects to the victims' families, and tried to grasp the new world being born before our eyes. For a time we were more serious and turned toward substance. And the press gave it to us: cable and network and print and Internet news all running daily reports and analysis on the international issues that bore upon the 9/11 attacks, the buildup to our invasion of Afghanistan, the progress and consequences of that war, and the threat of Al Qaeda and other terrorist groups. We discussed foreign policy at dinner. Even comedians were quiet for a few weeks.

But then slowly we began to shift back to frivolity. Celebrity "news" warmed up again. Tom Cruise and Nicole Kidman split, Winona Ryder was charged with shoplifting from Saks Fifth Avenue, JLo and P. Diddy split, and breathless coverage about pretty people and their petty problems resumed. I started getting calls again to come on national networks and talk about these stories. The public was ready, news directors told me. Doing so would help us all recover and get back to normal, they said.

So I was wrong on 9/11. Everything did not change. Within months we in the media returned to the status quo, enthusiastically peering into the personal lives of television and film stars. Within a few years news organizations, tired of war stories getting low ratings, completely embraced the fluff, which now generated more print inches, airtime, and web content than ever before. New tabloid shows aired; gossip sites like TMZ.com, PerezHilton.com and RadarOnline.com burst onto the web and became hugely popular, tabloid magazines sold millions of copies weekly, giving us "breaking news" on Jon and Kate's divorce or Octomom's brood or Ashlee Simpson's plastic surgery. We are now in the grip of a celebrity mania on a scale never before experienced in human history. No wonder one survey of children under ten found that they ranked "being a celebrity" as "the best thing in the world," followed by "good looks" and "being rich."[20]

Of course, there is a place for lighter stories. No one wants a life with only heavy, bleak headlines. I was certainly relieved when the comedians returned to telling jokes in the fall of 2001. We are all human, and we all need levity, perhaps especially after a tragedy. And sure, most of us have some petty urge to gossip about the rich and famous. But wouldn't the appropriate mix be to lead with what's most important and follow with what's next most important, throwing in an occasional silly story to keep us sane? Shouldn't we eat our vegetables before we have dessert?

Because the consequences of not knowing can be catastrophic.

BRITNEY SPEARS WAS ASKED in a CNN interview in September 2003, "A lot of entertainers have come out against the war in Iraq. Have you?"

"Honestly," Britney responded, "I think we should just trust our president in every decision he makes and should just support that, you know, and be faithful in what happens."[21]

Just support our president in every decision he makes? Brit, say it ain't so. Tell me that behind that pretty façade there is *some* brain activity going on.

I'm with former President Teddy Roosevelt:

> To announce that there must be no criticism of the President, or that we are to stand by the President, right or wrong, is not only unpatriotic and servile, but it is morally treasonable to the American public.[22]

But I'm not looking to pick on Britney, an easy target. She was and is, after all, a singer. Who cares what her political views are? If I were interviewing her, I'd ask her about her phenomenal music career because that's her area of expertise.

Asking Britney political questions only reflects the intense and absurd celebrity fascination of our time to which we returned with a vengeance after 9/11—even in matters of such dire importance as terrorism and war.

Somehow pundit Tucker Carlson, working for CNN in 2003, found himself conducting the interview with Britney that brought out her "our president, right or wrong" view. Maybe all the CNN political reporters drew straws for the interview. Maybe he banged on the assignment editor's door for it. Who knows? But once the interview was his, he conducted it like the hard-hitting political journalist he is:

> CARLSON: I was reading the *Star*. I know you haven't seen this, but in here, there's a picture of you coming out of a restaurant grabbing your stomach and it made me think are you shadowed all the time?
>
> CARLSON: Do you see photographers following you all the time?
>
> CARLSON: Give me the chronology of the kiss. How did you decide to kiss Madonna?
>
> CARLSON: Had you have ever kissed a woman before?
>
> CARLSON: Would you again?
>
> CARLSON: You're going to stay true to Madonna?
>
> CARLSON: What does your mom think?[23]

This was the state of American journalism, even on a serious news network, after 9/11. (And it still is.)

It's not about Tucker. We've all been assigned inane celeb stories and vapid interviews, including me. Because I have also covered Saddam Hussein's war crimes tribunal, the legal wranglings of the disputed Bush-Gore election, many Supreme Court cases, and other significant crime and justice issues, I told myself that there was nothing wrong with the occasional light story. But in my decade-long career as an American television legal commentator, I can see the decline: Celebrity stories are now the overwhelming majority of what I'm asked to analyze on air—probably 95 percent at this point. However we began, it seems—I'm a legal analyst—we are all on the celebrity beat now.

While we were scrutinizing Britney's kiss, here's what we weren't doing: demanding that our leaders give us verifiable facts to justify going to war. That our media failed to ask the tough questions they should have in the 2002–2003 buildup to the Iraq War is widely acknowledged now. "The mainstream Western media failed miserably in their coverage of the Bush government's reasons for invading Iraq and the 'gung-ho' way many approached the invasion," says the journalists' website, Journalism Today.[24] Gary Kamiya, writing for Salon.com, the rare independent news website, sums it up:

> It's no secret that the period of time between 9/11 and the invasion of Iraq represents one of the greatest collapses in the history of the American media. Every branch of the media failed, from daily newspapers, magazines and Web sites to television networks, cable channels and radio . . . the real failing was not in any one area; it was across the board. Bush administration lies and distortions went unchallenged, or were actively promoted. Fundamental and problematic assumptions about terrorism and the "war on terror" were rarely debated or even discussed. Vital historical context was almost never provided. And it wasn't just a failure of analysis. With some honorable exceptions, good old-fashioned reporting was also absent.[25]

The fallout from our distraction is that we didn't even notice until much later—too late—that the media failed us on this, our most monumental post-9/11 issue: the decision whether or not to invade a sovereign nation half a planet away, whether to shoot and bomb and reorder their world.

Why did intelligent reporters turn away? The answer comes back, as it always does, to consumer preference. We, the customers, didn't want journalists to dig deeper, to ask impertinent questions that sounded disloyal to our leaders. Kristina Borjesson, author of *Feet to the Fire*, a collection of interviews with twenty-one prominent American journalists about why the press collapsed in the run-up to the Iraq war, writes that ultra-patriotic consumers, who did not take kindly to criticism of the president in the time following 9/11, made many journalists feel constrained. Station managers and editors make business decisions daily about what the customers want, and the decision was made, in newsrooms virtually everywhere, that the American public did not want tough questions, hard-hitting analysis, or even real debate during the nine months we were gearing up to invade Iraq. We wanted more talk about Britney and Madonna. And so most of the press and the public, lined up, lemminglike, behind the Bush administration's choice to invade Iraq.

Our ignorance had devastating consequences. Just before our 2003 invasion of Iraq nearly seven in ten Americans believed that Saddam Hussein was responsible for 9/11, according to a *Washington Post* poll. By June 2007 when we were deeply mired in Iraq, we knew better: Only 41 percent of the American public believed that Hussein was involved in planning, financing, or carrying out the 9/11 attacks, according to a *Newsweek* poll.[26] The simple truth is that there never was any evidence that the Iraqi regime was responsible for the attacks, which were perpetrated mostly by Saudi Arabian hijackers. Ultimately, most of us realized that. The facts never changed, only our awareness of them did.

Over four thousand American troops lost their lives and more than thirty thousand have been injured in the Iraq war, one of the longest wars in U.S. history. Estimates of Iraqi civilians killed ranges from one hundred thousand to one million, depending on whether they are measured by hospital and morgue records or household surveys. Joseph E. Stiglitz, a professor at Columbia University, former chairman of President Bill Clinton's Council of Economic Advisers, and winner of the Nobel Prize in economics in 2001, puts the cost of the Iraq war at over $3 trillion—$3,000,000,000,000—a staggering amount that he claims added substantially to the federal debt (because the war has been financed entirely by borrowing), which caused, in part, the global financial crisis, made the crisis more severe, and prevented us from responding to it more swiftly and effectively. [27]

By September 2010, as American forces withdrew combat troops from Iraq, a Pew Research Center poll found that 62 percent of Americans believed that our Iraq invasion was "not worth it."[28]

In the case of post-9/11 coverage, the media failed to ask tough questions of our leaders, believing that readers, viewers, and listeners just did not want to know inconvenient facts that might militate against the invasion. This was a failure of courage, a cowardly refusal to live up to the noble job of journalists to ask impertinent questions of powerful people, to investigate claims the government PR machine made, to unearth inconsistencies and outright lies. The press failed us, and we, in our state of apathy and distraction, failed them.

Our press fails us in other ways as well. Most of us don't even notice that worthy stories outside our borders are rarely covered, even though America comprises only 5 percent of the world's population. Let me give you an example of how our press misses the opportunity to educate us on a glaring issue affecting millions of children worldwide.

Jaycee Dugard was an eleven-year-old pretty, blonde California girl who was kidnapped from her front yard in broad daylight, right under her stepfather's nose. Eighteen years later, Phillip Garrido and his wife, Nancy, were arrested for her abduction and charged with twenty-eight felony counts, including forcible rape, forcible abduction, kidnapping, and false imprisonment. Garrido had fathered two children with Jaycee when she was fourteen and seventeen. Jaycee and her children had not attended school or been to a doctor in eighteen years. They apparently had lived virtually the entirety of those years in a makeshift series of sheds and tents in the Garrido backyard.

This story, of course, horrified us. It was front-page news across the country, the top story on all the cable news broadcasts. I appeared on show after show on the two networks where I worked as a legal analyst, CBS and CNN, day after day, week after week, analyzing all the sickening aspects of the case. Months later, I even discussed it on *The Rachael Ray Show*. The biggest question was: How could this happen in our country, right under our noses? Phillip Garrido, we learned, was a sex predator who had previously been convicted of the abduction and forcible rape of a young woman in the 1970s. He'd been sentenced to fifty years in prison but was released after ten because he had been a model prisoner (probably because there were no women for him to assault in prison).

His wife, Nancy Garrido, was likely the woman Jaycee's stepfather saw jump out of the car and physically grab Jaycee on the morning of her abduction as she was walking to the school bus stop. Phillip Garrido had a parole violation in 1993 and was reincarcerated from April to August of that year. During that time Nancy Garrido was the sole captor for Jaycee. People often asked me how a woman could be an active part of the abduction, kidnapping, rape, and imprisonment of a young girl. This kind of crime is rare, but women commit crimes against children, even shocking crimes like this one, in order to get or stay in the good graces of their boyfriends or husbands.

As a paroled sex offender, Phillip Garrido was required to report twice monthly to his parole officer. His home was subjected to random home visits. During those visits law enforcement never checked his backyard. Even after a new neighbor called the police to say that her neighbor was a "sex addict" who had children living in his backyard, the police came to the house but never checked the backyard. How could law enforcement be so lackadaisical when children were at risk?

On show after show I discussed this case as the directors flashed Jaycee's pretty young face on screen. The morning shows used their prime real estate—the opening twenty minutes at 7 a.m., when they cover top stories of the day—to revealing any new details they could glean about the story. Jaycee's aunt says she is now a vivacious twenty-nine-year old and seems to be in good health, they reported. Jaycee had managed to teach her daughters to read and write. She and her kids knew how to use the Internet. Nancy Garrido's attorney said she missed her "family," that is, Phillip Garrido, Jaycee, and Jaycee's two daughters.

Psychologists opined on whether and how Jaycee could recover from her ordeal. This was a horror show, everyone agreed. Tragic, shocking—how could we prevent this in the future? Did we need tougher laws? Better monitoring of sex offenders? More oversight of cops?

Anderson Cooper asked me if I thought prosecutors might give Nancy Garrido a deal in exchange for her testimony against her husband. I explained that is how multiple defendant cases usually proceed: Get the little fish to flip and turn state's evidence against the big fish (assuming that Phillip Garrido had also victimized Nancy Garrido into submission, which, as of this writing, we still don't know). But I doubted prosecutors would offer that here. Why? Because of the extraordinary public outcry that had accompanied this case. Members of the public were burning up the phone and e-mail lines to the shows I was on about this story. My Facebook posts about Jaycee got one hundred comments immediately, compared to a dozen or so on an average day. This public outcry in turn translated into enormous ratings for the news shows that ran stories on Jaycee from morning shows through prime time and into late night. And that media saturation of the story fed more public outrage.

The only positive in this horrific story is that the high ratings the Dugard story garnered reflect, in part, the public's deep and abiding interest in protecting children. Once the shock of the initial and sensational tragedy wore off, the press stayed with the story and discovered the failure of the courts and the parole system to protect Jaycee Dugard, though they had ample opportunities to save her. More public outrage resulted, with citizens demanding to know how the system had failed. That outcry led to California's Inspector General, David R. Shaw conducting a detailed investigation followed by a scathing report that revealed more than a dozen failures on the part of the California Department of Corrections and Rehabilitation, with specific recommendations for reform. Citizen uproar produced results: a state agency devoting significant resources to review what went wrong, with a blueprint for reform. The combined outrage of both the media and the public they informed produced results.

If only the press had decided to stay with the story even further, to deepen and expand on the Dugard story to embrace children outside our borders—because this horror story of child abduction, false imprisonment, and rape plays out in a worldwide phenomenon that our media rarely covers. As a result, authorities sit on their hands—and the suffering continues, unchecked.

Three million women and girls worldwide are enslaved today in the international sex trade. Typically around puberty, and often before, they are kidnapped from their home village or tricked into thinking they are going to a distant city for a legitimate job, and then they are forcibly kidnapped. The standard operating procedure is for pimps, thugs, gangsters, and brothel owners to rape them immediately, beat them constantly, drug them into addiction, and threaten them with violence such as blinding, throwing acid in their faces, or viciously beating and even killing other girls in front of them.[29]

As many modern abolitionist groups do, I choose the word "slavery" rather than "trafficking" because "slavery" is more accurate. The girls are kept imprisoned under threats of violence and have no freedom to come and go or even visit their families. They do not receive payment for their work—all the money goes to the pimps. They must do as their captors say or they are savagely beaten. In rare cases they, or a benefactor, can buy their freedom. This is the very essence of slavery. ("Trafficking" also generally implies crossing borders, and roughly half of the abducted girls are enslaved in their own countries.[30])

The enormity of three million enslaved girls is hard to get our minds around. As Nicholas Kristof and Sheryl WuDunn explain compellingly in their groundbreaking book about third world women's oppression, *Half the Sky*:

> In the peak decade of the transatlantic slave trade, the 1780s, an average of just under eighty thousand slaves were shipped annually across the Atlantic from Africa to the New World. The average then dropped to a bit more than fifty thousand between 1811 and 1850. In other words, far more women and girls are shipped into brothels each year in the early twenty-

first century than African slaves were shipped into slave plantations each year in the eighteenth or nineteenth centuries—although the overall population was of course far smaller then.[31]

One of the biggest differences between nineteenth-century and modern slavery, Kristof and WuDunn observe, is early death. Many enslaved girls of our time die of AIDS by their late twenties. Although the male customers prefer young girls, believing them to be free of HIV, the opposite is often true, as sexually inexperienced adolescents are more likely to suffer lacerations and subsequent infection.[32]

A report by DePaul University's International Human Rights Institute found that 80 percent of those sold into sexual slavery are under twenty-four, with some as young as six. An estimated thirty thousand die annually from abuse, torture, neglect, and disease. Ten thousand children between the ages of six and fourteen—ten thousand Jaycee Dugards—are captives in Sri Lankan brothels alone. Two hundred thousand Nepali girls as young as nine have been sold into India's red-light districts in the last decade.[33]

Srey Nath was a fifteen-year-old Cambodian villager who decided to travel to a restaurant in Thailand for a promised dishwashing job in order to help support her poor family. Instead, gangsters kidnapped her to Malaysia, where she was beaten, drugged, and raped by brothel customers fifteen hours a day, seven days a week. She and the other sex slaves were kept hungry (customers didn't like fat prostitutes) and naked (to prevent theft or escape). Guards patrolled the girls' every move, from the brothel to the tenth-floor apartment where they were housed. One night some of the girls pried loose a five-inch-wide board and balanced it from their balcony to a balcony on the next building, twelve feet away. Srey and three others risked their lives crossing that rickety board to freedom.

Srey and the girls went to the police, where they were promptly arrested for illegal immigration. She served a year in Malaysian prison, and on her release, the policeman drove her to the Thai border and sold her to a trafficker, who sold her to another Thai brothel.[34]

This story comes to us from the stubborn pen of Pulitzer Prize–winning journalist Nicholas Kristof, who insists on telling the stories of the world's forgotten people. God bless the *New York Times* for regularly publishing Kristof's important pieces about third world poverty and, especially, the plight of women and girls in South Asia and sub-Saharan Africa. Small alternative stations like PBS, NPR, and BBC America also sometimes cover stories like this.

As a television journalist, I am sorry to say that seeing any coverage whatsoever of the world's three million currently enslaved prostitutes in the mainstream media is excruciatingly rare. Like Jaycee Dugard, these are girls kidnapped in adolescence, cruelly held captive, and repeatedly raped. They are held for years. Do their horror stories not shock the conscience on the same level as the Jaycee Dugard story? If not, why not?

Why do so many news outlets provide months of round-the-clock coverage of Jaycee Dugard but not even ten seconds for the three million others? This is a question that ate away at me as I continued to get booked on Dugard story updates. Are we so solipsistic? To me this seemed a clear example of the media once again failing to keep us informed about one of the most desperate and compelling issues of our time. And because we're not informed, there's no public outcry, no pushing our leaders to act while three million girls remain enslaved, imprisoned, and raped—daily.

I went right to the top and asked this question of Howard Kurtz, the country's foremost media analyst. He's a journalist's journalist who has covered the media's strengths and flaws on his Sunday morning CNN show, *Reliable Sources*, for eleven years, for the *Washington Post* for twenty-nine years, and now for TheDailyBeast.com. He told me:

> The truth is that American television has little interest in problems overseas, unless there's an earthquake, a tsunami, a war, or good ol' Americans are somehow affected. It's like local TV: the closer to home, the better. A murder in your hometown counts for more than one in the next state.
>
> But the neglect is more than that: television, far more than the print media, obsesses on having a single damsel in distress. A little girl who falls

> in a well is deemed a far more compelling narrative, in TV terms, than thousands of faceless victims of some faraway calamity. The missing-white-women plotline has become a cable- and morning-show staple. Even as heart-rending a tale as Jaycee Dugard is, a local crime story magically transformed into a national melodrama, complete with a cast of supporting characters that can be pursued for interviews. That doesn't make these stories important, but it does drive the ratings in a way that becomes addictive for television executives.[35]

Human beings love a story with an identifiable victim or protagonist. There is something hardwired in us that loves a story about a person—one person—we get to know. We can wrap our mind around it. I get that. We have a saying in journalism: One death is a tragedy; a thousand deaths is a statistic.

But then, I asked, why don't we tell individual "damsel in distress" stories about girls like Srey Nath? Racism? Bias against foreigners? Because news directors don't care, or they do care but have to care more about ratings, given that the business has to make a profit? Is it the programmers' fault or the fault of media consumers?

Kurtz replied:

> There's plenty of blame to go around. News executives are people, and they're not insensitive to mass tragedy. But their job is to put numbers on the board, and they have learned over the years what sells.
>
> The audience bears some responsibility too. The more that people drive up the ratings for missing-women stories, the more that news executives can claim they're just giving people what they want. As the Iraq war dragged on, producers would tell me that the numbers would nosedive every time they switched to the war.

We like stories about people like ourselves. Jaycee is the girl next door, an American girl we can relate to. But let's not kid ourselves. The story got the enormous, breathless coverage it did because Jaycee is fair, blonde, blue-eyed, and American.

I never imagined when I embarked on a career as a full-time television legal analyst nine years ago that I'd spend so much of my time covering what I call Missing Pretty White Girl stories. Of course it's horrendous that Natalee Holloway and Hayleigh Cummings went missing and are presumed dead. The sick murders of Danielle van Dam, Jessica Lunsford, and Caylee Anthony were devastating for their families. I had to study autopsy photos. The details haunt me, years after I've closed my files on these stories.

These cases sorely test my anti-death penalty resolve.

But if a missing child is not white or not pretty or is, God forbid, male, that story will rarely make air. I have personally tried to get more media attention for stories about missing children who were not pretty white girls. News directors have told me not to bother bringing them those stories. Viewers clamor about middle-class children who come into harm's way and become attached to stories with pictures of Missing Pretty White Girls. Others don't make it to national broadcasts.

The National Center for Missing and Exploited Children's website, www.missingkids.com, has photos of disappeared American children. They come in all shapes, sizes, and colors, and both male and female. I clicked on the website recently. The first three listed were all boys, Hispanic and African American. I hadn't heard of any of these three. Two of them had been missing for nine months, teenagers Oscar Garcia-Calles and Samuel Garcia-Calles. Perhaps they are brothers. They are listed as nonfamily abductions, the type the media is interested in. But they are brown skinned, male, and maybe too old to generate any national media interest. The third, Shalomiel Solel, a four-year-old dark-skinned African American boy, poignantly adorable in his photo, had disappeared five months earlier. Never heard of him. And I cover these stories when producers call and ask me to come on, as they do on a daily basis. No one had asked me to talk about Oscar, Samuel, or Shalomiel, and probably no one ever would.

The millions—*millions*—of mostly South Asian and African children on other continents who suffer from Jaycee Dugard–like abductions, rape, and imprisonment—usually for the financial profit of their pimps and with the tacit approval of local authorities—are not newsworthy here at all. And the "bottom billion" of the world's population who suffer from the unspeakable deprivations of extreme poverty—imagine the coverage if a cute young, blonde California girl starved to death in her own home—get no mention, much less resulting outrage.

I'm not saying we shouldn't cover the Jaycee Dugard story. The crime story was shocking, and as it developed, it became an important "keeping them honest" (as we say at CNN) story about law enforcement and parole officers failing to communicate with one another, failing to properly classify Garrido as a high-risk sex offender, failing to follow up on a neighbor's tips that children were living in his home, and failing to thoroughly inspect his property on home visits to discover an entire compound with three human beings living in the backyard. But wouldn't the news be powerful if we covered it this way?

> ABDUCTED GIRL JAYCEE DUGARD RESCUED AFTER EIGHTEEN YEARS OF CAPTIVITY WITH SEX PREDATOR; MILLIONS MORE ENSLAVED GIRLS AWAIT WORLD'S RESCUE

Can't we tell the stories of enslaved girls who India's Rescue Foundation and other abolitionist organizations have freed? Can't we run pictures of abducted South Asian girls alongside our American girls' stories? They too are fresh faced and adorable. Their stories are just as heart-wrenching and compelling.

Economist Jeffrey Sachs, who has spent his life fighting extreme poverty in the most miserable countries in the world—bless him—opens his book *The End of Poverty: Economic Possibilities for Our Time* with this:

> Every morning our newspapers could report, "More than 20,000 perished yesterday of extreme poverty." The stories would put the stark numbers in context—up to 8,000 children die of malaria, 5,000 mothers and fathers dead of tuberculosis, 7,500 young adults dead of AIDS, and thousands more dead of diarrhea, respiratory infection, and other killer diseases that

> prey on bodies weakened by chronic hunger. The poor die in hospital wards that lack drugs, in villages that lack antimalarial bed nets, in houses that lack safe drinking water. They die namelessly, without public comment. Sadly, such stories rarely get written. Most people are unaware of the daily struggles for survival, and of the vast numbers of impoverished people around the world who lose that struggle.[36]

Those stories don't get written because editors believe we don't want to read them. They believe this because we don't clamor for them and we don't respond to them. Is it the media's fault we're ill informed about the enslavement of children in our own time? Yes. Is our ignorance our own fault too? Indisputably.

I KNOW FROM PERSONAL EXPERIENCE getting serious international stories on American mainstream television is next to impossible.

In December of 2007, on my own nickel, I visited the international war crimes tribunal in Phnom Penh, Cambodia. Imprisoned there, awaiting trial, were five leaders of the Khmer Rouge. In the late 1970s this political party rose to power based in part on an anti-American platform. Our covert bombing of Cambodian civilians during those years led them, quite understandably, to hostility against us. How would you feel if another country dropped land mines in your backyard? How about land mines specifically designed to attract children—pineapple-shaped, bright yellow baubles?

Three decades later, incidentally, because the United States is one of the few countries in the world that has refused to sign the Mine Ban Treaty, even under the Obama administration, those bombs are still maiming children. I shook the sole remaining hand of one of those children, a reed-thin boy of about twelve, at the Cambodia Landmine Museum outside Phnom Penh. He smiled warmly at me. The world's poor, so often victimized, are endlessly forgiving. Some recovered, detonated land mines are now painted and sold as vases or planters in the Landmine Museum Gift Shop. Swords into plowshares.

The Khmer Rouge presented itself as a party of the people, promising to throw off the imperialist Americans. The Cambodian people believed it, and the Khmer Rouge rose to power. Instead, however, they installed one of the most vicious and repressive regimes of the twentieth century, the bloodiest in human history. Nearly two million Cambodians perished in four years, one quarter of the population.

In Cambodia today, every living person over the age of forty is a Khmer Rouge survivor. I asked a random man I met at a mass gravesite what happened to his family during the time of the Khmer Rouge. A curtain of pain lowered over his face. "They kill my mother and father!" he said. "My sister and brother too! Only I survive Khmer Rouge! Understand?" He began to yell. "Only I!" Yes, I said, yes, I understand. I am so sorry, I said, uselessly.

I talked my way past the guards—no easy feat, as they spoke little English and I spoke no Khmer beyond "hello" and "thank you"—and into the compound where the tribunal was underway. This was a first-of-its-kind operation, with three Cambodian judges—in recognition that Cambodians needed to bring justice to their own people—and two international judges who could bring international law and resources to the court. An international group of mainly European observers provided backup. They needed two decades for Cambodia to stabilize enough for the court to convene and then another decade to work out the details of who would preside, who would be accused, and how the novel tribunal would structure the trial. And now it was finally underway.

Japan, which had nothing to do with the Cambodian genocide, was the primary financial supporter of the tribunal. The European Union was second. The United States had not contributed a dime by the time of my visit.[37]

Equally disturbing was the fact that although over one hundred news outlets from around the world had attended some of the important early hearings, according to the public information officer, only one or two were American, evidence of our indifference to the world outside our borders.

As the tribunal moved slowly over the next year, conducting pretrial hearings and gearing up to begin, back home in the United States I pitched my story with everything I had to various shows and networks I worked with. I had taken some still photos and even a little video and had gathered names of people we could interview. Having been there, I offered stories recounting what I saw at the tribunal. I wrote a short, snappy, and, I thought, compelling pitch. No go. I got no takers. Some shows said they were interested, maybe next week, but then next week never came. I followed up and met with polite refusals.

Dith Pran, the Cambodian photojournalist and genocide survivor who was the inspiration for the movie *The Killing Fields*, died a few months after I returned to the United States in 2008. With that news hook, I pitched the story about the war crimes tribunal again.

Still nothing. I couldn't get it on the air. Later, a show I worked with often asked me for three legal stories I'd like to discuss for the following day's show. I passionately pitched the Cambodian war crimes tribunal. Nope. I couldn't even get it on as *one of three*. (I think we ended up with the Rihanna domestic violence story and a couple of celebrity divorces.)

By not informing us of major world events, such as a court attempting to bring justice to millions of genocide survivors, our news outlets keep us ignorant. As a student of international war crimes tribunals, I have often wondered whether these courts may one day help prevent future wars or genocides or deter future despots as they are intended to do. Courts, not killing fields. Courts, not battlefields. Civilization, not savagery. But our own mainstream media are not asking these questions on air, in print, or online. When I mention the Cambodian war crimes tribunal, even to friends who are attorneys, law professors, or judges, no one has heard of it. So is our ignorance of world affairs the media's fault? Sure, in part. But if we buy tabloids and watch celebrity gossip shows to the exclusion of serious news outlets that struggle to cover international stories, we too are to blame. The market will give us what we demand. Every dollar spent on a newspaper or magazine, every website click, every television show watched is a vote for the kind of media we want. And as things stand, news directors know that running coverage of Charlie Sheen's misadventures with porn stars or Kim Kardashian's bikini photos generates enormous profits because that is what we tune into and stay with, day after day. The media's—and our—priorities are skewed. Some of the world's most worthy stories are never covered while the silliest receive endless play. It's all about balance, about insisting that important world events get covered in depth before we hear a word—hopefully only a brief word at the tail end of the broadcast—about Paris Hilton's claim that she thought the cocaine in her purse was gum.

On the other hand, all of the research I've done for this book has come from . . . the media. There *are* many serious news sources that deliver hard-hitting international stories: in addition to the *New York Times*, www.nytimes.com; there's National Public Radio, www.npr.org; BBC America, www.bbcamerica.com; CNN International, http://edition.cnn.com; and Reuters, www.reuters.com, to name a few. So when we choose to blame "the media," which media is that, exactly? The fluff sites we're clicking on or silly shows we're watching? Then who is really to blame here? The clicker or the clickee?

Worst of all, and I can only give this to you straight, news directors tell me that they have to run stories on celebrity sex scandals, fashion,* and new plastic surgery techniques because doing so is the only way to capture the female market. Even though most journalists I know are dying to cover more serious stories, market studies and ratings breakdowns bear the suits out.[38] This is what women want.

I hope that's as painful for you to read as it was for me to write.

Wouldn't it be great if the only way for the local news to increase their female ratings were to cover climate change in depth, to report on the modern-day abolitionists who are struggling to free enslaved girls, to update us on the millions of girls who don't go to school at all, and to report any number of other real stories that are worthy of our attention?

---

*Fashion "news" spoiler alert: It's always going to be plaid in the fall, boots in winter, flowers in spring, sundresses in summer—every year until we die.

Wouldn't you like to see the day when, because of overwhelming consumer demand for worthy information about our world, Angelina Jolie's love life is squeezed out of the papers?

Because I have some news for you about Angelina Jolie.

Angelina Jolie and the Media Cult of the Absurd

What do you know about Angelina Jolie?

That she is movie-star beautiful? Drop-dead gorgeous? That has to come to mind first. The hourglass figure, the puffy lips, the green eyes, and sleek brunette mane—*People* magazine called her the World's Most Beautiful Woman in 2006 and then a British television station voted her the greatest sex symbol of all time. Okay. We are only human, and we all get a little stupid around stunningly lovely people. Fair enough. We can stop for a moment or two and stare. I don't begrudge any of us that, male or female. (In one poll, not only did men, lesbians, and bisexual women choose her as their top celebrity choice to sleep with, but so did straight women.)

But on my way to the New York City subway every weekday morning for the last half of the first decade of the twenty-first century, I walked by my corner newsstand. Brad and Angelina and Jen—there they were, week after week, in the screaming yellow two-inch block letters: They break up! They make up! They break their silence! Angelina's baby bump! Adoptions! Twins! Months turned into seasons, and the magazines still blared. Seasons changed, years passed, but the story raged on, somehow timeless.

If you live in America and have glanced at supermarket checkout racks in the last decade, you know that Brad and Angelina fell in love during the shooting of a film together, that Brad then left his wife Jennifer Aniston, that Brad and Angelina made a few babies together and adopted a few more, and then either they are or are not on the rocks, they will or will not split up, and she may or may not be pregnant again.

If you are ambulatory and breathe air, you know this. In fact, forget ambulatory. If you are paralyzed but have a television in front of you, you *still* know it. You can't *not* know it. My friend Rochelle does not own a TV, never reads glossies, never clicks on celeb news websites, and *she* knows this. She doesn't know *how* she knows, but she just does.

If you've opened one of those gossip magazines or watched "entertainment news" or clicked onto a celebrity website in the last decade, you know more: that there is speculation about whether her famous pillowy lips are the product of plastic surgery; that sometimes friends worry she is too thin; that she has a lot of tattoos; that she and Brad aren't married, but that maybe they will be one day, or maybe they won't; that she now has a large brood of children, some of whom were adopted from foreign countries; that Jennifer Aniston remains single, and although she is rich, successful, and gorgeous, she is sometimes also lonely.

I picked a random day and Googled each member of America's favorite love triangle. Here's what was being reported as "news" on that day:

Angelina went shopping at Toys R Us with two of her kids and bought them Spiderman-themed toys while wearing a Tom Ford skirt and tank top.

Brad texts, but does not talk on the phone, while urinating.

Jennifer was the winner in the "best arms" category in a poll of British women. Though they had to concede that Angelina had the "best boobs."

Alrighty then.

While the public and, let's face it, mainly the female part of the public, laps up this mind-numbing drivel, the real Angelina Jolie forges on. Perhaps you are vaguely aware that she is somehow involved with helping poor people in faraway places. The truth is that she has devoted a huge portion of the last eight years of her life—the same years the tabloid and the public obsessed about her appearance and her personal life—to educating herself and then doing everything within her power to raise consciousness about and directly aid those who Franz Fanon called "the wretched of the earth."

The contrast between Jolie's extraordinary devotion to humanitarian work on behalf of dispossessed people and our shallow fixation on her looks and personal life could not be more jarring. What is a throwaway line at the end of some stories about her—"Jolie also does some humanitarian work"—is the main event of her life. This work started when she was making the film *Tomb Raider* in Cambodia in 2000. Jolie says that while there, her eyes opened about third world refugees. She turned to the UN High Commissioner on Refugees (UNHCR), the UN's Refugee Agency, to educate herself about the issues, and she immersed herself in learning more about trouble spots around the world. (The UNHCR, which has won two Nobel Peace Prizes in the last fifty years, cares for twenty-two million refugees and other people that wars, famines, droughts, and other crises have uprooted in 120 countries.)

In the following months Jolie took it upon herself to personally visit refugee camps to learn more about the conditions displaced people faced. In February 2001 Jolie embarked on an eighteen-day mission to Sierra Leone and Tanzania, two of the poorest countries on earth. She then returned to desperately impoverished Cambodia to visit refugee camps there. Next she traveled to Pakistan, where she donated $1 million for Afghan refugees in response to an UNHCR emergency appeal. She insisted on covering all costs related to her missions herself, and she shared the same rudimentary working and living conditions as UN field staff.[39]

"I was shocked by what I saw," Jolie said. "We cannot close ourselves off to information and ignore the fact that millions of people are out there suffering. I honestly want to help. I don't believe I feel differently from other people. I think we all want justice and equality, a chance for a life with meaning. All of us would like to believe that if we were in a bad situation someone would help us."[40]

On August 27, 2001, at the UNHCR headquarters in Geneva, Jolie was named a UNHCR Goodwill Ambassador. This is not an empty title. Since 2001 Jolie has devoted herself to the issue, going on field missions and meeting with refugees in more than twenty countries. She knows that she can use the power of her celebrity to draw attention to the issue, and she hopes only for "awareness of the plight of these people. I think they should be commended for what they have survived, not looked down upon."[41]

Back at home, our media mostly ignored Jolie's refugee work, zeroing in instead on the urgent question of whether her breasts were real and how she got them large enough to resemble those of the video game heroine Lara Croft for her film. Serious interviewers wanted to know her bra size. C? D? Had she had breast enlargement surgery? Or did she just wear a padded bra? That year—2001—*Rolling Stone* magazine featured Angelina Jolie on its cover, leading with her then-marriage to actor Billy Bob Thornton. "Inside America's Most Dangerous Marriage," the cover headline blared, followed by, "blood sugar sex magic." She eats pumpkin pie in the bathtub, the article noted.[42]

In 2002 Jolie personally visited the Tham Hin refugee camp in Thailand, where tens of thousands of people had fled the repressive regime in Myanmar. These men, women, and children lived in squalid conditions and were legally forbidden to leave the camp, their lives put on indefinite hold. Jolie also met with Colombian refugees in Ecuador and Angolan refugees in Namibia, and she toured UNHCR facilities in Kosovo and a Sudanese refugee camp in Kenya.[43]

Back home, the possible reasons for her 2002 divorce from Billy Bob Thornton filled the media with breathless speculation. Did one or both of them cheat? Weren't they just *weird*? Were those amulets of each other's blood they wore around their necks?

But mainly, we talked about what she looked like. Ooh, she's so *pretty!* Gosh! Several polls ranked her as one of the "sexiest" women in the country.

In 2003 Jolie took a six-day mission to Tanzania, where she traveled to western border camps housing Congolese refugees. This trip was followed by a weeklong visit to Sri Lanka and a four-day mission to North Caucasus, Russia. That year, in an attempt to call attention to the needs of some of the poorest of the world's poor, she published *Notes from My Travels*, a collection of journal entries that chronicle her early field missions. During a private stay in Jordan in December

2003, she asked to visit Iraqi refugees in Jordan's eastern desert, and later that month she went to Egypt to meet Sudanese refugees.[44]

Guess what our media gave us that year in Jolie news? Details of Angelina's complicated relationship with her father, cover stories reminding us that she was "hot and single," reports on her new tattoos, and more "investigations" into the reasons for her divorce.

In 2004 Jolie went to Arizona on a UN trip to visit detained asylum seekers in deplorable conditions at four facilities right here in the United States, including one for children. She flew to the African nation of Chad, paying a visit to border camps for refugees who had fled fighting in western Sudan's desiccated Darfur region. Four months later she returned to Darfur. Later that year Jolie met with Afghan refugees in Thailand. She finished the year by visiting UNHCR's regional office in Beirut over her Christmas holiday, also taking the time to visit some young refugees and cancer patients in the Lebanese capital.[45]

Back at home we had next to no coverage of third world poor, refugees, wars not involving the United States, or Jolie's UNHCR work. In 2004 *Vogue* magazine did feature Jolie posing in some beautiful gowns, the kind of spread typical of what we asked of her: to smile for the camera and not talk too much about her humanitarian work. That year Jolie made the film *Mr. and Mrs. Smith* with Brad Pitt, and the media saturated us with speculation into whether or not Jolie and Pitt had hooked up and whether Jolie wore underwear during the film's sex scenes.

In 2005 Jolie visited Afghani refugees in Pakistani camps and met with Pakistan's president and prime minister. After the devastating Kashmir earthquake, Jolie spent her Thanksgiving weekend back in Pakistan to see the devastation and to attempt to focus the world's attention on the crisis. Seventy-nine thousand people had lost their lives.

At a National Press Club luncheon in 2005, Jolie announced the founding of an organization that provides free legal aid to asylum-seeking children with no legal representation. Jolie personally funded the center with a $500,000 donation. As always, Jolie's goal was to draw attention to the world's refugees.[46]

She got coverage in 2005 all right, but not the kind she hoped for. That year the media went into overdrive when Pitt left his wife, Jennifer Aniston, for Jolie. Tabloid and mainstream magazines, talk shows, and websites vilified her as a home wrecker and encouraged viewers to choose "Team Angie" or "Team Jen." In the fall the media whipped up frenzied speculation as to whether Jolie sported a "baby bump." Week after week tabloids featured cover stories on the love triangle, and sales boomed. Experts pored over pictures of Jolie and offered opinions as to whether she was pregnant or just "pooch-y."

Undaunted, Jolie flew to Haiti in 2006 and visited a school for impoverished children. In February Liberian refugee women sang songs of praise to Jolie and UNHCR as they graduated from refugee camp sewing classes that Jolie funded, each receiving a new sewing machine she purchased for them. The women rejoiced in their newfound skills, confident that they could return home to their war-torn country, Sierra Leone, able to support themselves and their families. "The sewing machine that I have received will help me and my family," said one new graduate. "I am a single mother. My husband was killed in the war in my country, Sierra Leone, and it has been really difficult for me to take care of our seven children. I am very grateful for this assistance."[47]

Later in 2006 Jolie then met with Afghan and Burmese refugees in New Delhi. She spent Christmas Day 2006 with Colombian refugees in Costa Rica, where she handed out presents and tried to bring attention to the needs of displaced people in our own hemisphere.

By now you know the result. Didn't happen. That year *People* magazine named Jolie its most beautiful female star, and *Maxim* named her hottest woman of the year, with a sultry Jolie cover photo featuring her seated, one leg up, with a dress strap slipping off her shoulder. Millions of gossip magazines were sold fulminating over the supposed Jolie-Aniston feud. "Team Jen" or "Team Angie" T-shirts continued to sell briskly. She announced her pregnancy in January 2006, and the story dominated the tabloid media and morning shows throughout the year: How did Jen feel about her ex-husband having a child? When was the baby conceived? Where would she give birth? Paparazzi photos of pregnant Jolie sold for tens of thousands of dollars.

In 2007 Jolie returned to Chad for a two-day mission to assess the deteriorating security situation for refugees from Darfur. Jolie and Pitt subsequently donated $1 million to three relief organizations in Chad and Darfur. Writing about the Darfur genocide for the *Washington Post*, Jolie bravely called for the perpetrators to be brought to justice in an international tribunal. Jolie also made her first visit to Syria and twice returned to Iraq to meet with Iraqi refugees as well as multinational forces and U.S. troops.

While she did, our media that year fueled round-the-clock breakup reports: Were Jolie and Pitts calling it quits? Photos of the stars looking away from one another at the moment a paparazzo snapped a shutter were analyzed to determine whether their body language meant the relationship was over. (It wasn't.) In one interview, Aniston called Jolie's public comments about the beginning of Jolie's relationship with Pitt "uncool"—just that single word. The media went into orbit, proclaiming Aniston's "utter contempt" for her "love rival." Would Jolie respond? *Should* she? Magazines drummed up sales by featuring split-cover photos of Jolie and Aniston cut and Photoshopped to look as though they were glaring at one another. Gossip sites ran headlines like, "Does Brad Pitt's Mother Hate Angelina Jolie?"

Throughout 2007, 2008, 2009, 2010, and 2011, as Jolie became a member of the prestigious think tank, the Council on Foreign Relations, which called her "part of the next generation of foreign policy leaders," she continued to tirelessly circle the globe, visit refugees, lobby and write on their behalf, and personally gift millions of her own money to assist the poorest of the world's poor. Yet the American media continued to deliver an endless feedback loop of the same old stories about Jolie, Pitt, and Aniston.

When Richard Haass, author of *War of Necessity, War of Choice*, appeared on Bill Maher's HBO show in early 2010, Maher gleefully showed him a photo of Jolie reading Haass's serious policy book about the lessons to be gleaned from the Iraq war. Haass, president of the Council on Foreign Relations, defended Jolie as a CFR member and a knowledgeable expert in foreign affairs and was, therefore, unsurprised that she'd read his book. Maher quipped that, to him, she was just a MILF.[48] Cue audience laughter.

In the twenty-first century our media still focuses on the most retro, stereotypically female images. One could entirely forget that women now have *careers* and, certainly in Jolie's case, tangible, meaningful *accomplishments*. Women's accomplishments are rarely celebrated in our media unless the "accomplishment" is in one of these five areas: appearance, romance, marriage, pregnancy, or babies. Women will get a cover for weight loss, breast enlargement or other plastic surgery, change in hair color, wearing the right dress, and, especially, for having a wedding, being pregnant, or giving birth. A male talk show host will mention her if he could imagine having sex with her, and he'll laugh at the idea that she could read a serious book, even if it's squarely in the field of her life's work. For the glossies, entertainment shows and sites, and talk shows, it's as though the women's movement never happened.

Jolie must feel as though she lives in an alternate universe, one of daily cognitive dissonance. She soldiers on, focusing on her humanitarian efforts, making films, raising her children. One-third of her income goes to savings, she has said, one-third to supporting herself and her family, and one-third to charity. For an actor commanding over $20 million per film, that is a generous annual donation to assist the world's poor.[49] She poses for provocative covers and gives interviews to raise her profile, hoping to divert some of the attention she gets to the needy and the destitute. She has one, and only one, persistent message to the world: Please, *please* pay attention to the millions who, through no fault of their own, have become refugees or internally displaced persons.[50]

After visiting a camp in Ecuador, Jolie said, "People's lives are truly in danger—not just in the sense that you feel your town is unsafe—their lives are actually being threatened and their houses are being burnt down."[51] How does she come home after visiting families without tents or clean water or access to medical care for their sick children to see cover stories now in their sixth year throwing around rumors about her supposed feud with Jen, television shows speculating about whether she's lost weight, and websites filled with vitriol about her decision to adopt international orphans?

As of December 2010 there was a Facebook group with more than 1,200 members entitled, "I Hate Angelina Jolie Because She's a Homewrecking Slut!"

Jolie has spoken before prestigious conferences, such as the World Economic Forum in Davos, Switzerland. She's personally lobbied Congress more than twenty times on behalf of refugees and children in extreme poverty.[52]

Most of us don't know about any of that. But we all know that in 2008 Jolie gave birth to twins. The media frenzy around the impending delivery reached a fever pitch. Rather than fight it, Jolie decided to harness it. She made a savvy business decision to auction off the first pictures of herself, Pitt, and the newborns to the highest bidder, which wound up being *People* magazine, for $14 million. Jolie donated all the money to her foundation to help third world refugees and, especially, displaced children.[53]

Wouldn't it be gratifying to live in a world where what happened to that $14 million was the story that garnered the big headlines in top-selling magazines? How many children got bed nets to save them from malaria? How many tents were purchased to give displaced families even that simple roof over their heads? How many classes were given so that widows could have marketable skills to use when they returned home, giving them the dignity of supporting themselves, paying their children's school fees, and providing their families with adequate nutrition? What kind of aid is working, and what isn't? What more can we do to follow her lead?

If only we had one-tenth the interest in Jolie's life's work as we have in her "beauty secrets"; if only we envied her compassion for the world's forgotten people rather than her appearance. If only we focused our attention on the tens of millions of luckless, displaced people rather than on a manufactured love triangle story that obviously bears little connection to reality at this point, if it ever did. If only ratings soared and websites crashed when the media covered real people with real stories of need and the simple fixes, like sewing classes, we can give them to get their lives back on track.

If only magazines flew off the racks when the inch-high yellow headline read,

> LIFE'S WORK OF ONE OF PLANET'S MOST ACTIVE AND GENEROUS HUMANITARIANS REVEALED!

Here's how depressingly bad the situation has become.

I once saw a major American news network promote an hour-long prime-time exclusive interview with Angelina Jolie. "Coming up tonight, Angelia Jolie opens up about Brad and motherhood," intoned the baritone voiceover guy, whoever he is, with a close-up of her pretty face. Throughout the day the network heralded its upcoming piece. Having worked for this serious, hard news network and appeared many times on this particular show, I knew they wouldn't devote an hour to a celebrity puff piece. I wondered what was going on. Would they really spend an hour asking her about how she felt about being half of "Brangelina," did she ever speak to Jen, or was she feeding her babies mashed peas?

Curious, I tuned in.

Bless the network, and bless her—it was an hour-long piece about African refugees, with Angelina explaining the heartbreaking need for humanitarian relief, the root causes of displacement of millions of innocent people, and the desperate conditions in which they were living. Toward the end the anchorman, an uber-intelligent guy who has traveled extensively himself, a man I know personally and who I doubt enjoyed asking these questions, threw her the requisite tabloidy questions that were required of him to live up to those promos. Was she pregnant again? Would she and Brad get married? She half-smiled and half-answered the questions. That part had to have been agreed to in advance and carefully choreographed.

Was it my imagination or was Angelina gritting her teeth, the cartoon thought bubble from her head reading, "Are you people such shallow morons that the only way you will learn about the suffering of millions of people is if I tell you whether or not I have a baby bump?"

That Q-and-A about Angelina's love life, thrown incongruously into a special about children literally starving in refugee camps, was for us. By "us," I mean the viewing public, and here, I mean primarily women. We won't watch a program about African refugees, so we have to be tricked into it. We *will* tune in if we know Angelina's going to "break her silence" about some trivial aspect of her private life.

The next day the media ran with the Angie-not-pregnant "news" from the special. Not a word about the refugees.

I HAVE TO GIVE YOU just one more example of our media's focus on the trivial to the exclusion of the meaningful.

In the American press, especially on cable news, former president Jimmy Carter has often been portrayed as a wing nut. In late 2009 the news shows and cable networks played over and over again his comment that race motivated some of the opposition to President Obama's health care reform. Race is an easy, emotional topic. Are we a postracial country? Is it fair to attack the opposition by calling them racists? Do some lawmakers and opposition activists treat President Obama more disrespectfully because he is African American? (Cable news is always better at asking questions than answering them.)

The obvious answer is that some extremists are racist, some pernicious racism still exists in America, and some conservatives had legitimate criticisms of Obama's health care plan that had nothing to do with race. After all, former president Bill Clinton was blasted to smithereens on health care too—and race, of course, did not motivate that opposition.

Hour after hour was spent handwringing about Carter's comment. It was a topic that got endless play for about a week.

As analysts discussed Jimmy Carter, some said he'd gone too liberal, too soft. Some didn't like his views on the Middle East. Others defended him as speaking plainly on an issue that others shy away from. A fair number dismissed him entirely as having gone around the bend.

In sizing him up, not a single pundit mentioned the greatest achievement of Carter's postpresidential lifetime. Did you know that through his philanthropic efforts, Carter has almost succeeded in wiping out guinea worm, a parasite that has afflicted humans throughout history? Guinea worm is a plague so ancient that it is found in Egyptian mummies and is thought to be the "fiery serpent" described in the Old Testament as torturing the Israelites in the desert. Here's how the *New York Times* described this hideous parasite:

> For untold generations here [in Nigeria], yard-long, spaghetti-thin worms erupted from the legs or feet—or even eye sockets—of victims, forcing their way out by exuding acid under the skin until it bubbled and burst. The searing pain drove them to plunge the blisters into the nearest pool of water, whereupon the worm would squirt out a milky cloud of larvae, starting the cycle anew.[54]

"The pain is like if you stab somebody," said Hyacinth Igelle, a farmer with a worm coming out of a hand so swollen and tender that he could not hold a hoe. He indicated how the pain moved slowly up his arm. "It is like fire—it comes late, but you feel it even unto your heart."[55]

Former President Carter relentlessly campaigned for twenty years to have guinea worm be the first disease since smallpox to be eradicated from our planet. And he's very nearly done it. There were three million cases of guinea worm in 1986. In 2008 there were just twelve thousand.

Carter did this by persuading world leaders, philanthropists, and corporations to get on board with the fight. His foundation sent volunteers to tens of thousands of African villages to treat the drinking water where the worms lived.

Twenty years of thankless, tedious work. Nearly three million people are spared that suffering this year and hopefully every year in the future because of him.

In light of this, who cares what his occasional semicontroversial comment was? Shouldn't his work to eradicate the guinea worm at least be mentioned in the stories about him? If we organized news by what's most important, wouldn't this compose 90 percent of any story about Jimmy Carter? Shouldn't this be the headline?

CARTER SPARES MILLIONS OF AFRICANS
HIDEOUS GUINEA WORM AGONY
(Oh, he also made a random comment some people disagree with.)

Desperately poor people on the other side of the planet had yard-long acid-spitting fire worms squirting out of their feet or eyes and now they don't because of this man's humanitarian work.

I wonder about the Angelina Jolies and Jimmy Carters, whether they sit at home and watch the breathless coverage of the most trivial aspects of their lives and think, "What has become of my country?"; whether they tire of trying to trick people into paying attention to diseases and wars and refugee camps where millions languish; whether former president Clinton groans at another Monica Lewinsky wisecrack while his foundation's focus on climate change, HIV/AIDS, and sustainable development has improved millions of lives here and abroad in just five years? In private, off-camera, unscripted moments, do they turn to their friends and ask, despairingly, "Have we become a nation of idiots?"

No. I don't *actually* think we're a bunch of idiots, and I certainly don't think women are. I do think we have lost a certain focus, and the problem with the media has become a chicken-and-egg question. It delivers crap to us; the crap mesmerizes us (i.e., it generates high ratings); the media gives us more, and—oops—we've all become dazzled and distracted and unfocused. I myself fall prey to it periodically, and although I may act like a damn fool from time to time, I'm not an idiot. And neither are you. And neither are our sisters and mothers and girlfriends.

I don't think that we are cold and uncaring about the world's suffering either—quite the contrary. When the media occasionally swarms a worthy story—say, the devastating January 2010 Haiti earthquake—we Americans quickly respond, digging deep, swamping charitable organizations with hundreds of millions of dollars of our compassion. This occurs during a recession, when times are very tight for many of us. We see images of neighbors in our hemisphere, though they are strangers in a country most of us have never visited, and we want to help. How many other needy pockets of the world could be lifted up if the media highlighted those problems in the same way?

And I know we don't want to be ignorant. In the year I spent researching and writing this book and speaking to girls' and women's groups about this topic, I was heartened to discover that all the girls and women I talked to about thinking *wanted* to be smarter, *wanted* to focus on what's meaningful. We all know on some level that we've gone off track. Even in a culture that too often values hot over smart—Angelina Jolie isn't the only one whose looks are admired while her accomplishments are ignored—*we still want to be smart.* A great accomplishment of the women's movement is that even if men want sexy women, even if the culture rewards attractive women more, even if every billboard and commercial and film touts beauty as our foremost defining characteristic, even if every magazine has One Hundred Beauty Secrets You Need to Know Right Now!—to hell with that, we still want to be resourceful, and clever, and wise. We want to outsmart the boys. We want knowledge. We want to change the world. We want to *think.*

After all, 75 percent of us would rather win the Nobel Peace Prize than win America's Next Top Model, and 78 percent of us would rather lose our figures than our ability to read. And I believe—I truly believe—that most of us want to spend less time reading about this season's "must-have" pedicures and more time understanding what we can do to combat genocide, reduce climate change, or take on any number of worthy global or local problems. We are sick of giving up an hour to blow-drying and makeup while our boyfriends have that time to themselves. We want to spend less time exfoliating and brow shaping and more time reading the news and engaging with our world.

We're sick of a culture that tells us that to remain boyfriend worthy—even job worthy—we need to spend thousands of dollars having plastic surgeons carve us up, risking our good health and even our lives. I believe that most of us want to look at our imperfect bodies and say, in the words of singer India.Arie, "What God gave me is just fine" and get on with what's meaningful.[56]

I believe that we already know that, as Indie.Arie says, "a lady ain't what she wears but, what she knows."[57] We just sometimes lose sight of it, tempted by our dumbed-down media and constant shiny distractions.

If the culture isn't going to give us a road map for how to reclaim our brains, how do we get there?

Let's get talking about solutions.

PART TWO

solutions

4

Reclaiming the Brains God Gave Ya

WHEN SHE WAS A LITTLE GIRL in the early 1920s, my paternal grandmother, Louise, helped her mother hand out homemade birth control devices to coal miners' wives in West Virginia. (She never told me what these devices were, and now I kick myself for not asking.) She told me this one day in a matter-of-fact way as we were jarring jam made from her backyard peach tree.

A small line of tired wives would form out her back door most weekday mornings, she said, many with small children clutching their skirts. Women would tell Louise's mama, with a catch in their throat, "I already have nine kids, and I just can't have any more. I hear you have something that can help me. Is it true? God bless you for helping me."

Louise and her mama never told Daddy what they were doing. It wasn't his business. He didn't need to know. They knew what they were doing was illegal at the time—not until 1965, when she was a grandmother eight times over, did the U.S. Supreme Court strike down laws against birth control nationwide. But Louise and her mama didn't care, and The Law, as she called it, never came for them. They had to help their neighbors, "those poor souls," as Louise recalled them decades later, her heart still full of compassion for their hard lives. So they set up shop and did what they had to do whether or not The Law and Daddy approved. And that was that. Pass the peach jam.

Later my grandmother, as a young woman, moved to Alaska with her military husband. She came down to the kitchen one morning and found a grizzly bear, reared up on his hind legs, big as a house. She swiftly grabbed her shotgun and fired it into the air, scaring him out the back door, and then she put the coffee on.

That military husband, my grandfather, turned out to be bipolar, or "manic depressive" as it was called in those days. Louise said, "He had spells." In 1963 he committed suicide. She was left alone, in her mid-fifties, with next to nothing and three young adult children, two of whom had major mental illnesses they'd inherited from their father. Louise knew that she was the one who had to take care of them for the rest of her life. My aunt was schizophrenic and my father severely bipolar. Louise wasn't about to leave their care up to the state, nor would she become a destitute widow. Those options were out of the question.

She looked around and assessed her options. She had just moved to a quiet little Southern California seaside town named La Jolla. Others were starting to notice the quaint, sunny charm of the place. Real estate, she decided, would be her business. She then set out to get her broker's license, learned the business, and founded her own real estate company. Louise went on to a three-decade-long career selling homes at a time when men dominated the industry. She hired a few brokers to work under her, rented prime office space smack in the middle of downtown, and became prosperous. She supported herself and her family and became active on the town council, opposing overdevelopment of her little beach community. Woe to the fat cat corporation that wanted to build a skyscraper in her town—wasn't going to happen on her watch. Nor could stores put up garish signs or fail to sweep their sidewalk. Town preservation didn't just happen, folks; it took vigilance. In 1980s La Jolla, vigilance was an old lady with sensible shoes and a clasp purse who patrolled the village daily. Everywhere we went in La Jolla, people would stop Louise and say hello, thank her for selling their home or saving the children's beach, and tell me how much they loved her.

Louise had a late-in-life name change. One of my cousins nicknamed her "Foxy Lady" when that term was in vogue in the 1970s, and the name became abbreviated to Fox, which is the only name I ever called her. She absorbed the name with glee, collecting silver fox figurines and grinning that she was "cunning"—one of her highest compliments to anyone—"cunning like a fox."

A great animal lover, Fox always adopted the ugliest pets from her local shelter, knowing no one else would. She had a misshapen gray mutt with an enormous head, scrawny body, and a hole in his palate that dripped saliva. She named him Cutty, generously comparing him to the cute terrier mascot of her favorite scotch. A scruffy, acerbic terrier named Margaret Thatcher yapped incessantly at a painful decibel. She'd smile and scratch her between the ears, "Oh, Meg! Honestly."

Fox wore no makeup but a little lipstick when she went out and was proud of her "laugh lines." "See these?" she asked me, pointing to her crow's feet. "I *earned* these!" She had her hair done once a week, and that was about it for her beauty routine.

She had her daily scotch on the rocks and cigarette on her deck every day at 5 p.m., thank you very much, and she taught my brother at age eight to prepare and bring her that cocktail. Later, when the health effects of smoking became undeniably clear, she announced that she was going to stop cold turkey, after decades of addiction. And that's precisely what she did.

My grandmother figured out her own life. She used her own brain to work out what she had to do. She didn't complain about what life had dealt her, ranging from her husband's cruel suicide to her children's mental illnesses to the dead birds her tomcat insisted on depositing on her pillow at night. As her daughter descended into severe schizophrenia, Louise found her a little fixer-upper house a block from the beach, bought it, and arranged for her care. Louise arranged for her son, my dad, to live in another small but clean house a stone's throw from hers where she could keep an eye on him daily as he battled frequent depression. In her typically understated style, she'd sometimes tell me that he just "wasn't feeling well."

Afflicted with ALS, a degenerative and fatal neurological disease (more commonly known as Lou Gehrig's Disease), in her eighties, she lost the use of her left hand. Then she couldn't move her left elbow, then her left shoulder. Her left arm lay limp. She continued to live alone, buttoning her clothes with her right hand—slowly, steadily, surely—making her own meals, taking care of her pets and herself.

When her right hand started to numb, she knew what lay ahead: loss of both arms and then total paralysis. "I'm not one of these people who will type with their toes, Lisa," she told me evenly. Her own mama had died from ALS in her thirties, and Fox had watched her mother's steady deterioration. "I will never live in a nursing home," she'd told me many times. "They're full of *old* people," she said, a twinkle in her eyes. They also didn't allow pets, and life without her beloved rescue dogs was not a life she considered worth living.

Fox took it upon herself to read end-of-life books. She was not afraid of the right-to-die group, the Hemlock Society, and figured they'd have something to teach her. She let me know that the end was near and that she was going to take control of it. Because she did that, I was able to write her a long letter thanking her for every life lesson she'd given me. I thanked her for not simply *letting* me jump off the cliffs into the ocean at the beach near her home but also for *encouraging* me, whooping and hollering and saying "go!" so I'd time the jump right to land on the crest of those big old waves. I thanked her for a lifetime of fussing with my hair, tying it up in old-fashioned strips of rags when I was a girl, producing firm ringlets in the morning, pulling it back tight over my forehead when she took me to church on Sunday mornings, and brushing it one hundred times at night when I was a teenager. I thanked her for the endless books she bought me from the beloved corner bookstore when I came to visit and for leaving me the unstructured time to wallow in them, lying in bed in the mornings with tangled hair, sun streaming in, my teeth unbrushed, my stomach rumbling for breakfast—just a few more pages, just until the end of the chapter, just one more chapter, only thirty pages until the end, ten more pages, oh! That was such a good book!

I thanked her for teaching me self-confidence, for always trusting me to make good choices about my life. She was the anti-worrier. My leaping off rocky escarpments into the roiling sea was terrific in her eyes. My marrying young and popping out my kids in my twenties—hey, why not? It would all work out. When I was accepted to Harvard and Yale Law Schools and my mother was pressing me hard to go to Harvard, my second choice, Fox picked up the phone and instructed her briskly, "If Lisa is smart enough to get into Harvard and Yale, she's smart enough to decide which one to go to." That ended *that* discussion.

Life, to her, could all be managed if you used your head and figured things out, relied on your own wits, and continued marching forward. Her life was one big no-whining zone. In the thirty years I had the good fortune to have a life that overlapped with hers, the only complaint I can ever remember coming from her lips was about women who went out in public with curlers in their hair. She couldn't abide them. Otherwise, life, and everything it threw her way, was just fine with her.

Fox left on her own terms at a time she chose. My heart was broken, but someone had to give the eulogy at her funeral, and I was the family public speaker. She never shirked from any responsibility, so on a windy cemetery hill overlooking her beloved blue Pacific, I gave it everything I had. Twenty years later, I still miss her daily.

If her life had played out in the twenty-first century, how would it be different? I suppose many would criticize a mother, her mother, who encouraged a child to break the law in their own little criminal conspiracy, even though birth control is no longer considered sinful. Risking jail to help strangers is unheard of now. After her husband's death, Fox would now be expected to undergo years of therapy to determine why she'd been attracted to such a man to begin with, to analyze whether she'd been codependent, addicted to love, or an enabler. Grief counseling, parenting classes, relationship counseling. She'd certainly be prescribed antidepressants, because you can't get out of an American doctor's office these days without a scrip for at least Valium or Prozac. Her mentally ill children would probably be institutionalized, and we'd all be paying for their care. Perhaps she'd undergo career counseling and take standardized tests to steer her into a job that matched her skill set. Then she'd work for five or ten years for someone else, learning the business from the ground up before applying for small business loans to venture out tentatively on her own.

Child protective services would haul her in for questioning when they found out she'd cheered for me to jump off cliffs and taught my little brother to make cocktails for her. Would animal welfare take a look at those deformed dogs of hers? And was the Hemlock Society entirely legal?* Shouldn't she at least have had a doctor assist her in ending her life?

Fox was the original Do-It-Yourselfer, as were all the women who came before us—those who rejected all the negative cultural messages about what women weren't supposed to do and instead just got on with their lives on their own terms. And Fox had bupkis compared to the resources and opportunities we have now.

Not only was Fox a great role model to me—a woman who worked out her own stuff, day after day—but she also gave me the gift of confidence in my own judgment. That's something overprotective parents unknowingly withhold from their kids. When I jumped off the cliff into the ocean, I learned that I could time the leap, hit the top of the wave, get pulled under, and pull myself up to air. It was scary, and I often got the wind knocked out of me, but even if I sputtered up onto the sand, I did it. *I* did it. And that lesson has buoyed me through many rough patches.

I meet too many smart girls and women who simper at the first sign of trouble in their lives—a boyfriend who cheats, a husband who won't do housework, an obnoxious teacher, the sadistic boss. I want to inject them with a healthy dose of my grandmother's *cunning* spirit. I want

*Fun fact from your author, the legal analyst: Suicide is the only crime that is unlawful as an attempted, but not a completed, act.

them to stand up straight, dust themselves off, come up with a plan, and march confidently forward.

I want them—you!—to reclaim your brain. Then I want to encourage you to use your newfound brain power for good, my friend, not evil; to refocus on what's meaningful; and to ignore everything else that is not.

I spent the first half of this book trying to grab you by the eyeballs and alert you to the horrors of what's happened because we let our brains fall into disuse. Are you ready to get back on track? I can't sugarcoat it. I have to get personal. I'm going to give it to you straight, like Fox's Scotch.

Step One: Reclaim Time to Think

The primary reason why we women lose track of what's going on in the world, why we rarely pick up a book or a decent newspaper, why we aren't more involved in our communities and our world, why we often have difficulty managing even our own lives is that we run ourselves ragged just maintaining our hectic schedules. We have less leisure time than ever before and significantly less than our male counterparts. Men slack off thirty-eight minutes more per day than women, which adds up to ten days off per year they take that we don't, according to the Organization for Economic Cooperation and Development.[1] Many women I know have virtually *no* leisure time whatsoever and haven't taken a vacation for years. "I *wish* I could be more up on the news," my friend Anna tells me on a wistful phone call, "I wish I could go to a school board meeting and tell them the curriculum is idiotic, but—Charlotte! Honey, put that down!" The phone goes dead.

In the tough economy we've lived in the last few years, many of us work longer hours for companies with fewer employees to churn out the product, looking over our shoulders at the competition nipping at our heels from the unemployment lines. Who dares to complain? There are a hundred others who'd be happy to have our jobs.

Sound familiar? We have become grunts, slaves to the needs of our employers and families.

And this applies not only to the working moms, though we have it the worst. College girls are so swamped with their course loads and part-time jobs that they can't imagine having free time to think globally, locally, or creatively, and young women feel overwhelmed with their new jobs, working long hours for low wages just to pay the rent in a tough economy. Thinking becomes a luxury to do later . . . when . . . I don't know . . . maybe when I'm on vacation? Or when I get a promotion and don't have to work so hard? When I find Mr. Right? Or when the kids are both in school? After my divorce is final?

Uh huh. Sure.

Reminds me of the elderly couple who go to the rabbi for a divorce. "A divorce?" says the rabbi. "But you're both in your nineties! You've been married for over sixty years! Why would you get divorced now?" "Because," says the couple, "we wanted to wait until the kids were dead."

Are you going to wait until the proverbial kids are dead—until every other responsibility and distraction in your life has magically disappeared—before you allow yourself time to think? Or will you commit to carving out thinking time for yourself every day because doing so is a priority? Wouldn't engaging your brain daily *help* you with all the other issues in your life?

I know that no one can think when life is nothing but work, laundry, kids, dinner, dishes, sleep deprivation, repeat, repeat, repeat. Don't you deserve better than just dragging your sorry ass from home to work and back again, sleep deprived, carelessly pouring baby formula into your coffee mug? (*Shudder*—a mistake I made only once.) Your first step must be to take a clear look at your life and unearth some fresh new time each and every day to call your very own: to dream, to imagine, to *think*.

When I speak to college and graduate women's groups, regardless of what I am there to discuss—high-profile cases, media, sexual harassment law, what have you—hands shoot up afterward and these earnest, adorable young faces always ask me for advice on "having it all." They seem so concerned about how they will juggle careers and family. Can it work? How did I do it?

At dinner with friends of my generation, the working moms have a couple of glasses of wine and just start weeping. The poor things are just beat, and they dread going back home to the 24/7 treadmill of work, kids, and housework that awaits them.

If "having it all" means having a family with kids, outside work, and enough "me" time to be able to shave both of your legs on the same day, I am here to say that it's definitely attainable. In fact, we can shoot higher. But to get there, I'm going to have to shake up some deeply held mindsets that are holding us back. We've talked about work-life balance for decades, after all, and *still* we're not progressing. This calls for some blunt talk and drastic action—because we can't focus on big issues like climate change or genocide or the sorry state of our kids' schools when we're exhausted from our own lives.

First, my credentials. I worked straight through my kids' childhoods, first as a civil rights attorney in the trenches of sexual harassment, race discrimination, and other hot-button areas of the law and then as a full-time television host and commentator. In 2001 Court TV hired me to anchor a national trial coverage show for two hours a day, live, for eight years. A few years in, ABC hired me as a legal analyst for *Good Morning America* and then CBS hired me as a legal analyst for *The Early Show*. Then CNN hired me as a legal analyst for its networks (CNN, HLN, CNN International) too. For the last five years or so, I've been on an average of a couple of times a day on one show or another. In addition to this, I now run my own busy law firm, the Bloom Firm, handling high-profile clients as well as everyday folks seeking justice in all types of family, civil, and criminal cases.

The point is that I have a busy work schedule. For the last five years I've had two or three jobs simultaneously, two biological kids, and, as I write, a beloved adolescent foster son.

Just like millions of other working moms, my kids were always my main concern. I was a single mother for much of their childhood.

Making a home-cooked dinner nearly every night was a priority because I wanted to get healthy food into them at least once a day, and sitting around the table over big bowls of pasta is the best way to get to know what's up in each other's lives. We laughed, we cried. Sometimes they laughed while I cried. We had an ornery, occasionally vicious rescue terrier named Whiskey who only we understood and loved, and we were distraught when she died. We still have our other family rescue dog, Soda, who we all adore so much we've become Crazy Dog People. I got married and divorced twice when they were little and vowed that would be it for me, and then I had a nice, long-term boyfriend and when we broke up, I felt guilty guilty guilty; my kids told me it was okay, Mom. And that, in a nutshell, was our family.

I ain't perfect. But this was life, and my kids and I kept ticking. The three of us, my kids and I, were a family unit, and we stuck together and stuck up for each other. They didn't rebel against me like most American teenagers, though I certainly had a boundless capacity to annoy them. Each of my kids did one Very Bad Thing during their adolescence, and if I reveal those things in print they'll stick me in the foulest possible nursing home when my time comes, so I can't. However, the very good things they did daily vastly outweighed their Very Bad Things, things like being home when promised, being kind, and only lying to me a normal teenaged amount. Mainly it was a rollicking good time for all of us, at least it was until my son beat me at Scrabble and my daughter started stealing my clothes in earnest.

Knock on wood, my babies turned into a young woman and a young man who are both bright, sweet-natured, hardworking people of character who think for themselves. I could not be more proud of them. They both got in to their first-choice colleges, and so far neither is an axe murderer or an Octomom. To the extent that I had anything to do with that, this section explains how.

The thing is that I *didn't* weep from exhaustion. I didn't have a nanny. I had time to read books and work out and talk to my friends, and without that, I'd have gone around the bend. Oh, also, during my single working mom years, I trained for and ran two marathons, prayed with Buddhist monks in Laos, sat in on the Prime Minister's Questions in British Parliament, saw Picasso's *Guernica* in Spain, volcano boarded in Nicaragua, slept in a mud hut with a Berber family in Morocco, practiced yoga on a cliff over a desolate beach in India, backpacked up thirteen of the highest peaks in the White Mountains of New Hampshire, canoe camped along the Delaware River, and skied down a double black diamond run in a Vermont blizzard, ripping my knee in half.* Geez, do I have fun.

I'm not saying this to brag; rather, I am saying it to persuade you that you can be a working mom—even a single working mom—and still *live*.

How? The biggest change you need to make is to your attitude. You have to toss out dusty old myths that hold us back. We're not in the 1950s anymore, homegirls. What is the heaviest yoke around our necks that is preventing us from moving forward? Housework.

Housework Is Not Your Job!

In the twenty-first century there are *still* commercials featuring women delightedly dancing around their bathrooms with their new soap-scum products, singing along with animated characters. In real life, we'd call these women deranged.

Any magazine that tries to sell you on the idea that scrubbing toilets makes you burst into song or that trying a new mop is a blast, or that you'll be giddy when you get your kids' pants whiter than their friends' clothing† should be lit on fire and hurled into the street.

We are the first generation of girls that beat the boys in school so soundly that they need affirmative action to compete with us! Hello!

---

*The secret upside to divorce: When the kids are with your ex, get out there and have adventures! I took these trips when the kids had summer or holiday time with Dad or Grandma. If you're willing to change planes a few times and sleep in a tent, you can travel abroad for peanuts.

†Seriously, who even *buys* white pants for kids? Or for themselves?

So how are we still swallowing the message that it is *our job* to polish and dust and vacuum?

According to the U.S. Census Bureau, when both a working wife and a working husband come home from their full-time jobs—that's *jobs*, plural—the wife does an average of one hour more of housework per day than the husband. And according to time-diary data from the federally funded Panel Study of Income Dynamics, when a single woman gets married, she shoulders an extra seven hours per week of housework while her new husband does an hour a week less than he did as a bachelor.[2]

This makes me want to hurt someone.

Why, oh why, is this still the case? There is only one explanation: because we women have deeply internalized the message from the days of pointy bras and thick girdles that housework is *our* job. Maybe the mindset came from your eternally dusting and sweeping mother, bless her. But she came from another era and didn't know any better, so I forgive her.

You, I don't excuse. Have you watched nothing but *Leave It to Beaver* for the last forty years? Are you enjoying being a martyr? Because it's not working for you.

I am here to deprogram you—because we are *not* passing this down to the next generation. It has got to stop with us. Your sons and daughters are watching you. You are not going to raise them to expect that men sit back and watch the game while the women scrub out bath rings.

Housework is not your job. It is not women's work. Let's call it what it is: repetitive, mind-numbing drudgery. Why should that job fall to the adult with the vagina? There is no logical reason whatsoever. None. If you really enjoy doing it, fine. If you have a spouse/partner who really enjoys doing it and does his/her fair share, fine. For the other 99.9 percent of us: You must look at it as not your job. This is an essential mindset. You don't fix your own car. Why not? You could. You could learn. Most women don't even change the oil in their cars. Why not? That's an easy job, actually. We don't because we don't think of that as our job. We have to put housework in the same mental category.

It is *a* job, but it is not *your* job. Say it loud, say it proud.

Many women change careers or jobs to get better, more "family friendly" hours. We'll go through all that trouble and then come home and slave away like automatons. Why do we fight for better hours and working conditions from our employers but not from our families?

Look at it another way. Why do men in our culture still not do their fair share of housework? Because they don't consider it to be their *job*. That's why they don't see the dirty socks and you do.

Men finish college and then get their first low-paying job and their first dinky little apartment. What do they do right away to fire up that bachelor pad? They call to set up their utilities—check. Cable—check. Hire a housekeeper to come bimonthly—check. Why? (Recite it with me.) Because they do not see housework as their *job*. How many single ladies do this? Very few.

This is the mindset we need to adopt.

I am not talking about child care here, only cleaning. There's a world of difference between time with the kids and time doing housework. Your kids will grow up fondly remembering the times you threw a ball with them, played Monopoly with them, and chatted around the dinner table with them. Your oven will not fondly remember any of the times you scoured it. The less time you spend doing housework, the more time you'll have with your kids—or for yourself, to read, to dream, to strategize, to think.

Housework is a job that, ideally, you are going to farm out. That is more doable than you may think. And if you are so strapped that you can't pay for a little help, then you are going to make sure that everyone in your home who sullies the kitchen and fouls the toilets shares that job equally.

I know women who can easily afford a housekeeper but do all the housework themselves. My friend Joni founded her own small business, a dance school, which grew by leaps and bounds to become the leading dance school in her state, with thousands of students and scores of recitals and performances every year. Her company earns several million dollars annually in revenue, enough to help pay for her beautiful large home as well as a lakefront vacation house. A working mom, she raised her son and daughter to be two of the loveliest people you could ever hope to know.

Joni always insisted on personally cleaning both homes herself. And they are spotless. And I am depressed. I don't think I've ever seen Joni sitting down. While her husband and kids kick back, watch movies, and catch up, she's off tidying up somewhere, missing out. What happened here? She feels that maintaining her homes is *her job*, and anyway, housekeepers don't do as good a job, she says. They don't clean as well as she does.

But guess what, Joni? You can train housekeepers. You can tell them how, exactly, you want the table dusted or the baseboards wiped, if that's important to you. (In my case, I wouldn't notice dust until it morphed into a troglodyte and started growling at me. But I understand other people have slightly more exacting housekeeping standards.) The housekeeper works for you. You can specify how you want everything, and she will do it your way.*

Then there is my friend Susan, working mom of three school-age daughters who are rambunctious and sassy and cute as puppies. She is a leftist type who is uncomfortable with the idea of hiring someone to clean up after her family, though she too could afford it. But doing so would make her feel elitist. Hey Susan! What do you think happens when you leave your office at night? People come and clean, that's what. Do you feel guilty about that? What's the difference between a professional cleaning your office and a professional cleaning your home?

Susan is always strung out, sleep deprived, and dog tired.

To my beloved pinko liberal friends: Don't you want to help out a female small business owner? Because that's what most house cleaners are. Don't condescend. She is an independent contractor looking for accounts. Pay her a fair wage, give her referrals to your friends and a nice holiday bonus, and feel good about helping a sister grow her business.

*No "he/she" here. We all know the housekeeper is usually a "she."

Maybe you are like my friend Janice, a working mother of two toddlers who feels so financially strapped she doesn't feel she can justify paying a housekeeper out of her tight budget. Yet Janice often comes home so bleary-eyed that she can't face making dinner, so they eat out frequently. That's the catch-22: The more wiped out you are, the more frequently you spend extra bucks at restaurants, and the less you feel you can afford help.

Look, you really only need someone to come and clean every two weeks. If you skip eating out two or three times a month, you can pay for it. Eat peanut butter and jelly now and then if necessary—the kids prefer that anyway—and relish that shiny kitchen floor that someone else mopped to perfection. In my case, I'd skip eating *altogether* twice a month if necessary to avoid doing my laundry, much less the reeking piles of teenaged boys' socks.

And don't you dare clean before the housekeeper comes. Do you shave before a bikini wax?

In between housekeeper visits, of course, light housework will need to happen. Although I've considered it, you really can't let dishes pile up for two weeks. When the baby throws up in the vestibule, you can't *always* count on the dog to lap it up.

This is why you put your family on a schedule. You sit all the humans over age two around the table. Everyone contributes to the schedule, and everyone adheres to it. Children like clarity, men like charts with vertical and horizontal lines, and you like eight hours of sleep at night. When it's all in print, everyone understands their part, the rooms and jobs they're responsible for, and the fundamental fairness of not working Mom to weepy delirium.

The chart is important because traditionally male jobs, like taking out the trash and doing home repairs, take nanoseconds compared to the hours of daily drudgery that traditionally women's chores like child care, grocery shopping, cooking, and cleaning suck out of our lives. The chart makes this clear without having to nag about it. The chart rules.

You and any other adults in the house then need only to enforce the chart.

Once they are walking and speaking in sentences ("*Mommy, don't!*" is a complete sentence), children are old enough to clean up after themselves. If they can expand photos on an iPhone, they can do chores.

Here's how it went down in the Bloom household:

"Mom, can I go over to Hannah's?"

"So your room is clean?"

"Uh . . ."

I go back to my book. Damn, but that Elizabeth Strout sure can write. What a *pleasure* it is to have my feet up on the coffee table, reading her short stories. Should I have a cup of tea? Well, I did have one about an hour ago . . .

Half an hour passes, marked by muffled thumping sounds in the kid's bedroom.

"Mom, can I go over to Hannah's?"

"So you took the trash out and fed the dogs?"

Sound of garbage being pulled out of can, tied, taken out. Door slams. Kibble plinking into metal bowls.

"Mom . . ."

"Hi honey! Sure, have fun! Call me when you get there!"

See how pleasant that was *for Mom*?

And kids are not allowed to kvetch about chores because that does not add to Mommy's bliss. And no whining or begging on your end. If they don't do their job, they don't get to have their fun. Here's a great speech to have ready when they try that standard adolescent mope:

"I have to do *everything* around here."

I smile. "Sit down, sweetheart."

Kid gets nervous. Sits.

"Here was my day. Got up at five to go to work so I could support you. Took a quick shower, got dressed, without anyone telling me to. Brushed my teeth without being asked. Took out the trash. Made coffee, emptied dishwasher. Walked the dogs. Went to work. Went to your parent-teacher conference to learn that you're not turning in all of your homework. [Dramatic pregnant pause, meaningful mom-stare into fidgeting kid's eyes.] Went to grocery store. Carried heavy bags of groceries all the way home by myself. Dragged them into the apartment and made us all a nice dinner. After dinner, went online and signed you up for summer camp and paid the deposit out of money I made working all day.

"Boy, there isn't room enough for all that on the chart, is there? Maybe we need a bigger one! Maybe we need to adjust everyone else's chores to catch up to mine!

"Now, what was that you said about having to do *everything*? Because you did what . . . one load of dishes?"

They will never, ever say it again.

Here's the corollary to *housework is not your job.*

It's Okay for Your Kids to Be Miserable Sometimes

Better *they* should be miserable than *you* should be miserable, that's for sure—as long as they've earned it. I'm not talking about child abuse or neglect. I'm talking about allowing them to suffer a reasonable amount for the natural and fair consequences of their behavior.

So little Zachary got busted for smacking his sister Chloe, and now he's screaming in wretchedness in his room because you grounded him. Ho hum. That's his problem, not yours. Turn up your music, have a cookie, call your best friend, read a book to Chloe. He'll be fine. This is how he learns and grows.

If you're always running to comfort the crying kid or trying to calm down the hysterical toddler, they don't learn to work things out themselves. And you have needlessly run yourself ragged. No wonder you never have a second to think.

Alone time is important for kids' proper development, and not just when they're wailing. Here's another piece of advice that saw me through:

Children's Entertainment Is Not Your Job

Many working moms unnecessarily drain themselves managing every minute of their kids' leisure time. Unless you're a professional clown, entertainment of children should not be a part of your job description.

By which I mean leaving the kids (safely) on their own is a good thing. Let them hang out in their room with books, blocks, paper, and crayons and figure out what to do. Some of my happiest memories are staring out the window from my grandmother's house as a child. I imagined myself jumping off the roof or building a secret fort or stringing a rope bridge over to the next house. I mapped out my first novel. My grandma Fox did not assume responsibility for my every amusement, and it would never have dawned on me to ask her to. She loved me. She fed me. She asked me to help her in the kitchen and around the house, and I did, proud to take responsibility like a big girl for shucking ears of corn, bringing in the groceries, or walking her poodle, Linus Pauling. Each time I came to visit, our first stop was the corner bookstore. I was allowed to buy one book, two if I begged (I became an outstanding beggar). Then she left me alone with gorgeous blocks of unstructured time to enjoy them. Those books and my imagination were my entertainment for the weekend, and it was heaven.

And Fox genuinely enjoyed my visits because she didn't run herself ragged dragging me from one child's activity to the next. She didn't sit on the floor nor did she pretend to enjoy games with me that weren't her cup of tea. I stretched by listening to her music (Bing Crosby) and watching her TV shows with her (*Masterpiece Theater*—to this day, the opening theme music still puts me right to sleep). She quietly left my favorite cake in the refrigerator and never commented in the morning that a giant slice had carved itself out and disappeared while she was sleeping, so long as the knife, fork, and plate had washed themselves and found their way neatly into the dishwasher.

I implored my parents to let me visit Fox as much as I could during my childhood.

Two economists at the University of California, San Diego recently conducted a time study and found that moms today spend more time on child care (an average of twenty-one hours per week for college-educated women and sixteen hours per week for noncollege-educated) than moms did a generation ago (twelve hours per week, on average). How can that be possible when there are significantly fewer stay-at-home moms today? After all, the stay-at-home moms had all that face time with their kids. They had the home team advantage! The only explanation is that my mother's generation left us to our own devices most of the time. Kids were expected to play alone or with siblings or friends. Parents were not expected—nor, frankly, were they *invited*—to play with us. Parents were, to a large extent, authorities to be rebelled against. Inviting them into the fort would give aid and comfort to the enemy.

My kids made this mistake only once: "Mom, I'm bored."

"Oh, great!" I said, eagerly. "Here's a list of things for you to do. Start with cleaning your room. Next, wash the windows. There's some crud baked on to this pan that really needs a good scrubbing to get it off. Did you rewrite that homework assignment to bring up your grade? How's that thank you note to Grandma coming along? Honey? Where'd you go?"

I always interpret "I'm bored" as "How may I be of assistance?"

When my kids were little and they weren't required to do anything right at that moment, I called it "free time" and bestowed it upon them like the glorious gift it was: "Okay, we're home, there's an hour until dinner, so you have . . . *free time*!" They saw this as a special treat. As I do. Free time for them means precious free time for you. And that's what it's all about.

In a landmark study called "Ask the Children," researchers asked 1,000 kids what one wish they had for their parents. Researchers expected the answer would be the children's wish for more family time. "I wish Mommy would play with me more"? Nope. The top answer? For their parents to be "less tired and less stressed."

In her warm and wise parenting books, *The Blessing of a Skinned Knee* and *The Blessing of a B Minus*, Dr. Wendy Mogel comes to the same conclusion: Back off and give your kids the chance to solve their own problems, to exercise the divine gift of free will, to learn not to panic over pain. In short, give them the freedom to fail. She comes at it from a different perspective—because it's better for your kids, as overprotective, overinvolved parents produce flaccid, nervous children who struggle to become independent, self-sufficient adults.[3]

From my perspective, I know that moms need some grownup mental space for ourselves, to daydream and problem solve and create and wander. We need, figuratively if not literally, Virginia Woolf's "room of one's own," a place without a changing table, playpen, or Sponge Bob.

Take a break, Mom. Even your kids want you to. And for heaven's sakes, sleep with grownups only.

Enforce Bedtime and Mommy's Sleep Time

You can argue with me until you're blue in the face that the family bed leads to closer parent-child bonds, that the children feel nurtured, that other cultures do it, yada yada. Talk to the hand. I'm not buying it. Show me a home with a family bed and I'll show you a mom so tired she walks into poles. Sure, if you sneak in *their* rooms to check on them for a moment, they are innocent little sleeping angels, so serene it's impossible not to smooth their hair back and kiss them one more time. Share the bed with that same child, though, and you'll learn something they never told you in the *What to Expect* books: A sleeping child is a sweaty, babbling, horizontal windmill, cartwheeling nonstop all night.

Oh, no, not in *my* bed, you don't.

For their own health, kids need a strict bedtime because statistically speaking, most American kids are sleep deprived.[4] And as a result, they perform poorly in school, which in turn is part of the reason we're breeding the next generation of nonthinkers.[5] And you need them to go to bed at a set bedtime (8 p.m. sharp for elementary school kids) so that you can—say it with me—have time to think. According to the National Sleep Foundation, working moms of school-age kids average less than six hours sleep a night, though the American Academy of Sleep Medicine says we need at least seven or eight. No wonder we're all a bunch of walking zombies. Let's fix this once and for all. They go in their bed. You read them a book. Lights out. And they stay in that bed.

In our house, my children learned the hushed, sacrosanct rule: Never Wake Sleeping Mommy. Never, unless it is an emergency. An emergency is defined as (1) prolonged, intense pain or (2) profuse bleeding. An emergency does *not* include (1) "I can't sleep" or (2) "hey! I just thought of something!" Write it down and tell me in the morning, kid, when I'll be peppy and all ears.

If you don't stake out your territory, your kids will walk all over you. They'll suck up every minute of your waking and sleeping hours. Yes, it's adorable that they want to be with you every minute. It's cute how bonded they are. It's true that one day they'll be sulky big postpubescent creatures who growl at you when you have the unmitigated gall to crack open their bedroom door to ask if they're ready for dinner. You have to savor the little kid times—just not at night, and not in your bed.

Cooking: Keep It Simple . . . Really Simple

Eating needs to be done, especially by children, and there is something wonderful about family dinners because that's when you have a chance to cross-examine your teenagers. Our house features home-cooked meals nightly, and yours should too. It's much cheaper, thereby freeing up money for your twice-a-month housekeeper. Homemade food is healthier than those giant lard-ridden portions restaurants serve and is prepared just the way everyone likes it. You don't have to worry about the baby's high-pitched scream alarming the other diners. People can have seconds. Your friends can come to dinner, relax, kick back, and join in the fun embarrassing your tweens.

Family dinners at home rock.

If you have a partner who cooks, give yourself a big smug pat on the back, do the dishes nightly, and skip ahead if you like.

In my house, I'm the chef. Though I like to cook, I certainly didn't relish the job every livelong day after tromping home from work. Nevertheless, it had to be done, so I learned how to make fresh meals from scratch that my kids would eat, averaging less than a half hour of my time nightly.

If you're the family chef, focus on the part that gets you accolades: serving up heaping bowls of hot food to happy, hungry family members. It's not the slicing and dicing. We wax nostalgic for Mom serving up that spaghetti sauce, not for her sweating and grunting in the kitchen.

So, here are a few suggestions:

Become intimately acquainted with the prewashed, precut section in produce. God gave us presliced mangoes, and I, for one, am grateful. Ditto for prewashed, bagged salads. This is a good use of your money. These products are only a few bucks more, and they will save you precious Unhappy Hour time—the witching hour between school/work and dinner when everyone is cranky and you have to pretend you're not. Because I always cooked vegetarian, I had to cut down on the endless veggie washing and chopping time or I would have become homicidal. That prewashed, presliced section was my salvation. Toss some toasted peanuts, chopped red pepper, tofu, and peanut dressing on a bag of prewashed salad, warm up some whole grain rolls, and you've got a fresh, healthy dinner in less than five minutes.* (For more quickie fresh dinner ideas, check out my "Un-Recipes" at the end of this book.)

Share the love! Tell the staff at your market that prewashed, prechopped stuff amazes and delights you. I literally embraced the produce manager when my market starting offering preminced carrot, onion, and celery all in one convenient container—the quick start to my soups and chilies. Sing hosannah!

If you have a spare man lying around, ask him do the chopping. They like big cleavers. I tell mine he does such a great job carving up a pineapple. I myself never do it as well. It must be those big triceps! Grr! He grins and does the kitchen jobs I hate. You get the idea. (I have a friend who's gotten her husband to vacuum for forty years by

*I have more of these superfast healthy recipes I couldn't fit in here at www.Think.tv. Post your own there too!

laying on the syrupy praise about what a terrific job he does. Use what works, ladies.)

Develop a short list of easy-to-make dinners that the kids like. Nearly every week we ate pasta, dinner salads, burritos, or veggie burgers at least once. They like 'em, I like 'em, they're cheap, and each of these dinners can be made in less than half an hour while I'm sipping my soy tea latte and listening to the mellifluous voices on NPR.

Cleanup is the kids' job. After dinner I push back from the table with the contentment of knowing that my day's work is done. Cleanup is a perfect job for kids because washing dishes and wiping the table is easy. In our house, the dishwasher on duty that night gets to be DJ in the kitchen and blast whatever music he/she chooses at the decibel of his/her choosing while cleaning up. Loud music makes scrubbing pots somewhat angry and violent, which older kids enjoy. You can walk by the kitchen and pretend to be shocked by their music, as if you didn't body surf at AC/DC concerts before they were born.

Go to the market once a week and buy a ton of food. If you're going more often than that, other than for a few fresh items midweek, you're not buying enough. And you'll save money buying in bulk.

Cook big once a week. On Sunday I cook a giant witch's vat of chili or a huge pot of stew. Though this takes over an hour, most of that is simmering time while you can do other things, and then when you serve these tasty concoctions up as leftovers during the week, the five-minute warm-up prep time still gets your average back down to under thirty minutes cooking time per night. Which leads to . . .

Eat leftovers often. My next door neighbors, Harris and Melissa, parents of four kids, don't believe in eating leftovers because that's not how Melissa was raised. Come again? This translates into many extra hours in the kitchen for Melissa. On our side of the fence, we eat leftovers about three times a week. It's the ultimate fast food. Why do you think God gave us Tupperware and microwaves? Think of cooking as *assembling* items that you are going to have lined up in your fridge in happy abundance once you start cooking regularly: a little of yesterday's leftover spaghetti, a prewashed salad, and BAM! Dinner. Kids like their meals simple anyway. Don't obsess about making children elaborate dinners. If left to their own devices, their favorite meal would be a pile of sugar.

I know that single women are reluctant to cook because doing so is a lot of effort for just you. So don't let it be a lot of effort. Make food preparation light and breezy, but still make large quantities. Even if you're cooking for one, you're going to need fourteen lunches and dinners this week, next week, and hey, probably the week after that too. Make a bunch of food, save the leftovers, take 'em for lunch, eat 'em again in a few days, freeze the rest. And when it's dinner for one, relish the joy of cooking for *you*—spicy if that's your preference, or extra guacamole or with Japanese plum paste slathered on your ear of corn. (I do this. It's tangy-sweet deliciousness, I swear. No one else thinks so, though.) Now's your chance to discover your own preferences. And you can relish your favorite meals with your favorite author. A book is a delightful single girl's dinner companion. When I was dating, I would think, "Hmm, would I rather have dinner with this guy or Ian McEwan?"

Let Others Have Your Kids Sometimes . . . Without You

If you are lucky enough to have extended family or friends who offer to take your kids occasionally, good God woman, take them up on it. My mother, bless her, took my kids every Sunday morning when they were little, freeing me up to go to the gym, read the *Times*, and pick up sailors.*

Single moms! If your friend says, "Hey, I could watch your kids sometime," most of you respond, "Hey, that would be nice . . ." and then nothing comes of it.

No! Ixnay! Let's try this again.

Your friend says, "Hey, I could watch your kids sometime."

*If only.

You say, "Wow, that would *really* help me out! How about every Wednesday night from 6 to 10?"

Make it a regular weekly date with little Mika or Diego. Why shouldn't your friends and family have the joy of bonding with your kids, and your kids with them? However, for this to work, you must allow others to do things their way with your kids. It's a big world out there. Your kids may as well learn early that some people eat Sugar Smacks and watch QVC. It's okay, I promise. Breathe. And lay the appreciation on thick for your free babysitter. You can't thank them enough, but you can try.

Work-life balance? In short, don't be a martyr. Instead, work out the hours of your day just like you aced eighth-grade algebra. Solve for *x*, where *x* is your need to be a human with a little time to sit down and eat like a civilized person, to breathe, to read, to have friends, and to sleep. You're not living in a gulag. You make the rules. Change them as necessary in order to grant yourself the time you need to think.

Time Savers for Single Girls

Single girls, I haven't forgotten you.

If you're childless now and have kids one day in the future, you're going to look back on these years as your heyday of free time. You come home from work and then have several hours to do with as you please! No second shift focusing every moment on little people whose very survival depends on you! That you now consider yourself busy will blow your mind.

And yet most single and childless women I know do feel time pressured, squashed by the very real demands of their lives. (I did.) They put off their big plans for another day.

Single ladies, you too need *time to think*. What's eating up your time?

First, too much mental energy wasted on the guy who got away, the guy who didn't call, inability to meet the right guy, yada yada. This used to be me. What did he *mean* when he said, "See ya"? Did that mean "Goodbye forever"? Did that mean "I had a great time and I'll call you in five minutes"? Did it just mean, "Hey, I'm leaving now, so toodle-oo"? I'd call my best friend and deconstruct the entire evening. Then I'd call another friend and replay it for her point of view. Then I'd call the first friend back and bounce the second friend's advice off of her. Hours and hours wasted each week on this craziness.

All the single women I know do this. It saps the life out of us.

There's a better way to live. Here's what I suggest.

Be happy and busy. From the retro book *The Rules*, which teaches women to deceive men and other fun dating tips, I picked up this *one* piece of sensible advice: Be happy and busy! Happy and busy means you're not obsessing over your love life. Hotties will flock to you because you're such a blast to be around, yet often inaccessible, you fascinating creature. And if they don't, it doesn't matter much because you're . . . happy and busy.

Once you've decided to get out of a relationship, get on with it. That prolonged moaning and groaning, reconnecting, breaking up again, another hookup, late-night calls with your girlfriends—*look* at yourself. Do you look like a confident, thinking woman? Would your grandmother be proud of you, sniveling like that? Bite the breakup bullet. After a week or a night or five minutes, get back out there and have some fun. You are *busy*, and busy girls have no time for whimpering over the one who got away.

I have single girlfriends who still eat, sleep, and breathe their romantic dramas, who want to spend every conversation slicing and dicing their last date. Really? We're not living in a romantic comedy, in which the perfectly coiffed and nattily dressed actresses do nothing but plot to get the guy. We have educations to put to use; careers to tend to; friends, family, and community to engage with. And you'll be a more alluring catch when you are more engaged in all aspects of your life, not just your latest crush.

Then there's this: Not to get too personal, but how much time are you spending at bars and parties?

Young women mope that they don't have enough time in their lives, but if they added up their late-night partying several times a week (or more), most would magically find plenty of shiny new hours they could reclaim. Look, going out is fun, I know. You don't need to eliminate it entirely. I danced my youth away in New York and Hollywood clubs, and that was more fun than I care to detail in a book I expect my kids to read. But consider how much time it absorbs. For some reason, young people don't count the hours after 10 p.m. as *time*. If you're partying until 4 a.m. and then sleeping until noon or 2 p.m.—you know who you are, Gen Y—you've lost half a day. And because I know you—I *was* you—I know you're not honest with your boss or your mother or even yourself as to how often this is going on. And as far as I'm concerned, if you're barhopping frequently, you've lost the right to complain that you never have enough time for the things you really want to do. What if you limited the big blowout night to once a week? Or two hours, twice a week? What could you then accomplish?

Finally, take a hard look at your time spent on social media and texting. We spend twice as much time on social media than any other online activity, according to Nielsen. Facebook and Twitter will suck the life out of you. Push back. And, good grief, American teens average eighty texts per day, which means one every few minutes for every waking hour.[6] In my experience, young adults are no better. You think each text only takes a second, but in the aggregate they are diverting your attention and devouring your time. I know the iPhone is amazing, that the Blackberry's BBM function is lightning fast and fun, and that connecting with your friends constantly makes you feel loved. But put down the electronics regularly and free up time for your brain to breathe. You are stealing time—precious, valuable time—from yourself.

No matter where you are in your life—single, in a relationship, "it's complicated," kids or no—you need to grab chunks of time from all the other demands and temptations pushing for your attention. Some things cannot be changed. You're in a career you love, and it requires long hours. Your significant other needs quality and quantity time. Young children demand constant attention. You gotta eat and sleep.

You have family obligations. You need to take the dog to the vet. I get it. But too many of us don't carve out any mental space for ourselves at all, and as I've outlined earlier in this book, the consequences of that are becoming disastrous.

I've offered these suggestions to show that pushing back against at least *some* of the forces at play in your life, so that you can create some real time to get smart and think, is possible. I have big plans for what you are going to do with that those fresh new hours you've just discovered. Hint: You're not going to be watching back episodes of *Jersey Shore*.

Step Two: Read Constantly, and Read the Good Stuff

Those who do not read are no better off than those who cannot.
—Chinese proverb

That's the reason Asians leave us in the dust in college, folks. We don't have any proverbs advocating reading. Do you think the fact that we are currently $1 trillion in debt to these people is just a coincidence?

The best advice I can give on how to get smart can be summed up in this one piece of advice: Read. Read until your eyes are sore. Then read some more.

How much? Oh, only about ten times more than you are now. I know, I know. The time! The expense! I'll destroy those weak arguments in just a moment. But first, the case for reading.

Reading is mental fitness. It is a workout for your brain. Don't tell me you're a visual learner. You just cannot get enough intelligent information to rise out of ignorance without a steady diet of written articles, commentary, and, most importantly, books. If you want to distinguish yourself from your hairy ancestors whose knuckles scraped the ground, you must read books regularly, frequently, constantly. If you are a slow reader, all the more reason to step it up. As with anything, the more you do it, the better and faster you become.

Books, smart magazine articles, and world-class newspapers have taught me nearly everything I know. Mostly, however, it was the books. Phil Graham, former editor-in-chief of the *Washington Post*, called newspapers "the first rough draft of history." Newspapers (and I include hard news websites here, of course) are critical, and I'll swoon over them in a minute. But you have to read not only the first draft but also *the final draft*—and that's books. Books put all the pieces together and give us the long view, the analysis, and the lessons. I learned about America's shameful response to genocide from Samantha Power's *A Problem from Hell*. I learned about the pain of living in a rigidly misogynist fundamentalist Islamic society in Ayaan Hirsi Ali's *Infidel*, Carmen bin Laden's *Inside the Kingdom*, and Geraldine Brooks's *Nine Parts of Desire*. God bless Jonathan Kozol for writing book after raging book about the quiet, desperate lives of poor American children, books like *Rachel and Her Children* and *Savage Inequalities*. I was moved to significantly step up my charitable giving from Peter Singer's *The Life You Can Save*. Nicholas Kristof and Sheryl WuDunn's brilliant *Half the Sky* connected so many stories about the oppression of third world women and girls and motivated me to contribute significantly to projects to help them—from my support of a hospital that repairs obstetric fistulas to funding girls' scholarships in Ethiopia to supporting female entrepreneurs on Kiva.org.

Don't tell me you've learned some important things from other media. Weighty subjects can't be covered thoughtfully and comprehensively in a clipped television segment or even a short print article, nor can they be read on a computer monitor while your Facebook friends beckon you to play Mafia Wars in another open window. The average word count for a book is seventy-five thousand words. The average word count for a half-hour local news program is a thousand words, and most of that is the anchors' "happy talk."

And word count matters. Not everything can or should be reduced to a sound bite. Can I give you one sentence about the severity of women's suffering in the third world that will drive home the message of my favorite book of the last decade, *Half the Sky*? No, I can't, and I don't want to try. Doing so would diminish the subject, which is worthy of several hundred pages as well as our attention during the hours it takes to read the book. A sustained narrative, the building of a case, references, storytelling—these require a book. And we, the reader, are better for sitting down and letting our minds actually focus on a topic for a real stretch of time.

Television and Internet and, to a lesser extent, newspapers and magazines deliver quickies to our ADHD culture. When I am on television, it's usually a three-minute segment, and part of that is the anchor asking me questions. I have to cull a large amount of information down into a tiny number of words. I always walk away knowing that there was so much left unsaid. Books are where I turn to get the full story.

Without reading regularly, we sink into a swamp of ignorance. But when we do read, we transform ourselves in ways that may surprise you. In November 2007 the National Endowment for the Arts surveyed and analyzed all the best available data from academia, business groups, foundations, and government studies about the reading habits of Americans for its comprehensive, book-length report, *To Read or Not to Read: A Question of National Consequence*. The NEA's chairman wrote,

> When one assembles data from disparate sources, the results often present contradictions. This is not the case with *To Read or Not To Read*. Here the results are startling in their consistency. All of the data combine to tell the same story about American reading.
>
> The story the data tell is simple, consistent, and alarming. Although there has been measurable progress in recent years in reading ability at the elementary school level, all progress appears to halt as children enter their teenage years. There is a general decline in reading among teenage and adult Americans. Most alarming, both reading ability and the habit of regular reading have greatly declined among college graduates. These negative trends have more than literary importance. As this report makes clear, the declines have demonstrable social, economic, cultural, and civic implications.[7]

We saw in part 2 how American fifth graders compete well against their international counterparts, but by high school they lag far behind. This occurs just as American kids stop reading and as our teens spend thirty, forty, even fifty hours a week in front of "screens"—computers, television, video games.[8] So what are those alarming "social, economic, cultural and civic implications" that have befallen us as we've stopped reading? The NEA explains,

> How does one summarize this disturbing story? As Americans, especially younger Americans, read less, they read less well. Because they read less well, they have lower levels of academic achievement. (The shameful fact that nearly one-third of American teenagers drop out of school is deeply connected to declining literacy and reading comprehension.) With lower levels of reading and writing ability, people do less well in the job market. Poor reading skills correlate heavily with lack of employment, lower wages, and fewer opportunities for advancement. And deficient readers are less likely to become active in civic and cultural life, most notably in volunteerism and voting.[9]

This report blew me away primarily because we don't often hear big government agencies like the NEA sounding the alarm bells quite like this. Ordinarily their reports are peppered with qualifiers and disclaimers, but this is not the case in *To Read or Not to Read*:

> All of the data suggest how powerfully reading transforms the lives of individuals—whatever their social circumstances. Regular reading not only boosts the likelihood of an individual's academic and economic success—facts that are not especially surprising—but it also seems to awaken a person's social and civic sense. Reading correlates with almost every measurement of positive personal and social behavior surveyed. It is reassuring, though hardly amazing, that readers attend more concerts and theater than non-readers, but it is surprising that they exercise more and play more sports—no matter what their educational level. These cold statistics confirm something that most readers know but have

mostly been reluctant to declare as fact—books change lives for the better.[10]

Reading is the cure for what ails us: ignorance. Readers do better in school, earn more money, are better citizens, have happier personal lives, and are more actively engaged in the world around us. We may think we're cocooning alone under a reading lamp, sheltered from the world, but the opposite is true for most avid readers. We connect. Books get our minds out there, into the world of ideas, and where our brains go, our bodies follow. So naturally music and art books will get us to concerts and galleries, and political treatises will get us into the voting booth. And nearly any book, even a book you hate, will stir your brain and make you think. Knowledge expands us.

C. S. Lewis said this about the transformational power of great literature:

> Literary experience heals the wound, without undermining the privilege, of individuality. There are mass emotions that heal the wound; but they destroy the privilege. But in reading great literature I become a thousand men and yet remain myself. Here, as in worship, in love, in moral action, and in knowing, I transcend myself; and am never more myself than when I do.

Most of us can remember at least one transformative book we've read, though for many it's been too long ago. So what, then, is keeping us from this magnificent, expansive, enriching experience? Cost is one reason people tell me they don't read more. Haven't books gotten expensive?

No. In fact, other than staring at the walls, books are, hands down, the cheapest form of leisure and entertainment available to you. You can get piles of free library books probably less than a mile away from your home. You can buy one-dollar used books at your neighborhood thrift shop or used book store, and thus support a good cause—a charity or the bookstore owner who's probably one step away from relying on the Salvation Army herself. If you're willing to step it up to, say, five bucks for a work that probably took the author *five years of her life* (no, but don't feel guilty, really—how much do you spend for your monthly cable, Tivo, and Internet access bill, by the way?), you can buy any of roughly forty bazillion used titles on Amazon.com. You can swap books with your friends or check out a book swap site like SwapTree.com or PaperbackSwap.com or BooksFree.com. Trade books for free and reduce your carbon footprint by recycling old books! (Because I am *sure* that the reason you're not reading more is concern for the environment.) Mosey over to your friendly but lonely independent bookseller—you know, the one everyone cries over when it goes out of business. How about actually patronizing it before it goes under?

And last but not least, steep discounts on new bestsellers await you at the giant chain bookstores every livelong day. Oh, those meccas of the written word, with their hundreds of gleaming aisles, the fresh, pulpy smell of newly bound hardcovers! I am a sucker for enormous bookstores. If you take me to the mall, I'm going to the bookstore while you piddle around looking for the latest fashions (let me know when the skull motifs and peep-toe boots go out of style). I hope you get lost and take the long way back to me. As this book went to press, 675-store Borders teetered on the edge of bankruptcy.[11]

You could even—I hope you're sitting down here—pay *full price* for a book. For twenty bucks or so, you are getting, what, roughly twenty hours of entertainment? Thirty? Where else do you get that much bang for your buck? I just spent $25 for two tickets to the latest *Twilight* movie, and that's two mind-numbing hours of my life I'm not getting back. I didn't get to check out the first section of the movie like I do with books; I went because my daughter wanted to go. If I bought a book for that price and didn't like it, I could put it down, give it to someone who would enjoy it, donate it to a charity that could get some value out of it, or swap it online. But I can't do any of that with a movie ticket to a clunker, and no one complains about money wasted at the multiplex. In fact, the American film industry had banner years in 2009 and 2010, when we were in the deep recession pit, because consumers felt that movies were a good entertainment bargain compared to concerts, sporting events, and even dinner out. And that is true. But none of that compares to the dollar-an-hour, bargain-basement price of a book, which you can then pass along to someone else for their free enjoyment. The average American family spends $27 annually on books, the price of one new hardcover book for four people for one year. Come on. Cost is not what's holding you back.

Movies have made me laugh (*Despicable Me*) and cry (*The Notebook*, good Lord), and some have even left me stunned for the rest of the evening (*Life Is Beautiful*). Documentaries, a genre that's really taken off with Michael Moore's trenchant satires, vividly teach (*Sicko, Pray the Devil Back to Hell, Food, Inc., The Cove*). Bravo.

But there is no film that's made me change my life, that's rocked me to the foundations of what I believe, though I have read many books that have done just that. After Peter Singer's classic *Animal Liberation*, I went vegetarian (thirty-three years ago). J. M. Coetzee's poignant *The Lives of Animals* and Rory Freedman's hilarious, pushy *Skinny Bitch* convinced me to go vegan (two years ago), reinforced by Jonathan Safran Foer's exposé on animal cruelty, *Eating Animals*. And after Barbara Kingsolver's *Animal, Vegetable, Miracle*, I'm persuaded to eat local, organic, and seasonal. Has any film or TV show radically changed your behavior three times a day for life?

And I'm not just talking about nonfiction. The sweeping Canadian historical novel *Fall on Your Knees* so moved my friend Doria Roberts that she carried it around with her for two weeks after she read it, clutching it to her, mournful to have finished. Anyone who's ever reluctantly turned the last page of a brilliant novel has experienced this bittersweet feeling. I want to give the book a state funeral or erect a shrine to it; instead, I press it earnestly into the hands of a reader-friend, the best kind of friend to have. *You have to read this! Right now!* Reader-friends understand. Doria understands. Lisa See's *Snow Flower and the Secret Fan*, with its wrenching descriptions of the rigid nineteenth-century world of Chinese rural women, their feet and psyches cruelly bound, swept through my family in just this way. My daughter Sarah would not relent. Every time she visited me from college, she'd ask, "read *Snow Flower* yet? Huh? Huh? Have you? Why *not*?" Finally I did, and then I became a proselytizer, crowing about it on my Facebook page. My son Sammy swooned over Gabriel Garcia Marquez's magnum opus *One Hundred Years of Solitude* and insisted that I read it. That introduced me to the Spanish-language classic and a heretofore unknown-to-me genre, magical realism, where time expands and contracts and switches direction unexpectedly. Who knew? Cool.

Memoirs can pack the emotional, storytelling punch of a novel and give us the factual awakening we get reading nonfiction. Jeannette Walls's loving and maddening portrayal of her chronically refusing-to-be-employed parents in *The Glass Castle* made me rethink homeless people. Every time I pass an old man in rags, I think of her father in that book, and the old man in rags becomes less stereotyped and more humanized.

Of course readers are more engaged in our communities, of course we volunteer more, and of course we're more compassionate. We have opened ourselves to the world in all its blazing complexity—the villains with hearts of gold, the heroines with their fatal flaws. We sit with the long story, we hear out the full argument. We understand subtlety, and we yearn for depth.

Reading books takes us out of our heads and connects us to the lives and experiences of others in a way no other media can match. That connection makes us more engaged and empathic. At the very least, books improve us and make us smarter. Books keep us out of prison; get us better, higher paying jobs; and even get us to go to more concerts and work out more. (Who knew?) Plus the right ones are a hell of a lot of fun. So why aren't we reading more?

WHY DIDN'T 80 PERCENT OF US read a book last year? Probably because of bad memories of high school English teachers making us read *Moby Dick* or some other excruciatingly inaccessible tome. High school English was my favorite class, and I was an English literature major in college. I thought it was a scream that I could read novels, plays, and poetry—reading that I always did for fun, off duty—for four years and then I'd get a degree for it! Really? Where's the hidden camera? What's the catch?

Still, I did not enjoy Thackeray or Milton. I just didn't. *Vanity Fair, Paradise Lost*—not feeling 'em. They didn't speak to me.

Because I went to high school and college during the Pleistocene era, we almost never read anything by a woman or by a man who wasn't white. That has changed, but I can see why some people got turned off from reading because of school assignments. One bad English teacher can keep you out of bookstores for life. (This applies to any subject, really. My kids once had an elementary school violin teacher who responded to their giggling in class with, "Music is not fun!" That ended their string instrument avocation.) So maybe you couldn't relate to the books you were assigned in school, and that turned you off from books entirely.

I was a little miffed to discover the world of books my teachers had kept from me—books by women like Amy Tan or Sandra Cisneros or Jhumpa Lahiri that opened my eyes to the color and richness of the lives of immigrant families.

Reading as an adult, for pleasure, is infinitely better than reading the stuff assigned to you back in school. You get to *choose* what you want to read. Read three or four at once! Why not? I do. Something heavy, something light. Nonfiction, fiction. Mix and match. It's nobody's business but yours. You have no deadlines, pop quizzes, or book reports. Read at your own relaxed or engrossed pace.

The pleasure difference between the books you were forced to read in school and those you select for yourself now is the difference between prison food and a gourmet meal at a four-star restaurant in which you select each course.

As adults, we can seek out books that specifically answer our nagging questions about life. For me, I wonder about the age-old question of why there continue to be so many starving and suffering people in the world and what I can do about it. If this eats at you too, stop wringing your hands and start reading. *The Bottom Billion* by Paul Collier is a smart economist's explanation of why the poorest people in the world stay poor and how we can help them break out of the cycle. If you want concrete proof of how one person can truly make a difference, pick up Greg Mortenson's *Three Cups of Tea*. What do we first-worlders do with the guilt any decent person must feel as we go to sleep at night, warm in our beds, secure in our homes, and bellies full while one billion of our fellow humans do not? *The Life You Can Save*, a short book by Peter Singer, gives a brilliant, satisfying answer to this question. Read it if you dare to have your world truly rocked.

There are books with answers to every question your heart and mind have asked. There are books that ask questions you have never thought of. There are books to churn you and books to settle you. All you have to do is pick them up and allow the benefits to spill into your life. To get you started, check out my Recommended Reading List at the end of this book.*

No one offers a class on *how* to read once we're out of school, so here's my advice, a few of my big secret rules about reading:

Rule 1: If You Don't Like It, Put the Damn Thing Down and Move on to Something Better

Immediately if not sooner! Stop reading it.†

Most people I know buy a book, and whether they like it or not, they feel they have to stick with it until the bitter end. Phooey. You're not in high school English anymore! Fly and be free!

There are too many good books out there to read, and I figure if I'm *very* lucky I have forty good reading years left. If I can read fifty books a year, that's 2,000 books out of the roughly 200,000 new titles

*We'll be regularly updating our recommended book lists at www.Think.tv/books. Chat about your favorites, join a reading group, and post your thoughts on our picks there.

†Not this book, of course—other books.

that come out every year in the United States alone and the 501 must-read books already on my list. That means I have no time for the clunkers. I give a book fifty pages. You can give it less or more; that's up to you. After those fifty pages, if I'm not eagerly reaching for it, I say good-bye and move on. Ba-bye.

They are inanimate objects. They don't actually care if they're in your hands or on the shelf or in the incinerator. There's no need for guilt. You are the customer, so you get to say no.

Rule 2: Read Promiscuously

Some people go to a bookstore, wile away an hour or so, and leave with a book. They go home, read that book, maybe, and then wait three months until they get to a bookstore again.

No.

If you want to step up your reading, you must use your time more efficiently. When you go to the bookstore, library, online, or to your friend's bookshelf—it makes no never mind where you get your books, so long as you get them—load up! Leave with heavy bags! You can go to bed with a big heavy tome tonight, a skinny little light one tomorrow, and two others on Saturday night, you tart. Don't limit yourself. You're not required to have monogamous relationships with authors. Be a wild and free woman when it comes to your reading.

I raided libraries throughout my childhood and college. At UCLA I was once summoned to a stern-faced administrator's office to answer questions about why I had so many overdue library books. (Oh . . . I was supposed to *return* them?) Throughout law school and my early adulthood, and certainly when my kids were young, I was the library groupie, hauling around arms full of books for all of us.

Somewhere around my second or third television contract, when other women would celebrate with shiny diamond earrings, I decided my gift to myself for moving up in the world would be that henceforth, whenever I see a book I want, I can have it. Just like that! I don't drive an expensive car and I don't spend a great deal on clothes, but I gave myself permission to buy books wherever the mood struck, such as in previously off-limits places like airport bookstores, where they are, regrettably, full price. It's okay, I can buy it if I want it. I gave myself permission.

Now along comes technology. For years friends told me I would love the electronic reader. I ignored them, though a little voice told me that these particular friends had never yet steered me wrong. When I went on a trip of a week or more, I always brought at least five books. One for each long flight, two for the trip's reading, and one throwaway—the one that seemed like a winner in the bookstore, but, remember, if it doesn't grab me in the first fifty pages, I show it the door. If it puts me to sleep more than twice, it's out.

Five books crammed into my carry-on roller bag meant very little room for clothes and shoes. I would usually offload them as I read them, handing them to the seatmate on my plane ("I saw you sneaking peeks over my shoulder. This was a good book! Take it! Read it!") or leaving them at hotel libraries. In the third world, I'd donate my finished or jettisoned books to the neighborhood bookstore's English section, to the surprised smiles of the proprietors. Still, all those books were weighing me down, especially on the outbound flight.

Then, I got the Kindle and, later, my iPad—light little e-readers that fit in my purse and can carry thousands of books plus all my newspapers and magazines. Now all the books I buy are about ten bucks, leave zero carbon footprint, and upload anywhere in less time than it takes to think, "I want to read Jeannette Walls's *Half-Broke Horses*." Ta-da! There it is! I can adjust the font size if I'm too lazy to get my reading glasses from the other room, and I get dictionary definitions of unknown words instantly. I swear I read books faster on the e-readers too. I took fifty-five e-books on a two-week trip to China—I'd already read many of them, but that's how many went with me—and I could pack all the shoes I wanted. On a trip to Ireland, I uploaded a bunch of James Joyce books between "fasten your seatbelts" and "turn off your electronic devices," and they were free! Honestly, can life get any better than this?

Rule Three: Cross-Read

Not choice, but habit rules the unreflecting herd. —William Wordsworth

Neuroscientists have found that new learning such as studying an unfamiliar foreign language or stretching your mind to discover new concepts actually creates new neural pathways in the brain. If you don't continue to learn, your brain literally begins to atrophy, at which point you're on your way to Alzheimer's, dementia, and other diseases associated with old age, diseases that are increasingly being seen as caused (at least in part) by being in a mental rut. In a recent study published in the *Journal of Economic Perspectives*, for instance, researchers found a straight-line relationship between early retirement and memory loss.[12] So use it or lose it. Stretch it or watch it go limp. And there is no better way to turn your brain on to new ideas than by reading stuff that's unfamiliar or that you don't expect to agree with. I call this cross-reading.

My favorite kind of book is one that upends my point of view and makes me think, "Whoa. I never thought about it that way." For example, I was of the opinion that we overmedicate kids today, especially on psychiatric meds, until I read Judith Warner's *We've Got Issues: Children and Parents in the Age of Medication*. Warner herself admits that she got her book contract and began writing a book from the conventional wisdom point of view: that we overdiagnose normal kids with phony psychiatric disorders in order to drug them up and make life easier for lazy parents. After interviewing many parents of disturbed kids, however, what she found was quite the opposite: that there are surprising numbers of children with severe, legitimate mental illnesses who are profoundly helped only through medication, which their loving, hardworking parents used only as a last resort. In fact, she reports, there are many undiagnosed kids who could benefit from modern medication and psychiatric treatment but who aren't getting it because their parents can't afford it, insurance won't pay, and because of the cultural shaming that says parents who drug their kids are bad parents.

Warner's evidence and narrative were so compelling that I now have a completely different attitude on this issue.

Though I'm not Christian, I cross-read conservative pastor Rick Warren's *The Purpose-Driven Life: What on Earth Am I Here For?* because I wanted to hear what this highly influential man had to say. I already knew that his anti-abortion, anti-gay marriage, fundamentalist religious views differed sharply from mine. Still, this book is one of the best-selling nonfiction books of all time, and it might have something to say to me because, after all, finding purpose in my life is important to me. The book turned out to be pure Christian evangelism, which didn't speak to me, but I did learn what all the fuss was about and maybe warded off Alzheimer's a few more days at the same time.

I read another book by another popular American cleric, Rabbi Shmuley Boteach. Shmuley and I became unlikely friends after he appeared on my Court TV show and dazzled me with his razor-sharp mind, Talmudic wisdom, and passion for substance. Most of that friendship consists of me going to his home for Shabbat dinner and arguing politics and culture with him in front of his wife and nine kids. Good times. For example, he tells his eldest teenage daughter that he expects her to marry soon, as is the orthodox way, and I beg her to wait at least until she's finished college. I tell her that I live happily unmarried with my man Braden and that she has options. Shmuley then rails against my fornicating lifestyle. We eat hummus.

When Shmuley sent me a manuscript for *The Kosher Sutra: 8 Sacred Secrets for Reigniting Desire and Restoring Passion for Life*, I thought, really? This hairy little conservative orthodox rabbi is going to teach me how to jazz up my sex life? Well, knock me over with a feather, if it wasn't the most compelling book about human eroticism I've read.

Cross-reading can not only make you smarter, expose you to new ideas, and ward off disease, but it can also sex you up. I rest my case.*

---

*Check out my recommended cross-reading list and post your own recommendations at www.Think.tv/books.

Those three reading rules are enough. I don't want to load you up with rules. Reading should be free, exhilarating, and a place you crave daily. Make your own reading rules—and then break them. But read. Just read—frequently, constantly, daily.

I HOPE I'VE CONVINCED YOU that you can seriously ratchet up your reading intake for little or no cost. Reading will smarten you up, fill you with information you can use immediately to improve your life and the lives of those around you, and shake you up with new ideas. It is, as I said, mental fitness, and some form of fitness needs to happen every day. So how can reading become part of your daily life?

I hear you. You are saying, "Sure, maybe when I go on vacation I can fit in some reading time. But I have a job, kids, school, a busy life. How can I find time to read?"

How? We've already talked about housework and child care, carving out significant chunks of time for yourself that you can devote to your brain. What other time suckers are draining you of time to think? How much time are you spending in front of screens? We all need downtime, but most of us get it at the end of the day by zoning out in front of the TV or poking around online. How much time do you spend doing this? On average, people under fifty-five spend two hours a day watching TV. There's fourteen hours a week! If you swap TV time for book time, you can finish a full-length book in about ten days.

And if you're like me, jumping into action every time the Blackberry beeps, please, put the damn thing down—for hours at a time. Yes, even during the day. Our electronic devices and their incessant trilling eat away so many hours that could be productive. Here's a rule few Type-A people follow: *Just because it beeps does not mean you have to respond.* The device works for you, not the other way around. Not only do you not have to respond to every e-mail, text, and instant message within five seconds, if you do, you look like you are sitting around with nothing else to do, and this encourages people to continue to engage with you. To start weaning yourself off this time waster, start with an auto-reply that says, "I'm not available from 4 p.m. to 7 p.m. today due to a pressing project. If your matter is urgent, please phone me. Otherwise, I'll respond after 7 p.m." After a week or so, expand your unavailable hours. Eventually, you can work up to responding to all nonurgent messages only once or twice a day. And when you do respond to e-mails, put all relevant information in your response to discourage more back-and-forth discussion. The recipient will appreciate this and you will have bought yourself more time to yourself, to think, to read.

If you have the opposite problem—too many phone calls for matters that could be handled much quicker by e-mail—try this outgoing message on your voice mail: "Hi, it's _____. Sorry I missed your call. I only check this voice mail occasionally. For the fastest response, please e-mail me at _____. Thanks!" I hate going through voice mails, so this has saved me many wasted hours—hours I can devote to reading.

Americans spend an average of almost an hour a day surfing the web—"surfing" being a euphemism for looking at porn (men), shopping (women), and spinning our wheels on Facebook (yes, I mean you). Your time does not have to be spent this way. There is nothing compelling you to participate in this much computer activity. According to Neilson Online, we lead the world in hours per month online, at almost twenty-eight. France is next with nineteen hours per month, Spain at almost eighteen, the UK and Germany at seventeen, and Italy at fifteen. Australians spend half the time we do online, at fourteen hours per month. Don't tell me you're reading something important at your computer. Among Yahoo's top five search terms for 2010 were Miley Cyrus and Kim Kardashian.[13]

Next, do what we women do best: multitask. I don't mean read while watching TV. No, no, no. Always have a book in your purse and then take advantage of those down-time minutes that come every day by whipping out your book and turning a few pages. I read while commuting, at the TV studios in between takes, when I'm miked up and waiting my turn to be questioned, and during the commercial breaks. Of course I read in dentist's and doctor's offices but also when standing in line for anything, when at the car wash, when holding on the phone for customer service, and nearly always at bedtime. I read while working out, either the old-fashioned way or via an audiobook. I've cooked many a dinner to audiobooks. Boy, does that make slicing and dicing more fun. I always have a book—now my e-reader—in my bag, ready to pop out. (The only downside to the e-reader is that everyone interrupts me to ask if they can play with it. *Shh! I'm trying to read.*)

If you think *I'm* obsessed with carving out time for reading, you should meet Nina Sankovitch. Shaken after the death of her beloved sister, Nina believed (as I do) that answers to all of life's great questions—why am I here, why do we suffer, how can I go on, how can I find meaning—can be found in great literature. She started reading heavily. Then she decided to do something big. She announced that she would read a book a day for a year. This is a mother of five, four still at home, who reads while waiting to pick up the kids, reads for fun, reads for knowledge, reads late at night, reads whenever she has a moment, reads, reads, reads, mainly because she loves it. She posts a review of the previous day's book on her blog, www.readallday.org.

How'd she do it? Sure, she generally chose shorter books, 250 or 300 pages. Though in one day she powered through all 560 pages of C. J. Sansom's *Revelation*, a murder mystery. To find the time, she said, she cut out time swallowers like diddling around online and clothes shopping.

But wait! Is she ignoring her kids? What about them? How have they reacted to mom's obsession? Stop the presses. According to the *New York Times*, they have followed her lead and become avid readers themselves. Peter, at sixteen, reads Thomas Pynchon; Michael, fourteen, Ayn Rand and Al Franken; and George, eleven, says he prefers "long books."[14]

This is a key point. When mom reads, she is a bookish role model for the kids. Reading is good—not bad—parenting.

The great horror writer Stephen King says he's a slow reader, so he reads "only" seventy or eighty books a year. How?

> I take a book with me everywhere I go, and find there are all sorts of opportunities to dip in. The trick is to teach yourself to read in small sips as

> well as in long swallows. Waiting rooms are made for books—of course! But so are theater lobbies before the show, long and boring checkout lines, and everyone's favorite, the john. You can even read while you're driving, thanks to the audiobook revolution. Of the books I read each year, anywhere from six to a dozen are on tape. As for all the wonderful radio you will be missing, come on—how many times can you listen to Deep Purple sing "Highway Star"?
>
> . . . Where else can you read? There's always the treadmill, or whatever you use down at the local health club to get aerobic. I try to spend an hour doing that every day, and I think I'd go mad without a good novel to keep me company.[15]

This is an excerpt from Stephen King's *On Writing*, and he's giving advice to aspiring writers that they should read, read, read. You may not be an aspiring writer, but if you're still reading the book at this point, I hope I've convinced you to become an aspiring *thinker*. And so the advice is the same. If you're motivated, you can find the time.

Make Reading a Social Activity

> *Outside of a dog, a book is man's best friend. Inside of a dog, it's too dark to read.* —Mark Twain

If you're now geared up to make books your new best friends, and now that you've found some time to enjoy the act of reading, what about your flesh-and-blood BFFs, kids, and families?

I believe that one of the big reasons we don't read as much as we, say, watch TV or go to the movies or socialize on Facebook is because reading feels like an inherently antisocial activity. When you're in a relationship or you have a family, to go off by yourself with a book for an hour or two every day seems selfish or, as we used to say in high school, "stuck up." (*What, she's too good to hang out with me in front of the* TV?)

When my kids were little, I did worry that if I sat and read a book of my own, I would be ignoring them. Then I read (naturally) that in fact I would be modeling healthy, brain-enhancing behavior for them. A kid who sees Mom reading for pleasure quickly gets the message that reading *is* a pleasure.

So I made it a joint activity. I made a "book nook" at their level, which is to say that I threw a futon and a bunch of big cozy pillows on the floor in the corner by some nice windows. I put some low bookcases filled with kids' books along with some of mine next to the cushions. Of course we had a good reading light there too. That's all we needed. After all the dishes were done, I'd announce, "cozy reading time!" and we'd all flump down together with our books, our legs wrapped around one another, and open our books. I'd read a story or two to them, and then we'd sink into our own books. Sometimes we'd read choice passages to one another, but mainly we'd be quiet and absorbed in our own pages.

For my kids, books were always a reward, never a punishment. For a job well done, *a new book*! When we went to the mall, we stopped first (when they were most alert) at the bookstore or library. At bedtime, we read a story . . . or two or three. When they were babies, there were plastic books that went right into the bathtub and, inevitably, got gnawed up by their teething gums. As toddlers, there were the pop-up books and hard cardboard affairs they colored on. I didn't care. I don't believe books should be treated as delicate, precious objects. They exist for our pleasure. If my rug rats got more pleasure out of them by enhancing their pictures with their own artwork, they were allowed to go for it. I myself dog-ear and write in my books (and now underline and highlight with reckless abandon on my e-reader). I want to remember the choice bits later. I want to make notes on things that pop into my head next to the provocative paragraph. So I do.

By their tweens, my kids were recommending books to me. *Harry Potter*, of course, but also *Holes* by Louis Sachar, allegedly a kids' book, but honestly, I think that masterpiece was written just for me. When they told me to read a good book, I'd read it, even if it wasn't my style. Why not? I like diversity in people as well as in my reading materials. I felt that being exposed to something new, something that affected them and was rattling around in their brains was always good. I tell my kids the main reason I had them was to have a steady source of book recommendations in my old age.

And I reciprocate. In their early teens, I'd wonder aloud if a book was "too adult" for them, a surefire way to pique their interest. (Mwah hah hah . . .) My daughter loved one of my favorite books, *The Glass Castle* by Jeannette Walls. My son read all 656 pages of the dense, intense *Amazing Adventures of Kavalier and Clay*, Michael Chabon's Pulitzer Prize–winning magnum opus he had seen me reading a few years before. We all cried over Alice Sebold's haunting *The Lovely Bones*. Say that title in front of any of the three of us and we'll say, "oh!" and clutch our hearts.

If I have passed along a love of reading to my kids, I have done something right in this life. Great literature has sustained me and answered some of my persistent, nagging questions about meaning and the universe. Nonfiction has opened my eyes to the world. Though I travel overseas often, life is too short to be able to get to every country on the planet unless I didn't have to work and had a hefty trust fund. Doesn't look like either of those is happening any time soon, which is probably better for my mental health anyway because I believe grownups need to work (and I think being a full-time child caretaker counts double for "work"). So because I can't travel to every town on God's green earth that I'd like to in the time I have left, I can read about them. There are, especially, some new books coming out of places that the English-speaking publishing world had forgotten, like *Say You're One of Them* by Uwem Akpan, achingly beautiful first-person stories narrated by West African children, or *A Long Way Gone* by Ishmael Beah, a twelve-year-old soldier in Sierra Leone's bloody civil war.

Making books social requires only a little creativity. I know a family whose annual holiday card is a list of each family member's favorite book from that year, from grandma's historical novel down to baby's favorite teether. I know a man who asked twenty-one smart friends the most meaningful book they'd ever read and then gave his son each of those books for his twenty-first birthday. There is no end to the imaginative ways that you can make reading social if you put your mind to it.

So, kids, reading, check. What about husbands, wives, or significant others?

The principle is the same: Lots of love and positive reinforcement gets lovers to do just about anything.

I live with my boyfriend Braden, and I don't want to be the solitary girl cocooning with my book, giving the poor guy the cold shoulder. However, I'm not about to give up reading. So here are my strategies for making reading time couple time.

Say, "Hey, let's snuggle up on the couch together with our books" and then bring him a steamy cup of hot cocoa, a green tea latte (my guy's fave), or a cold beer to instill positive reinforcement. When he's reading something and reacts (laughter, sighing, grunting), express intense interest and have him read you the passage.

Rub his feet while he's reading. Remember, men and Pavlov's dogs are not so different. Tell him he's so sexy with a book in his hands. Grr. Smart guys are hot. Remind him of that.

Share books. Braden, a brilliant entrepreneur, likes business books—not really my genre—but I've read some of them so that we can have that shared experience, and I did want to rush out and start my own Internet company after whizzing through *The 4-Hour Work Week*. If nothing else, sharing books gives us new topics to discuss over our seitan tacos. And he reciprocates by reading some of the books I'm passionate about. He has become my in-house reader-friend, and he knows that means the world to me.

Read books, or at least the good parts, aloud to each other. I confess that I go bananas for my hot boyfriend reading to me from a good book because it combines two of the best things in my life. We read *The Immortal Life of Henrietta Lacks* to each other on a long car trip upstate. I know an intellectually curious couple that reads particle physics books to each other at bedtime. Geek out, people. You only go around once.

Make dates out of author readings or bookstore outings. We once spent a three-hour layover in the Atlanta airport in the bookstore—a pretty nice one, with comfy chairs and a coffee place next door. When we drive through small towns, we stop in the local bookstores to say hello to the proprietor and check out the stock. I like to see what's selling well there and what they're recommending. Most people stop at a McDonald's or Howard Johnson's—why? They're the same everywhere. There's no better place to get a sense of local flavor than at the little independent bookstore, and there's no better business to support.

And if you're single, what better place to meet your friends or to meet intelligent like-minded prospects than at your neighborhood book store, a la Julia Roberts in *Notting Hill*? Or try a book reading, a book club, or a dating site like Alikewise.com that pairs folks based on book tastes? Sure beats enduring another beer-breathed guy at the local bar.

IF YOU CAN'T NAME THREE AMAZING BOOKS you've read in the last year, you're not reading enough. (Mine are, off the top of my head, *The Warmth of Other Suns: The Epic Story of America's Great Migration* by Isabel Wilkerson, *Freedom* by Jonathan Franzen, and *Olive Kitteridge* by Elizabeth Strout.)*

Have you opted out of checking out what the world's great thinkers have to say on subjects that matter to you? Have you wimped out because you let a few bad experiences in high school scare you away from lifelong learning? (*The Great Gatsby* didn't speak to me, either, even when I gave it a second chance as an adult. There, I said it.) Have you bought hook, line and sinker our culture's overwhelming message that downtime means sitting in front of a flickering screen in which someone's always trying to sell you something? Internet ads get freakishly more specialized to our individual tastes daily; TV commercials shout at us louder and for more minutes each season, so much so that Congress had to pass a bill that lowered their volume; movies, even DVDs, require us to sit through pregame commercials and then bombard us with product placement. Music? Lady Gaga, notwithstanding

*An updated list of top reads in fiction and nonfiction are at www.Think.tv/com.

all her over-the-top fabulousness in song and costuming, set a new low in her "Bad Romance" video with *eight* product placements, including Parrot by Philippe Stark, Nemiroff vodka, Heartbeats earphones, HP Envy lap top, Nintendo Wii, Burberry, and Safari sunglasses. Books are the last frontier of entertainment without any ads at all. They only want to sell you some ideas.

Above all else, are you missing out on one of the truly great pleasures of life, now more available to you at a lower cost than ever before? Are you denying yourself the exquisite treat of a moving book, chosen by you, that speaks directly to what you need at this moment? Is your life ticking by without daily moments of elevation, inspiration, and provocation?

Not reading, to me, would be like a vow of chastity. Giving up pleasure is not how I roll.

Reader-friend, stop depriving yourself. You've run out of excuses. Give your brain what it aches for, what it loves: Give yourself the joy of reading.

Listen to my girl Virginia Woolf. She knows. She said,

> I have sometimes dreamt, at least, that when the Day of Judgment dawns and the great conquerors and lawyers and statesmen come to receive their rewards—their crowns, their laurels, their names carved indelibly upon imperishable marble—the Almighty will turn to Peter and will say, not without a certain envy when he sees us coming with our books under our arms, "Look, these need no reward. We have nothing to give them here. They have loved reading."

I'M NOT DONE.

You also must read newspapers. You must read the *New York Times* plus your hometown paper, daily. At least skim the headlines online every day and read in depth the stories that are important to our world and to you. If you push back, I'll let you skip the Saturday edition because it's usually light and big news rarely breaks on Fridays. But that's all the slack I'm cutting you.

Watching TV news will not substitute. All of the actual news in a nightly newscast fits into one-quarter of the front page of a newspaper. This is why everyone I know in TV news—the producers, anchors, reporters, and commentators like me—*reads* their news before they trim it way down to the barest of bare bones and deliver it to you on air. TV news is also heavily video driven, which means it will lead with, say, a life-sized Jiffy Pop balloon floating across the sky with, maybe, a little boy in it.* No network could resist that "balloon boy" video, over and over again. Don't get me wrong, I love TV news. I've watched the morning shows and cable news all my life while I'm doing mindless tasks like getting dressed or making dinner. But these are no substitute for the reams of information you can get only by reading your news daily. TV news is an add-on.

Local television news justifies its existence (and its FCC licenses) by claiming to bring the public important stories about local politics, law enforcement, budgets, and education. However, the Norman Lear Center at the USC Annenberg School for Communications and Journalism analyzed nearly eleven thousand news stories contained within a thousand half-hour segments on local Los Angeles stations during a recent summer. Out of a half-hour nightly show, guess how much time was allotted to these worthy local issues? Out of the twenty-two minute (not counting commercials) newscasts, would 10 percent be too much to ask—2.2 minutes?

Correct answer: twenty-two seconds. The vast majority was crime stories ("if it bleeds, it leads"), sports, entertainment, "lifestyle pieces," and weather.[16] (Do we really need several minutes on the barometric pressure system moving in, or the Doppler radar, whatever that is? I always think of comedian Jackie Mason: "Just tell me, will it be hot or cold? Will it rain, or not?") Teasers ("*coming up: is your toothpaste killing you*?") got nearly ten times as much airtime as any real news.

What a waste. Read your news.

The *New York Times* has hundreds of intrepid journalists all over the globe and the most fearless, intelligent op-ed page of any American

*Oops! No it didn't!

paper. Do you think it's too liberal for you? Then fine, skip the op-ed page. You should be forming your own opinions anyway, so this is the least important part of a paper to read. But you must read the rest, which is unbiased, hard-news reporting, especially the "World" section's comprehensive international coverage. When I lived outside the subscription zone, I used to get up early to try to flirt and cajole my newsstand guy, who always claimed he'd sold out, pleading for the one last *Sunday Times* I knew he kept under the counter, heavy as a toddler. Those days, of course, are over, and we can now read the *Times* in all its glory daily for free online—in color, zipping around the links, even watching video. Free knowledge, free app on your digital device, right there for the taking. It's almost criminal.

The *New York Times* has prominent international coverage of stories that matter, every day: climate change updates, genocide in Darfur, the plight of America's poor, government corruption, the suffering of third world women, devastating pieces on Iraqi civilian casualties. They don't shirk from the hard stuff nor do they pander to our lowest instincts by spooning us tabloid drivel. This should be your first stop every morning.

Other national American news sites contain worthy stories and solid reporting too, but they contain significantly fewer articles overall, shorter pieces, and significantly fewer hard-news and investigative stories. Smaller papers have shorter pieces, far less international coverage, and less coverage of the arts and books. There is really no comparison. The *New York Times* has won 101 Pulitzer Prizes—more than any other paper. Read it for a few weeks and you'll be ruined for anything else.

Oh, of course the *Times* has its faults. It's run by humans, and our species makes mistakes. But what other organization trumpets those mistakes prominently on a daily correction page *and* on a Sunday "public editor" page? They hired a guy whose sole job is to criticize them in print, in their own newspaper, and on a regular basis. Top that.

In the lovely, sprawling novel *Cutting for Stone*, an old Bronx junior high school teacher, Mr. Walters, is described this way:

Mr. Walters read the *New York Times* every day. That and a Bible were a constant at his bedside. "I could never afford college. Just Bible school. I tell my students, "If you read this newspaper every day for a year, you'll have the vocabulary of a Ph.D. and you will know more than any college graduate. I guarantee you."

"Do they listen?"

He held up a finger. "Every year *one* does," he said, grinning. "But that one makes it worthwhile. Even Jesus only did twelve. I try to get one a year."

If you only have ten minutes, you can skim all the headlines and catch a few lead paragraphs on important stories. You'll at least have a general sense of what's up in your world.

But do more than that. This is your life, and you should always do the extra credit reading. If you take a half an hour each morning while you're sipping your coffee, you can skim all the headlines and read a few articles in depth. If you run out of time, you can mark a few for later. You can e-mail articles of interest to your friends, as I do daily, to stimulate their brains and make reading social. If you get revved up, add a comment at the end of an article and stir the pot. Why not? Why should everyone else get their opinion in but not you?

Make Mr. Walters, and me, proud. Be our disciple of the year.

If you have a crazy week and fall behind—this happens to all of us—I have just the thing for you. *The Week* is a little-known weekly news magazine that concisely summarizes what you need to know, striking just the right balance of priorities: international hard news first, then domestic, then features, a page of celebrity fluff, and pictures of homes you can fantasize about living in—mostly important stuff that grownups like you need to know and a little light stuff because, hey, we're only human. You can read every word of *The Week* in an hour on the exercise bike. I know this because my boyfriend does this and then struts out of the gym physically fit and mentally stimulated, ready to face anything.

After the *New York Times*, you need to read your local paper daily to find out what's going on in your community. At least peek at the headlines. How's your mayor doing? Are the police corrupt? Is your water clean? Doesn't all this matter more than what some druggie reality show star did in Hollywood last weekend? And, *wait*. *What*? The local library is closing for lack of funding? They're going to charge ten bucks to get into the parks? Doesn't that just make you itch to get involved?

Read This, Not That: Kick Your Tabloid Media Habit

All reading is not created equal. I really don't have to tell you this. The *New York Times* is not the *National Enquirer*. Duh.

"But I'm so *tired* after working all day," you say, clutching your glossy nervously. "Don't I *deserve* to kick back with a tabloid? It's my me-time. I don't take it seriously. Aren't I allowed a little *relaxation*?"

Yes, my dear, you *definitely* deserve a break—but a better, healthier, happier break.

We've seen previously in this book how tabloid media, if I may speak freely, makes you a vain, self-centered idiot. Garbage in, garbage out.

But, you say, you *know* the glossies and celeb shows and sites are dumb fluff, but it's your *relaxation*. What if you promise not to become narcissistic, self-loathing, and shallow? Can't you still have your guilty pleasure?

I hear this everywhere I go. Women feel so threatened, so scared of the idea of giving up their daily "fix" of sleazy celeb gossip. *I need it! I deserve it! I can't relax without it!*

Say what? Girls, let's think about this. It's been only in the last decade or two that tabloids ascended to selling millions of copies weekly, (dis)gracing the tables in every doctor's office, gym, and waiting room. Before that, guess what? Women hardly ever read them. Nevertheless, we *relaxed*, and we did it without reading about the sordid, anonymous-sourced dirt about Brangelina's latest alleged tiff. Imagine that. How on earth did we do it?

We listened to music—loud music.

We talked on the phone with our girlfriends.

We watched or read comedy.

We flirted.

We had sex.

We took a nap.

We made, and ate, cupcakes.

Not necessarily in that order.

"Oh, but that was in the olden days!" I can hear my daughter saying. "Come on! It's the digital age! The gossip sites didn't exist then!"

Hey, I enjoy my computer as much as the next girl. Fine, then, here are some more *modern* ways to relax, because for sure, we multitasking, overworked, underloved modern women deserve some downtime, and the Internet is fun.

Connect with your friends on Facebook. Comment on their pictures and post cute ones of yourself. Flirt with the guy from high school who just found you there by writing on his wall or sending him a private message.

Tweet, retweet, play with Twitter hashtags.

Play Lexulous or other online games that challenge your mind or, at least, don't impair your ability to think.

Watch funny YouTube clips of your favorite comedians (mine are Jim Gaffigan and Kathy Griffin).

Download new music on iTunes, or create and enjoy new stations on Pandora. Watch your Tivoed comedy show or Netflix flick.

Play Wii Fit games with your kids or live out your adolescent fantasies by jamming to "Rock Star" with your family.

Are you sensing a theme here? *Connect with friends and family, music, and comedy.* These are my top-three ways to unwind that aren't reading a book, as I've already made that case. Maybe you have others. That's your business. The point is, when did our culture decide to redefine downtime for women *solely* as consuming celeb media, which, as we've seen, dumbs us down and makes us think the plastic surgery secrets of the stars cosmically matter? I know you and I were not consulted about this.

Isn't that pretty insulting and narrowing—the idea that the only way we can unwind is by reading gossip about people who have nothing to do with our lives?

I know that single girls bond with each other over tabloids. But "all my friends do it" was a losing argument when you were eight, and it still is. Lead your homegirls in another direction—for your sake and theirs.

Some of my friends say they look at celeb mags because they're fun and light, and life can be so heavy. They just want a little diversion because they work hard all day long. They say they actually *laugh* at the dumbness of the tabloid media.

Hey, that's a step in the right direction. But if that's the case, instead of "they breathe air—just like us!" how about going for some *real* humor writing—writing that you're laughing *with*, not *at*? Humor is an essential component of life. We all need a break, a laugh, a moment on the lighter side. That's why God gave us David Sedaris, Augusten Burroughs, Dave Barry, Justin Halpern, and Nora Ephron. I read Carrie Fisher's *Wishful Drinking* on a plane, giggling through the safety instructions, chuckling as the drinks cart rammed into my knee, sniggering through the turbulence, trying to be quiet all the way through prepare-to-cross-check and wheels-down. Name me one movie you've watched on a plane that was that funny for that long. And unlike finishing celebrity magazines, when I closed the book, I had no desire to dash out for silicone injections.

ONE MORE TINY LITTLE POINT about tabloid media: It's often lies.

Michelle Williams, former girlfriend of the late movie star Heath Ledger, gave a moving interview to *The Week* in which she confessed that she had once been an avid reader of star magazines herself. When she found herself the object of vicious tabloid lies, however, she had an epiphany and decided to stop reading them.

In the celebrity cases I've handled, I've watched as tabloid news sites report rumor, speculation, and gossip that is often demonstrably false. Generally, reporters don't even call us for our side of the story.

Sometimes I can persuade the editors to correct misinformation, but often not. They just don't care, especially when the lie is more salacious than the boring truth. One of the worst tabloid lies about one of my clients was the hoax perpetrated on Michael Lohan, father of actress Lindsay Lohan. A blogger posted a screen grab, a purported copy of his Twitter page, making it look as though Michael had posted that his daughter was HIV positive and had sex with a music executive when she was a minor. On his behalf, I immediately objected that these were lies and that Michael had never said any such thing. Nevertheless, dozens of mainstream outlets ran with the story, many without even giving our denial. A few days later the original blogger confessed that the screen grab, and the entire story, was a hoax. We demanded retractions from every outlet that ran it. No one issued one. And Michael's reputation along with his relationship with his troubled daughter was shattered.[17]

Tabloids know that if stars sue, it only amplifies the rumor, so smear victims have a huge incentive to look the other way as they are publicly lied about. Lawsuits cost hundreds of thousands of dollars, or more, and take years. And the media can't be sued simply for mistakes—the plaintiff has to prove *defamation*, a tough legal standard that's even tougher for stars who are "public figures" within the meaning of defamation law. So the subjects of even vicious falsehoods usually just try to ignore them and wait for the public to lose interest and move on to the next faux scandal.

What is relaxing about reading nasty gossip and outright lies?

No Cake for One Month

So they're insipid, they make you dumber, they threaten your emotional health, and they are often pure fiction. Aren't these reasons enough to get tabloids out of your life?

If you have been relying on the tabloid media for a significant chunk of your "me time," if you have been counting entertainment news as news—you know who you are—if you know more about

Snooki and JWoww than how America's troops are faring overseas, it's time for a drastic change.

Just as kids aren't allowed to have dessert until they eat their healthy food, your brain is not growing big and strong on a diet of junk. Until you have amped up your reading of the *New York Times* plus your hometown paper plus a couple of good books a month, you're not allowed *any* celeb news.

That's right. You may have to go cold turkey and give them up entirely at first.

How can you tell what's junk reading? Here's a failsafe method: Any magazine with yellow headlines on the cover in a font size bigger than your pinky is off limits for the first thirty days of your media diet. If you find yourself reading something that uses any of these phrases, drop it and run:

Baby bump
Star babies
Plastic surgery nightmares/secrets
Bikini body
Stars without makeup
Just like us!
Breaks her silence
Who wore it better?
Who'd you rather?
Combined couple names, like Brangelina or Bennifer or Speidi

For thirty days you may not look at anything that has pictures of celebrities with drawn-on circles and arrows that are calling attention to flab or boob jobs. You may not look at anything that has photographs in it that paparazzi have taken while stalking people as they went for a cup of coffee or to take their little kids to school, which is how those photos get taken, put into the glossies, and delivered into your hands.

After that, you get a small break. You can *occasionally* take a peek. Celeb shenanigans are part of our culture, and you can dip into what's going on, enjoying the fashion and hairstyles *once in a while*. I just want you to keep the time spent with this stuff at a reasonable level. How much is too much? Think of the universe of tabloid media—shows, websites, gossip magazines—as a big, frosted, buttery, sugary cake. Tempting, for sure, but too much will make you puke. You wouldn't have cake for breakfast, lunch, and dinner day after day. How often do you eat cake, actually? I'd say I do about once a month, when it's someone's birthday or a special occasion. The cake eating lasts maybe fifteen minutes. That's about the right amount of time for celeb media consumption.

If you consume any more than that, you'll be filled with empty calories. "Wait!" you say to me, "How can you say this when *you* are sometimes *on* the celeb shows or quoted in the tabloid press?" Guilty as charged—because I am. Mostly I make a living representing ordinary people and talking about meaningful justice issues (or so I like to think) on air, but yes, I do the celeb shows too, usually to give a legal opinion on a divorce or an incident of domestic violence.

My conscience is clean. Sure, once in a while, I deliver the fluff. But even if I owned a bakery, I still wouldn't want you to eat cake 24/7.

IF YOU ARE DILIGENTLY FOLLOWING along with the program, by now you've carved out some mental time and space for yourself daily and you're reading smart stuff regularly. You've turned the volume way down on the tabloid media. Feeling brainier already? Wondering how you ever lived without intellectual curiosity, connection with the world's great minds, and information about your world?

Great. Now that you're so smart and fired up, we're going to put that fat brain of yours to some good use, right there in your own life.

Step Three: Use Your Newfound Time and Knowledge to Take Charge of Your Life

It is easier to live through someone else than to become complete yourself. —Betty Friedan

Once you have eliminated the time wasters in your life and acquired a solid base of knowledge through reading, you are ready to put that bright mind of yours into action. Your life is too important to outsource to someone else, no matter how well meaning those someone elses may be. You have one life. It is yours. You own it. When the muscles of your brain are flabby from disuse, just going along with the crowd may seem easier, but you know that you shouldn't just go along with what your friends say, what your husband or partner says, what your therapist says, what the majority says, or, hell, with what *I* say. In this section, I want to encourage you to think for yourself, without the crutch of leaning on the thinking of others. The more you use your wits to work out your own stuff, the easier it becomes and the more confidence you'll inspire in yourself.

When it comes to important aspects of your life—your mental and physical health, your money, your career, your family—you need to run the show using your own head. Good news! It's so easy to do.

Check Your Own Facts

> *One's own confidence in the rectitude of his opinion is no substitute for facts that only research can produce.* —Walter Cronkite

My friend Candace, thirty, is the mother of an adorable three-month-old baby girl, Bonnie. Candace has been putting baby Bonnie in one of those mechanized baby swings. The fussy baby settles right down as the thing jerks her back, forth, back, forth.

Candace's mother harps on her that the swing isn't good for the baby, that it will jumble her internal organs, and that she should stop using it. "Nah, mom, she likes it," Candace says, looking at the results, her contented baby. Back, forth, back, forth, goes the swing, as Bonnie, indeed, starts to nod off.

Turning to me, Candace asks, "Did *you* use a swing for your kids?" I search back through the murky recesses of my memory because, as

Candace well knows, about two decades have passed since I've needed a baby swing. But wait, the memory starts to come into focus. In the micro-mini Brooklyn apartment I lived in when my kids were babies, yes, yes, there *was* a squeaky swing, which took up 95 percent of our living room. I remembered the ee-eek, which harmonized so nicely with the quiet of baby Sarah blissfully sleeping. Read: not screaming.

"Sure," I said, visualizing slumped-down baby Sarah, mushy in her swing like a blob of mashed potatoes, going back, forth, back, forth.

"See, Mom!" says Candace. "Lisa used the swing. Lisa's kids turned out great!"

Say what?

"But Candace," I said, as gently as possible, "that was twenty years ago. We barely had the wheel rounded out back then. Don't rely on what *I* did. Find out what the latest research is on baby swings. What do unbiased health professionals say?"

"Oh, I'm sure they wouldn't be allowed to sell them if they harmed children," she said, dismissively. Bonnie lurched forward and back.

"But a lot of products *have* been on the market that harmed kids, until they were pulled. Just Google 'safety baby swings' and you'll get an instant answer. You don't want your baby to be the guinea pig."

"Sure, ok . . . " Candace said, losing interest.

To swing, or not to swing? A brief digression before we return to Bonnie, who we'll leave peacefully jerking back and forth in mechanized slumber, cute droopy baby face bobbling around on her soft neck.

First, can we have a little appreciation for the Internet and all of its wonders? I'm not talking about porn or shoe shopping. I am talking about the magic of Google.

For those of you born after 1980, let's take a quick stroll down Auntie Lisa's Memory Lane, to that distant time when All Knowledge in the World was *not* instantly accessible with a quick click. Put down your iPhone, step away from your incessant online chat, and travel backward in time with me, before Wifi on planes, 4G networks in your pocket, and TV shows on iPods.

Still with me?

When I was in college, I was on the debate team. This was before personal computers, much less the World Wide Web. We were still working with microfiche, and if you don't know what that is, believe me, you don't want to. Research was the key to our victories: We needed *more* facts—*better* facts—than the other teams we debated every weekend. When I wanted to research, say, the effect of Jerry Falwell's Moral Majority on the American political process (that was one of our debate topics), here's what I did:

> Step 1. Physically go to library during the hours they are open. Oops! Closed when I went first time, Monday night. Copy down library hours from sign on door. Put slip in purse, never to be seen again.
>
> Step 2. Try again. Back Tuesday afternoon. Yep! Library open. Go to card catalog. Look up issue from various angles: religion, politics, voting, constitutional issues. Wait impatiently (is there another way to wait?) while someone else leafs through the cards in the drawer I want. Finally, using a pinky-sized nubby pencil (were these required by law at every library?) scratch out zillion-digit Dewey Decimal System codes for books that might fit the research project.
>
> Step 3. Find map of Dewey Decimal book codes in library.
>
> Step 4. Go deep down into the stacks and hunt for the code.
>
> Step 5. Find maybe one out of the five books. Hope it was one of the good ones, but it never was. Sit in carrel in stacks and skim through it.
>
> Step 6. Make brief eye contact with twitchy guy sitting across from me, partially obscured by row of books. Oh, gross, he's . . .

oh, no . . . oh for God's sakes. Stop everything, run upstairs, report flasher to campus police.

This actually happened to me. I waited for a half hour for the police to come and then I made them follow me down into the stacks, where miraculously, he was *still there*. Police stopped him. Did I want to make a citizen's arrest? Hell, yes! The cops tried to talk me out of it. This was in Southern California, a few years after Roman Polanski's probation officer shrugged off his alleged rape of a thirteen-year-old girl on the grounds that the "situation was provocative." That was the thinking then. Guess the police similarly felt that I was "provoking" the flasher by reading books alone down in the stacks. Argh. After another hour consumed by raising police consciousness on the seriousness of sexual assaults, noting that flashers are obvious precursors to rapists, and then reviewing and signing the paperwork, I return to my research project. What was I looking for, again?

Sigh.

Step 7. Right, religion in politics. Well, that dusty old book about eighteenth-century British politics wasn't on point at all. Time to start over in the periodical room. And then the newspaper room. And then . . . the dreaded microfiche.

Whole days of research resulted in nothing but frustration. Looking back on it, that I gleaned anything of value is amazing. The library was like a fortress, jealously guarding her treasures. If you didn't have the secret code, the golden ticket, or if you didn't come on the right time on the right day, you were out of luck. That was me most of the time.

Out of the darkness, into the light: Along came the Internet. Before it, let's be honest, we were like apes. And now we stand upright.

Comedian Louis CK says,

> Everything's amazing right now, and nobody is happy. [In the past] if you wanted money, you had to go in the bank. It was open for like three hours, you had to stand in line and write yourself a check like an idiot. If you ran out of money, you'd just go, well, I can't do any more things now.[18]

Yes, kids, it's true. We had to take out paper checks and write them to ourselves and hope the bank teller would fork over some cash.

And we had to wait in line to get into the card catalog and then poke around dusty library stacks hoping against hope for some lame book that might shed some light on our research question.

Louis CK goes on:

> Now we live in an amazing, amazing world and it's wasted on the crappiest generation of spoiled idiots. I was on an airplane, and there was high-speed Internet. It's the newest thing that I know exists. And I'm sitting on the plane and they go, open up your laptop, you can go on the Internet. And it's fast, and I'm watching YouTube clips, it's amazing. I'm in an airplane. And then it breaks down. They apologize that it's not working. And the guy next to me goes, "Ugh, this is bullshit!" Like, *how quickly the world owes him something he knew existed only ten seconds ago.*"[19]

Everyone complains about air travel—the delays, the hassles. Louis CK asks,

> Oh really, what happened next, did you fly through the air, incredibly, like a bird, *did you partake of the miracle of human flight, you noncontributing zero?* Everybody on every plane should just constantly be going, *Oh my god! Wow!* You're sitting in a *chair* in the *sky*.[20]

This is how I feel about the Internet. Every time I do a Google search, which is about a hundred times per day because I always want to know stuff, plus I need to confirm everything I am saying on air and writing, I want to yell, WOW! WOW! WOW!

You used to need an advanced degree in library science to find tidbits of information squirreled away in the dark recesses of the stacks. You had to overcome sexual predators, and even then, it wasn't the right book. Okay, there are *more* sexual predators online. You've got me there. But they're in chat rooms. I've never met one on Google or my *New York Times* app.

Back to Candace and baby Bonnie lurching to and fro. Mom raised a legitimate question. Are baby swings safe? If Candace had done a quick Google search, she would have immediately come upon a *Consumer Reports* piece. *Consumer Reports* is a good, solid, unbiased source of information, well established for decades, reputable, independent, and nonprofit. Clicking on that page, Candace would have learned that in a recent year eighteen hundred babies were injured from swings and an average of one baby per year died. She would have seen the recommendations for increasing Bonnie's safety if she continued to use the swing: Don't let her swing for more than half an hour at a time, don't let older kids push the baby in the swing, don't put it on an elevated surface, and use the lowest setting for infants.

This is what's cool about research. You often find out things you didn't even think to ask. Here, there was a compromise I hadn't thought of: Use the swing, but use it only for short periods, at the lowest setting, and follow the safety recommendations.

Certainly this ten-second search yielded more current, reliable information than I could have told Candace. The two "experts" she consulted, her mom and me, knew next to nothing about her topic. We had only some vague instincts. Had she gone right to Google and *Consumer Reports*, she'd have received free, instant, expert information that she could then use to make a smart decision about her baby.

WOW! WOW! WOW!

When it comes to your health or the well-being of your family, you need answers, not shoot-from-the-hip opinions from a nonexpert friend like me. And you need to look it up yourself, to analyze the facts yourself, to follow the research to where it might lead you. Get in the habit of double-checking even your own opinions, which may be scientifically outdated or just based on how you were brought up. The more you look up the data yourself, the smarter you'll become on the issues that matter most to you.

For the first time in human history the universe has conspired to give us all the vital information we need instantly, for free. Make a habit of tapping into that amazing resource on any subject that matters to you. Look for reliable, unbiased sources (i.e., not random bloggers or companies trying to sell you something). Cross-check your findings against what other credible sources advise. Because no one will be more diligent in getting to the bottom of important questions in your life than you, this is a job you should do yourself, not delegate.

Be your own fact checker. You'll get the double benefit of making yourself smarter each time you do your own research, and you'll be taking charge of your own life.

Face Those Facts Head On

To do research, go right to the source, and get the facts is one thing; to truly accept them is another. If you want to get smart, get comfortable living with uncomfortable facts. There should be nothing about your life that you don't want to know, honestly and openly. You want to encourage everyone around you to give it to you straight so you can tackle it head on.

There's something hardwired in us that doesn't want to coolly stare down the facts when they are ugly or when they'd require us to change our worldview. Psychologists call it minimizing or denial. This is true even when a straightforward look at the hard, cold facts directly affects our own health, even our own mortality.

Consider this: How many times have we heard that two-thirds of us are overweight or obese? "I know, I know!" you may want to shout when you hear another one of those local news reports about the latest fat survey, accompanied by that video of chubby people cut off at the necks. Yet remarkably, we don't think it applies to us individually.

In 2007 Harris Interactive conducted a National Consumers League survey and found that Americans consistently consider ourselves to be less overweight than we actually are. Eighty-two percent of obese people surveyed identified themselves to be simply overweight; among those who were in fact overweight, close to one in three believed that they were normal weight.[21]

Part of the blame goes to doctors. Even when physicians do screen for obesity, many don't discuss the importance of weight loss. The Centers for Disease Control and Prevention released a 2005 study that found that only about 40 percent of obese people are ever advised by their health care professional to lose weight.

"Physicians are reluctant to bring up weight because it's such a loaded issue," Dr. William Dietz, director of the Division of Nutrition, Physical Activity and Obesity at the Centers for Disease Control, told the *Los Angeles Times*. "It's a difficult and often emotional conversation to have with patients, so some doctors just avoid it."[22]

But if doctors won't tell us about our health because they don't think we can handle it, we are in trouble, especially given the serious diseases obesity causes: heart disease—the number one killer of American men and women—diabetes, hypertension, and some cancers.

I think feeling good about oneself and also hearing the straight truth about being overweight is possible. Our size is only one part of us. Our brains; our ability to love; our creativity; our service to others; our connection to our families, communities, and the world; our ability to give back—these are far more important. We can learn to make healthier food choices, work out regularly, and feel good about ourselves every day as we do it. To think that knowing that our weight is a health problem that we need to correct will destroy us is a false assumption. But if we give the impression that we are hothouse flowers who will wilt in the harsh glare of uncomfortable facts, those facts won't be delivered to us.

We all know people who live in major denial. My beloved real estate broker, Kathleen, chain-smoked. She'd light her next cigarette from the nub of the one that was about to go out, one to the next, all day long. I guess she saved on matches. Given how intolerant I am of smoking—I gag if someone lights up in the next town—you know how much I had to adore this hard-working, can-do woman to let her represent me for both the purchase and then the sale four years later of my beloved country house in the Pocono mountains of Eastern Pennsylvania.

I asked Kathleen not to smoke when we were driving around in the car together looking at houses and when she was in my house. Breathing actual air without her customary side of nicotine wasn't easy for her, but she did it for me. And oh, did she cough. "The comps are running—cough cough!—about 15 percent lower—cough!—than we'd expected," she'd say. "The buyer—*cough*!—is asking that you—*cough*!—replace the—*ahhh*!"

"You okay, Kathleen?"

She'd nod yes and then say that it was "probably just the dry air."

"Or the chain smoking," I said.

Oh no, it wasn't that, she insisted with a straight face, then wheezed and spit phlegm into a tissue.

"*Seriously*? Seriously, Kathleen, you don't think this has to do with your smoking all day long?"

"I know someone—cough cough—who smoked for years, and when she stopped, she got cancer!" she said triumphantly.

This was not a woman interested in the facts. Giving her the straightforward information was not going to change her behavior. She'd rather contort her mind to believe that *quitting* smoking causes cancer.

For nicotine junkies to have excuses for smoking is one thing. My dad's was "it's a labor-intensive American industry!" Sure, so is cancer treatment.

Addicts deny reality. They are negative role models for the rest of us. We can't tackle the world until we stare at it head-on, unflinching.

We all know people who are protected from information others think they can't handle. They are always the last to know when there's an illness or someone's moving or lost their job. "*Don't tell Mom!*" Everyone contorts themselves to keep that person in the dark. I never wanted to be that person, the one who's perceived as unable to handle the facts or contribute to solving the problem, the one who's kept in a childlike state of naiveté by their friends and family, because that's the person who's unable to think clearly, lacking all the critical information.

Garbage in, garbage out.

Facts may be slippery things, but we've got to try to grab onto them. As science fiction writer Phillip K. Dick said, "Reality is that which, when you stop believing in it, doesn't go away."

I want you to have a fact-based life. I want you to be the one among your friends and family members who is known to be capable of taking in and processing difficult information. Become known as the person who coolly assesses facts, verifies them, acquires all relevant information, and then acts. That is my definition of a grown-up, thinking, take-charge woman. When you can handle the facts, you can take care of the necessary business in your life.

Here's an exercise that will force you to stare down some facts in your life that you may have been avoiding. Do your own taxes every year. Oh, yes. Doing this is a simple, wonderful way to learn nearly everything you need to know about your earnings and spending. Too many women are in denial about our own money, and as a result, men save more, invest better, pay off credit cards sooner, and overspend less. This must stop. I can't stand it when the boys beat us at anything besides arm wrestling. (And even then, it's irritating.) Doing your own taxes couldn't be easier via online tax programs, cheap at www.TurboTax.com or free at www.irs.gov, and it will force you to sit down, pull out your records, and spend a few hours working through your financial year. Little girls take a bag of receipts to some random CPA and pay hundreds of dollars for them to maybe do it right. Grown-up women take charge of their finances and think through their money world once a year with their own Form 1040s. I do it. Do I enjoy it? Hell no! I'd rather . . . do housework. But doing it forces me to face the facts of what I've earned and spent the prior year, and it forces me to learn about my little economic universe.

You can't do your own taxes without thinking, "I should have given more to charity last year"—because you get a sweet tax deduction for it. And you can't do your own taxes without learning something about how our economic system is set up to reward you for certain behaviors (buying real estate, for instance, or investing in green technologies). This is stuff you need to know to be a functioning grown-up.

The more you stare down the real facts in your life, the more you take charge of your own business, the more competent you will become. If you don't understand something, research it online, buy a book, or ask an expert. Knowledge is power.

In this area, and in all areas, you've just been promoted to CEO of your own life.

At first this can all feel awkward and uncomfortable. *Research baby safety? I'm not a scientist! Do my own taxes? But I'm not an accountant! Read my own closing documents? I'm not a real estate lawyer!* Resist that kind of thinking. When it comes to your life, *you* are the expert, and you are capable of reading and deciphering data. If professionals work for you, make them explain the jargon in plain English, and if they don't, look it up yourself online and keep asking questions. As with any muscle, the more you use that brain, the easier and more natural thinking for yourself will become. There is no end to what you can do. You may find yourself starting your own business, writing your own blog, and critically reading your mortgage documents—line by tedious–but-important line—on the purchase of your first house. As well you should, my friend. You may find yourself asking pointed questions of your dentist, your kids' teacher, your divorce lawyer, your government officials, your news sites. You may find yourself ordering books by experts to check the answers you got.

Yep, thinking is habit forming—and a hell of a lot of fun.

Best of all, you may find yourself passing it on to the next generation. When you see an adorable six-year-old girl, instead of telling her how much you like her party dress (our culture's standard talking-to-little-girl icebreaker), you'll look into her eyes and ask, "What are you reading?" Listen intently to her response, ask respectful questions about her opinions on that story, and tell her about your latest favorite book and why it means so much to you. Skip the talk about sparkly nail polish—she gets plenty of that from everyone else—and model for her what an adult female who has an active mind looks like.

Because we want her to aspire to win a Nobel Prize, not a ditzy reality show.

Take Charge of Your Own Happiness

> *You have brains in your head. You have feet in your shoes. You can steer yourself any direction you choose. You're on your own. And you know what you know. And YOU are the guy who'll decide where to go.*
> —Dr. Seuss, *Oh, the Places You'll Go!*

I can't talk about taking charge of your own life without addressing the importance of taking charge of your emotional state. To fire on all cylinders, you need emotional stability and, dare I say it, regular joy in your life. Happiness doesn't just happen. I'm convinced that for the most part, those who focus their minds on it, obtain it. I believe that you can think your way through to your own contented—even blissful—life, that it's up to you to use your brain to produce your own emotional health, and that to get there, you'll need to travel off the beaten path a bit.

Too many of us today are walking around in a funk. In 1972 and annually through 2009 researchers at the University of Chicago administered their General Social Survey asking thousands of men and women: "Taken all together, how would you say things are these days, would you say that you are very happy, pretty happy, or not too happy?"[23]

Despite all the gains women have made in the last generation—control over our own fertility, huge strides in education, access to jobs, a cultural shift to an expectation of equality across the board—sadly, women's happiness has significantly *declined*. In 1972 women reported more happiness than men. In 2009 that had reversed—men were now more contented with their lives. Women have become significantly less happy over time, in absolute terms and relative to men.[24]

Ouch. How can this be? Is this another case of paradox like we saw earlier, when women are getting smarter in school but dumbing ourselves down after graduation?

I posed this question—how can we have gained so much yet become so unhappy?—on my Facebook page, and I was bombarded with answers. Most of the women who wrote in said they were less happy because they worked harder, both at work and at home, than they perceived their mothers did in their childhoods. Having it all is a big fat recipe for exhaustion and late-night teary misery for many women (which is why I devoted an earlier section of this book to reclaiming time for yourself).

Rochelle Schieck is the founder of Qoya, a program designed to amp up women's joy on a physical, mental, and spiritual level.* Rochelle has made a life's work of studying women's happiness, and she knows more about the subject than anyone I know. She spends her days learning what makes women tick and how we can find joy in everyday experiences. (Hate your long commute? Use that time to listen to beautiful new music or an audiobook. Better still, call your husband and detail for him every erotic thrill you intend to have with him tonight. That's Rochelle's way of thinking.)

I asked Rochelle why women are losing the ability to experience joy. She said,

> One of the best things about men is their confidence, their rightness, their ability to go with their gut and produce. I rarely overhear men in cafes talking about how differently they could have or should have done something.
>
> However, one of the most paralyzing things for a woman is her doubt. Do I have the right job? Did I pick the right partner? Are these the right shoes? Did I pick the right place to go on vacation? Doubt is like an anchor that keeps women rooted in murky waters of disapproval.

---

*Learn more by visiting her website at www.RochelleSchieck.com.

> I believe men are happier than women because of their sense of self-approval. There is a sense of entitlement that men have and a sense of women always feeling like they need to prove themselves, instead of reveling in and enjoying who they are, as they are.[25]

No doubt men do have more confidence in their "rightness." So, Rochelle, why do you suppose women's happiness has declined when, on the surface at least, it seems that so much about our lives has improved?

She answered,

> My favorite quote about happiness is from Gandhi. "Happiness is when what you think, what you say, and what you do are in harmony."
>
> Each woman needs to take total self-responsibility for her happiness. Happiness is all perspective and what you look for is what you see. If a woman is committed to finding the golden thread through her stories, she will see it. If a woman is looking for ways in which she is victimized, she will find that too.

I couldn't agree more that we need to take responsibility for our own happiness. I suspect the happiness deficit is rooted in our failure to do precisely this. And clearly a miserable woman is not a thinking woman, a woman not engaged with her community or her planet. Misery doesn't love company, actually. Misery generally wallows alone. Misery disengages. Misery believes that any action is futile, so why bother?

If my mission is to get us standing on our own two feet and thinking, it has to include a happiness prescription. Yes, you could go to a therapist. But before you do, try these three free—and more fun—suggestions first.

Happiness Solution #1: Get Moving

Show me a grouch and I will show you a couch potato. When I was in law school, I went through a slump, so a counselor said to me, "How much exercise do you get?"

Uhh . . .

I was in New Haven, Connecticut. It was *cold*. After growing up in sunny, endless summer California, the winter there felt like eleven months a year. To get all bundled up, go to the gym, get unbundled, suit up, work out, shower, rebundle. . . . I just wasn't going to the gym much. It was true. She had me.

I got over it and started swimming. Swimming, during the freezing winter! Yale had a beautiful, enormous, free-to-students indoor pool. I grooved to the zen of stroke, stroke, stroke, breathe left, stroke, stroke, stroke, breathe right. Afterward, I never had the patience to blow-dry my hair all the way dry in those days (or now). So I'd throw on a wool cap and walk around with icicle hair. So what? Who cared? And the counselor was right. Stirring up those endorphins gave me a spring in my step.

You have so many options, and they don't have to involve a gym membership or anything expensive. Put on some sneakers and walk around the block blasting "It's a Beautiful Day" on your iPod and wave at everyone you see. Dust off your bike and ride around the park, doing wheelies like a goofy kid. Braden and I whack tennis balls at free public courts surrounded by aromatic pine trees a few blocks from our home. My friend Judith rents Bollywood movies and, after her kids go to bed, plays them on her home office computer and dances along with the cast. Try to do *that* without cracking up.

What you do to exercise really doesn't matter as long as you work up a little sweat, have fun, and do it regularly. You'll improve your general health, and you'll eat better because who wants to ingest disgusting fatty foods after a good workout? Not you, you vibrant, glowing thing.

Exercising makes you smarter, and smart people exercise more. It's a positive feedback loop. In one study, women who did weight training for just an hour or two a week scored higher on intelligence tests. "I like to say that exercise is like taking a little Prozac or a little Ritalin at just the right moment," says John J. Ratey, MD, a psychiatry professor at Harvard Medical School and author of *A User's Guide to the Brain*. "Exercise is really for the brain, not the body. It affects mood, vitality, alertness, and feelings of well-being."[26] So working out gives you the double whammy of making you smarter and happier, and those are only the mental benefits. What are you waiting for?

Exercise is a great excuse to listen to your personal tunes. I sweat to the Zac Brown Band, Taylor Swift, and other country music stars. There, I said it. And if I find you shaking a leg while listening to an audiobook, I swear I'm going to bear hug you right then and there.

And if you're single, don't turn your nose up at meeting potential dates at the gym. After all, at least they're healthy and you can get a good look at them in the light. And if they're interested in you sweaty and in yoga pants, they're going to love you trussed up for an evening out. Apart from that, you can join a runner's club, a soccer league, or any number of groups for people who are physically fit or who want to be, getting together to get the heart rate up on a regular basis.

Happiness Solution #2: Have More Sex!

We live in an odd culture that both glorifies and shames us for our sexuality. Ignore all that, and understand that as a matter of simple science, sex is good for your health and your mood.

So if you've got a main squeeze, go to town! Statistically, sex makes you not only happier but also healthier.* Frequent (once or twice a week) sex is scientifically proven to lower your blood pressure. Sex reduces stress so that you perform better at work and you're happier at home. Sex produces an antibody called immunoglobulin A, which reduces your susceptibility to colds and other infections. Sex burns 170 calories an hour, reduces the risk of fatal heart attacks, *and* boosts your self-esteem. Regular sex increases your levels of the hormone oxytocin, the so-called "love hormone," which helps us bond and build trust, gives us the urge to nurture, and makes us more generous. Surges of this wonder hormone also significantly decrease pain, as any woman with menstrual cramps will tell you after a good orgasm or two. And

*To state the painfully obvious: If you're having unprotected sex with a bunch of random people, you're risking all kinds of disgusting, oozing, itchy, burning, and even fatal diseases, and none of this applies to you.

oxytocin released during orgasm promotes sleep, and a good night's sleep keeps your blood pressure and weight down as well as helps you concentrate throughout the day. If you do Kegels during sex (or any time), you minimize your risk of incontinence later in life.[27]

Hey hey! See how *useful* it is to read the science section of a national newspaper?

Sex is better for you than vitamins! No lie. In large-scale studies vitamins E and C have been shown to have no effect on cancer rates or heart disease. A few vitamins have proven health benefits: vitamin B_{12} for vegans and the elderly, folic acid for women who want to have children, and vitamin D for those who don't get enough sunshine. But otherwise, high doses of vitamin E slightly *increases* heart failure and death rates; beta carotene *increases* lung cancer rates among smokers; high levels of vitamin A *increases* risks of women's hip fractures; and vitamin C does *not* prevent colds, according to all the most recent studies. But regular sex reduces your susceptibility to colds and strengthens your immune system.[28] I kid you not.

If you really want to snap out of your stupor, you don't need pills in any form, not even multivitamins. Just lock that bedroom door, put on Norah Jones, and jump your husband's bones.*

Happiness Solution #3: Girlfriends

Girlfriends are critical to long-term happiness. I'm sure I would have been committed and forcibly medicated by now if not for mine.

One American in four now reports having *no close confidants*, up from one in ten in 1985, according to the American Sociological Review.[29] How sad is that?

My friend Julie and I have whinged, exulted, and vented to each other for twenty years. We both lived in Los Angeles, where we met. I was an attorney, she was a paralegal in my firm. I immediately realized that (1) she had a big fat brain, (2) she was a fellow vegetarian and animal lover, and (3) she had a MacGyver-like ability to create and fix

*Or the bones of your boyfriend, girlfriend, wife, what have you.

things. I'm pretty sure she made her husband out of paper clips and Elmer's glue. But mainly she had a wise-ass sense of humor that made me laugh so hard I popped buttons.

Julie is the most supportive person on the planet. I could tell her that I'd taken a machine gun and mowed down a playground full of preschoolers, and she'd say evenly, "Oh Lisa, you've been under a lot of stress. You *needed* to do that." However, she'll also tell me honestly that the rainbow platform sandals I wore on *Dr. Phil* did not enhance my credibility as a legal analyst.

I love Julie. I attached myself to her like a tick. Julie is the one I called at 4 a.m. when I was staring down my first Father's Day without my father, when I was stupid lonely after my divorce, when my perfect children engaged in less-than-perfect behavior (*my* kids? How was that possible?). Julie talked me down out of the tree more times than I can count. We e-mail daily. If employers really do read their employees' e-mail, then some IT guys somewhere have gotten some graphic eyefuls about our trials, tribulations, and sex lives. With Julie by my side (if only by e-mail), misery is only trifling unhappiness; joy is ecstasy.

I told my kids that as teenagers, the choice of who your friends are is probably the most important choice you will make. Kids' friends have an enormous influence on them, especially now that they are electronically connected to them 24/7.

Choice of friends is just as important for adults and possibly even more important than a choice of spouse. In my case and in Julie's, spouses have come and gone, but BFFs are forever.

Do your friends raise you up, make you a better person, and inspire you to be the person you want to be?

My friend Lauren Lake is a knockout singer, a brilliant attorney, a creative interior designer, a savvy real estate developer, and a feisty television commentator and talk show host. Honestly, she is good at all of these things. Oh, she also just authored a terrific relationship book for single women, got married, and started a family. Strong, successful women like this intimidate some people, but I say, *you go girl!* Bring it on! Let me hang out with you and bask in the presence of all that brainpower and creative energy. I love it. I want to absorb some of that vitality. *I want what she's having.*

I mentioned my friend Rochelle Schieck, who teaches yoga and inspired movement to women and is one of the most brilliant voices in America today on the subject of women's joy. Nothing gets Rochelle down, and I mean *nothing*. Her phone was stolen. Now she gets to buy the new iPhone she's been wanting! Her beloved grandmother passed away. Rochelle was heartened that she arrived in time to spend her final hours with her.

When something is on my mind, I can call Rochelle to get a fresh look from her unremittingly optimistic, life-affirming perspective.

I met Rochelle in Kerala, India, at 5 a.m. one December morning when I arrived after traveling solo for over twenty-four hours to attend a yoga retreat. We got to chatting over predawn breakfast in the hotel's outdoor café overlooking the Indian Ocean. When I went to see if my room was ready, I was told in that uniquely South Asian way that tries to avoid saying the word "no" that, yes, my room was ready, and I could get the key at 3 p.m. "So, it's not ready?" I asked. "Yes, please come back at 3 p.m." We cracked up.

I later learned that Ro's luggage was missing, so I loaned her some clothes. Many people would carp about not having their suitcase when they are half a planet away from home, but she didn't miss a beat and actually seemed to enjoy trying on my yoga gear.

You can tell a lot about a person by how they react to travel inconveniences. Some people moan and groan over flight delays, gaps in translation, and hotel rooms that are not ready. Rochelle chooses humor over frustration. In fact, most frustrating experiences are funny, and you will laugh at them later. Why not laugh at them while they are happening—with a friend?

Ro's default state of being is happiness. She is a joy to be around and elevates everyone around her. I learn so much from her.

This is the kind of friend we all need. When the going gets tough, as it does for all of us, I can call one of my compassionate, funny, sunny, wise friends and be listened to, get good advice, or, when needed, smacked upside my head. They just give it to me straight, and I always feel better.

And, of course, I do the same for them.

For thousands of years—all of human history—we humans talked to our families, our neighbors, and our friends about the challenges in our lives. However, as we become more isolated and spend more time online, we lose that connection. If you don't have enough—or any—close girlfriends, pick a woman you know and admire and ask her out to lunch. Tell her why you respect her. Ask her advice on an issue in your life. (Everyone, I've found, likes being asked for advice.) Join a local women's book group and make a new friend. Even if you mostly keep up by e-mail, that bond will enhance your happiness, ground you, and help you laugh through the hard times. As Aristotle said, "The antidote for fifty enemies is one friend."

Have you noticed that all the happiness prescriptions I've offered require you to act on your own behalf rather than waiting for someone else to wave a magic wand and bestow emotional health upon you? I want you to get in the habit of making things happen in your own life. You can create the time, you can acquire the knowledge, you can check the facts, and you can create your own joy. When all is running smoothly, you're ready for the final step as a true thinker: engaging with your world.

Step 4: Engage, Connect, Take a Stand, Act

> *The hottest places in hell are reserved for those who in time of great moral crises maintain their neutrality.* —Dante

All of this shaking away of silly habits; letting go of the trivial, the silly, the gossipy fluff; increasing your font of knowledge and shoring up your own emotional foundation has a larger purpose. Now more than ever, your world needs you. It needs your first world education put to use. It needs your sharp mind to spring into action. It needs a little of your time, your creativity, your spunk, your stubbornness. It needs you to connect, and you need that connection too.

The first step is volunteering. Volunteering gives you the double benefit of amping up your personal happiness and it gets you out there engaging with the lives of others. Read to homeless kids, serve soup at the mission downtown, or sit and chat with a lonely, wheelchair-bound octogenarian in a convalescent home. Volunteering is a guaranteed spirit booster because you *need* to contribute, and it will make you feel peppy and alive. Make your life a blessing to others and you will glow.

University of Virginia psychologist Jonathan Haidt, who has extensively studied happiness, says that if you are hit by a truck and end up a paraplegic or if you win the lottery, a year from now neither will make much difference on your happiness scale. In fact, there are many studies about lottery winners who end up divorced, lonely, miserable, broke, and even suicidal a year or two after the initial high. Poverty is miserable. But after our basic needs are met, money does not buy happiness.[30]

What has been shown to consistently make us happy is "a connection to something larger"—a cause, a religion, a purpose. People who are connected and engaged with their world on a deeper level consistently score the highest on happiness scales. As Nicholas Kristof and Sheryl WuDunn write, "We are neurologically constructed so that we gain huge personal dividends from altruism."[31] Helen Keller, deaf, blind and mute, said it best: "Many persons have a wrong idea of what constitutes true happiness. It is not attained through self-gratification but through fidelity to a worthy purpose."

Even simply *talking* about bigger subjects, like the state of the world or the meaning of life, seems to produce more happiness than superficial chitchat. A University of Arizona psychologist got college students to consent to wearing mini-voice recorders for a few days, recording random snippets of their conversations throughout the day. The happiest people in the study had the most substantive conversations (current affairs, philosophy, religion, education). The unhappiest people had the most small talk (the weather, TV shows).[32]

Here's what I know. I have volunteered dancing with seniors in nursing homes, ladling chili in soup kitchens, running with disabled runners, and embracing kids crossing the finish line at the Special Olympics since I was in junior high school. Though I have often been tired and not in the mood when I dragged my sorry butt to the volunteer activity, I always left happy and energized. You never regret volunteering to help someone less fortunate than you.

All the old saws about volunteering are true. The volunteer gets a greater benefit than the recipient. Our "guests" at the New York Rescue Mission, where I cooked and served meals for eight years until I moved to Los Angeles, buoyed me with their friendliness, gratitude, and optimism. I smiled until my face hurt boogying with mostly wheelchair-bound elderly folks at the New York Home for the Aged as they grinned and bobbed their heads to the music, waved around their one good arm, or howled in fake protest as I wheeled them around the auditorium, which we trussed up to look like the ballrooms of yore.

I double dare you to go into that room and not come out happy to be alive, tapping your foot to the music and smiling back at the faces of giddy seniors.

Volunteering is free. (In fact, the costs of getting there and back are tax deductible.) It is an in-your-face reminder that this life is not all about you, and in fact, your problems are kind of lame compared to people who have to stand in line at a soup kitchen or who sit in their rooms at the nursing home all day hoping someone might come talk to them. Volunteering raises your self-esteem because you've actually *earned* the right to feel good about yourself by lending a hand to a needy person—by giving back, by joining the world.

My boyfriend, Braden, through the Jewish Big Brothers of America program, volunteers as a Big Brother with an adorable eleven-year-old boy named Daniel. That Daniel's father was out of the picture or that his single mom, a hard-working, smart Russian immigrant, could barely make ends meet was not his fault. Braden takes Daniel miniature golfing, shooting bows and arrows at the park, and to the bookstore. They appreciate fart jokes together far beyond my capacity to do so.

Neither Daniel nor his mom is Jewish. Why, then, did she choose the Jewish Big Brothers program to find a good male role model for her son? "Because Daniel's father is Jewish," she said. The guy who once beat her up, the guy she had to get a restraining order against? "I didn't want Daniel to become anti-Semitic. I wanted him to have a positive Jewish role model in his life," she said.

Come on. If that doesn't make you want to volunteer, to lend a hand to a big-hearted single mom like that, I don't know what will. If you don't feel like working with kids or the elderly, you can plant gardens, build houses, answer phones, teach computer skills, have conversations in English with new immigrants—the list is endless. Online clearinghouses will link you to local organizations that need you right now, like VOA.org, a faith-based volunteer organization; serve.gov, the president's service site; or NYCares.org, the brilliant New York City volunteer site that every city should emulate. Or just Google "volunteer" and your city and you'll find plenty of opportunities.*

If you still need a kick in the pants to engage with others to improve your world, consider the example of those with the best reason to do nothing yet who somehow find the strength and moral courage to act. I have noticed that people who have endured personal tragedies are often the most active and engaged in their communities. Their inspirational stories make me feel like a slouch. If they can get out there and improve the world, what the heck are we waiting for?

Matthew Hunt was a seventeen-year-old high school senior who suffered two horrific tragedies. He was in a car accident that left him paraplegic, bound to a wheelchair. Six months later Matthew and three other kids were murdered in a senseless, brutal drug killing.

Matthew's sisters were guests on my Court TV show ten years after the slaying, when the killer's trial took place. I tried to imagine what these young women had gone through: losing their baby brother so suddenly and violently followed by the excruciating decade-long wait for his killer to be brought to justice.

---

*Chat about your favorite volunteer organization and see others' picks at www.Think.tv/volunteer.

Matthew's sisters chose to honor and celebrate his life. In Matthew's memory they donated his wheelchair to another disabled young man who went on to use it in the Paralympics, an international competition for disabled athletes. They raise funds for chairs for wheelchair athletes in Matthew's honor. They smile and are positive in their memories of him.

So many families of murder victims I interviewed during my eight years at Court TV were active in this way, contributing via charities they started, getting legislation passed to help other crime victims, making their communities safer. Time and time again, the families stunned me with their composure, their grace under pressure, their decision to put their energy into a worthy cause.

In 2008 I covered the case of Florida college student Ryan Skipper. On March 14, 2007, Skipper was just walking down the street, minding his own business, when he was picked up by two young men and then murdered because he was gay. Ryan's body, with nineteen stab wounds, a severed carotid artery, and a severe cranial contusion, was found on a dark, rural road in Wahneta, Florida, less than two miles from his home, dumped along the side of the road like garbage. The killers drove Ryan's blood-soaked car around the county and bragged of killing him. According to a sheriff's department affidavit, one of the men stated that Ryan was targeted because he was a "faggot." In trial testimony, the killer was quoted as saying that he felt he was "doing the world a favor by getting rid of one more faggot."

I covered this trial in depth for a few weeks, and it took its toll on me. As a mother, I went home wiped out, upset, exhausted. Ten years after the murder of Matthew Shepard, boys were still getting picked up and killed simply because they were gay, right here in my own country! I could not bear to think about this case, and yet, for two hours a day as we followed the trial, I had to. The trial turned me inside out with grief for Ryan, who was like so many young gay men I knew and feared for.

My distress reached a point when a friend had to sit me down and remind me that not everyone is a homophobic killer. Listen to a gorgeous piece of music, he said. Watch some comedy. Read a nice book. Remind yourself that not all humans are evil. (He had heard that a judge in a genocide tribunal, who listened to stories of rape and murder all day long, stopped at a museum and gazed at a beautiful painting every day after the trial proceedings to cleanse his mind of the brutality.)

Still, covering the case made me physically ill. But of course, the trial wasn't about me at all. It was about Ryan Skipper and his family. One day Ryan's mother was a guest on my show. She was friendly and straightforward. She told me about when Ryan came out to her. She'd never cared that Ryan was gay. When he told her, it was like him saying he liked the color blue, she said. So what?

Devastated after her young son's murder, Ryan's mom had put her life back together after the local gay community rallied around her. She came to learn that many moms are not as accepting as she was of their kids' homosexuality. So she'd "adopted" the local young gay folks whose parents had disowned them. They were all welcome in her home. She now had an entire group of young people to mother, people she'd met only after, and because of, Ryan's death. These motherless gay men and lesbians now had Pat—and she had them.

You go, Pat. She chose to make her life a blessing to others who need her instead of isolating herself into darkness and anger. She forged her own path out of her tragedy, sweeping in others in her inclusiveness.

I saw this constantly when I interviewed families of murder victims. These people rose to the occasion, conducted themselves with dignity, found causes to rally around, passed legislation to help others, and fought for justice. Matthew Shepard's family, for example, chose not to ask the prosecutors for the death penalty for their son's killer—a man who had tied their son to a fence for over eighteen hours and left him to die. They chose to grant mercy to the young man who had no mercy for their gay son. And then they lobbied Congress for eleven years until federal hate crimes legislation included sexual orientation.

Faced with a wave of gay teen suicides in the fall of 2010, columnist Dan Savage wanted to reach out to lesbian, gay, bisexual, and transgender (LGBT) youth. Knowing that many school administrators and parents wouldn't let LGBT adults talk directly to their children about their futures, he decided to not bother getting permission to tell kids that life gets better after all the bullying in adolescence. He compiled a moving online video archive, www.ItGetsBetterProject.com, to share the stories of LGBT folks who are overcoming bullying and finding happiness. The world flocked to the site in support. A month later he had one hundred thousand supporters, thousands of inspiring videos from ordinary people and celebrities, and even one from President Obama, all in support of Savage's vision to tell LGBT kids that we love them, we are here for them, and no matter what abuse and intolerance they may be suffering now, it gets better. Within two months of the project's launch, five thousand people had uploaded messages of hope, and over fifteen million people had viewed the site.

All he needed to start that surely lifesaving campaign was a bold idea, a webcam, and an Internet connection. One man started, and thousands jumped on the bandwagon, because the cause was righteous and urgent. Out of the ashes of heartbreaking teen suicides arose a groundbreaking, clever online movement of hope.

FINALLY, CONSIDER THIS.

If you had been born in a remote village near the world's second-highest mountain, K2 in Pakistan, your "school" would have been an open-air platform—no roof, no walls. As winter came, you were freezing all day long, exposed to the elements, shivering among the glaciers. In the summer you baked in searing heat. Even worse, the village couldn't afford a full-time teacher, so you and your friends were expected to sit on the platform eight hours a day, several days a week, and go over your lessons quietly, on your own, with no supervising adult.

If you had been born a girl in that village, you'd consider yourself lucky, very lucky, to have the privilege of sitting on that open-air platform among all the boys to receive lessons at all. When American mountain climber (and now author and humanitarian) Greg Mortenson visited that Pakistani village school a few years ago, seventy boys and four girls were in attendance.

Girls were culturally forbidden to attend school, so only a few brave families, those willing to buck the trend, sent their girls to learn how to read, to add and subtract, to learn something about history and science and their world. The rest of the village girls would remain ignorant and illiterate all their lives.

If you were a girl trying to go to school in Kandahar, Afghanistan, in the fall of 2008, the local Taliban thug could have stopped you, asked if you were on your way to school, and, when you said yes, pulled your burka back and thrown acid in your face. This happened to Shamsia Husseini, age fifteen, her sister, and thirteen other girls. Months later, after their burns were treated, the girls returned to school, with painful scars and blurred vision. Shamsia suffered some hearing loss in the attack and had to cup her hand to her ear to hear the lessons. "My parents told me to keep coming to school even if I am killed," said Shamsia, at seventeen, in a moment after class. "The people who did this to me don't want women to be educated. They want us to be stupid things."[33]

After the Taliban, the most violently misogynistic organization on earth, seized control of the Swat Valley in northwest Pakistan in 2008, it decreed that girls were forbidden from being educated. Some four hundred private schools, enrolling forty thousand girls, were shut down. To make their message absolutely clear, the Taliban bombed or burned more than 150 girls' schools to the ground between December 2008 and the summer of 2009. As of November 2010, though it had brought peace to the area for over a year, the Pakistani government had yet to rebuild a single girls' school.[34]

If you had been born a girl in the Swat Valley, you might be sequestered in your home night and day, afraid to venture outdoors, just as girls were under Taliban rule in Afghanistan from 1996 to 2001.

If you had been born in a hill tribe in Laos, your school might have been two open-air rooms, each with holes in the roof the size of Volkswagens. Without money for books or paper, much less computers, your lessons would consist entirely of repeating after the teacher as he or she occasionally wrote something on the blackboard and you sat on the dirt floor. When it rained, as it does often there, school would not be in session.

I have seen this school.

If you had been born a girl in the southern African country of Zambia, after puberty you would likely stay home one week per month because you could not afford sanitary pads. Initially you might try to use and reuse old rags during your period, but because your school probably lacks running water and a place to rinse the rags, you wind up simply staying home and waiting out your periods while the boys go on learning. Missing this much school would probably cause you to fall so far behind you just give up on school entirely.[35]

If you'd been born a girl in Nepal, instead of going to school an aunt or trafficker could have taken you across the border, selling you into prostitution at age ten. Border guards would look the other way as you were trucked into India and sold into sex slavery, where you'd be drugged, raped, and forced to prostitute yourself seven days a week, without ever seeing a penny of the money you were producing for your pimps and traffickers.

We first world women have privileges that surely seem like impossible dreams to girls born in many places around the world. We all had a free, public education that was an entitlement, a right that no one could take away from us. The law required our parents to send us to school, and probably more importantly, our culture does not even contemplate any option but sending both boys and girls to elementary, middle, and high school. If an American kid, male or female, stopped showing up for school, a social worker or truancy officer would come looking. And the friends and neighbors of any parent not sending a child to school would shame that parent.

Girls have been legally barred from schools in Afghanistan and Pakistan and violence there has terrorized them out of their educations. They are kidnapped and sold into sex slavery in South Asia, where missing school is the least of their problems. Seemingly mundane issues like lack of access to feminine hygiene products keeps girls out of many African schools. And in Rwanda and Ethiopia, school fees as low as $20 a year are required for children to attend public schools. For a family earning only a few hundred dollars per year, these school fees often mean that they send their boys but not their girls. That is the cultural norm. Some girls attend school for a few years until the day they get the news that they will now sit at home doing menial labor all day long while their brother continues his schooling. These girls describe this day as the worst day of their lives. After that, they sit by, longingly, sometimes sneaking a look at their brothers' schoolbooks in the evenings.[36]

When I pick up a book or newspaper or freely click around on information sites on the web, I often think of all the girls who are consigned to being, as Shamsia put it, "stupid things." I imagine what my life would be like without the privilege to think. Had I been born in another place—not another "time and place," because these girls are trapped now—how would I cope with a lifetime of forced ignorance and illiteracy? Would my mind chew on itself in the way a caged animal gnaws on its own limbs?

As first world women, our freedom to wander intellectually, to read whatever we choose, to look up solutions to our life's challenges, and to debate the issues of our time come to us thanks to generations of feminists who fought for women's education and our full participation in our country's affairs. These freedoms come to us thanks to our country's founders who fought for the First Amendment and our core values of intellectual liberty, transparency, and openness. And they come to us—let's be honest—because of an accident of birth. We had the great good fortune to be born here in America, in a country that expects females to become educated and to contribute.

I am profoundly and constantly grateful for the solid education I received and the delicious privilege I have that allows me to spend a significant chunk of my life with my nose in a book. How lucky I am to have a career in which I am asked daily to join in the public discussion on television, to have smart people debating me on the other side of the issue or in a courtroom, testing my ideas.

I wonder how the girls whose cultures want them to be "stupid things" view us in the first world. Surely in their eyes, we all carry around invisible magic wands. We have the power to convert tiny bits of money (for us) into life changers (for them). Nearly all of us, for instance, could choose to pay a girl's school fees and educate her for one year. If the little girl living next door to you could not go to school because of a $20 fee, you'd immediately take that money out of your pocket and send her, wouldn't you? Is this reflex any different if the girl is on the other side of the globe?

Isn't it our solemn moral responsibility as educated first world women, we who have so much, to reach a hand across the planet, to wave those magic wands and raise up our third world counterparts? Because I'll tell you one thing I do know for sure: Ain't nobody going to do it but us. Girls and women are always the lowest priority for world leaders. They profess a belief in equality, sure, but they'll get around to it, oh, say, after world peace comes. I covered Pakistan's takeover of the Swat Valley as a nightly CNN panelist during the summer of 2009. World leaders wrung their hands over the political implications and military maneuvers. Third world girls cowering in their homes, terrorized, were not even on their radar. I waited for just one president or prime minister to talk about the bombing of the hundred and fifty girls' schools or the tens of thousands of girls who violence had intimidated and law had barred from going to school. It didn't happen.

For several years I have donated money to send girls to school in Rwanda, Ethiopia, India, and elsewhere.[37] Doing this is one of the most gratifying aspects of my life because I know that actual girls—girls who wouldn't otherwise—are going to school because of me. If we don't do it, it won't happen. Girls just don't matter in many cultures where they are last on the list to receive everything, including food, clothing, and medical care.

They matter to us, though, don't they?

One of the most radical acts you can do is to send a girl to school in a country that devalues her. Doing this is a way of spreading our egalitarian values without dropping bombs. It is subversive because the most misogynistic cultures are also the most violent. It is dazzlingly beautiful to read about educated girls growing up to become teachers of other girls in their villages or doctors who save mothers from dying in childbirth or lawyers who represent ten-year-old girls seeking a divorce from an arranged marriage, which is often little more than legalized child rape.

It's also a great deal for your philanthropic dollar. For very small amounts of money—$20, $100—you can do so much. I met a hardworking young man in Laos who told me his college tuition was $100 per year. For the price of a pair of shoes that you don't need, you can change a life. An Indian girl can be rescued from a child marriage for three dollars. Give up one latte, change a life.[38] Think of the possibilities.

I implore you to use that fat new brain of yours for self-improvement, sure, but also for the good of others. Use it for improving the world around you. Let me be specific: Use it to help desperately needy girls across the planet, the ones who didn't have the good fortune to be born us, the ones who yearn to be more than "stupid things," the ones who wish they had the privilege of complaining about the reading assignment, the mean science teacher, or the pop quiz.

For some of you, I know that my causes aren't your causes. Maybe your sharpened mind can now make a killer argument to bring about peace in a hot spot or feed the world's hungry or combat climate change. Maybe you want to help closer to home and improve conditions for our own battered women or veterans or homeless folks. Maybe you'll be sending me book recommendations on issues that call out to you.

Bring it.*

Regardless of what area of the planet you choose to work on, your bright mind should no longer be able to turn away entirely from what you need to do. It should smack down the excuses that lesser minds offer up for not helping: futility, possible corruption, the government or someone else should handle it. It should become knowledgeable

*Bring it at www.Think.tv.

about the best way to help, fact-check each organization's claims, figure out financially what's appropriate for you (luckily, you do your own taxes!), and then contribute your time, skills, money—whatever makes sense for you. Go right to the source and ask incisive questions of the group that you pick. If you're entrepreneurial, start your own organization that will address the issues important to you. Now that you can handle the facts, you are ready to actively connect with the issues that inspire you.

I don't believe that a woman can fail to become connected to her world when she takes time to think regularly, reads constantly, and is the CEO of her emotional health and all other aspects of her life. I am confident that once you've experienced the pride of meaningful connection with those who need you, you will never again disconnect and return to fluff and distractions.

The time to embrace your responsibilities as a privileged citizen of the first world is now.

Because your mind is a terrible thing to waste.

recommended reading

How do you find great books to read?

Go to the library, raid your friends' bookshelves, swap or buy books online in areas *you* are interested in.

When in doubt, read Pulitzer Prize winners, book award winners, Oprah books, and books that a like-minded passionate reader friend has recommended. Kindle and other e-bookstores will recommend books to you once you buy a few and they get to know your taste. Indie bookstore proprietors like nothing more than suggesting reading materials for you.

Here are some of my all-time favorites to get you started. I have eclectic taste, but I do zero in on certain passions, namely women in other cultures, especially the third world, and our relationship with animals and vegetarianism. In fiction, I love vivid, quirky novels with offbeat characters and just anything, anything at all, with beautiful prose, which gets me goose-bumpy and giddy.

Nonfiction

Half the Sky: Turning Oppression into Opportunity for Women Worldwide by Nicholas D. Kristof and Sheryl WuDunn. The most important book of the last decade, this book details the compelling, page-turning true story of the lives of hundreds of millions of women and girls who are little more than serfs and objects in brutally misogynistic cultures, and it provides specifics on the programs that really do make a difference in combating sexual slavery, mothers dying in child birth, female genital mutilation, bride burnings, and other horrors our sisters around the world endure daily.

Infidel by Ayaan Hirsi Ali. This is a vivid, personal account of a girl growing up in several extremist Muslim countries, her daring escape from an arranged marriage and rise to prominence as a Dutch member of Parliament, and her furtive life lived under death threats after she rejected Islam. Ali challenges us to be intolerant of any belief systems that crush women's spirits and restrict women's choices.

I am Nujood, Aged 10 and Divorced by Nujood Ali and Delphine Minoui. A little girl risks her life to walk into a Yemeni courthouse, all alone, and asks to be freed from the rapes and beatings her husband inflicts on her. That's the first page of the book, a moving, short memoir about this brave child and a culture that allows arranged marriages of girls to become little more than legally permitted sexual assault and child abuse.

Inside the Kingdom: My Life in Saudi Arabia by Carmen bin Laden. The rotten core of the cloistered world of wealthy Saudi women is revealed here by a woman who married into Osama bin Laden's family and then struggled to get out before her daughter grew up to become confined in that gender prison too.

Nine Parts of Desire: The Hidden World of Islamic Women by Geraldine Brooks. How did it come to pass that fundamentalist Muslim women are veiled, married off sometimes before puberty, and subject to such harsh restrictions on education, work, and travel? Brooks breaks it down in straightforward, accessible language.

Three Cups of Tea: One Man's Mission to Fight Terrorism and Build Nations—One School at a Time by Greg Mortenson. A hapless mountain climber makes a wrong turn coming down off K2 and, by building schools across remote sections of Pakistan and Afghanistan, spends the rest of his life thanking the villagers who saved his life. Somehow Mortenson shows deep respect for local culture while also getting girls to go to school in droves for the first time in many villages. His follow-up, *Stones into Schools: Promoting Peace with Books, Not Bombs, in Afghanistan and Pakistan*, is also worth a read.

Nothing to Envy: Ordinary Lives in North Korea by Barbara Demick. North Korea is the most closed, repressive country on earth, yet it shares a boundary with one of the most prosperous, open countries in Asia. What is life like for regular folks falling in love, supporting their families, and going to university in a land of deprivation, famines, and severe censorship? What do they know about us? How do the brave few escape, given the risk that escapees' families can all be sent to labor camps? After this riveting read, I now view news stories about North Korea with keen interest, as if I have friends there. The issues surrounding North Korea are not just about the leaders and the military moves; they're about ordinary folks like Mi-ran and Mrs. Song, and my heart goes out to them.

The Warmth of Other Suns: The Epic Story of America's Great Migration by Isabel Wilkerson. This book made me grit my teeth in frustration that I didn't learn this gigantic part of American history in school. Millions of African Americans fled from the Deep South during the years of lynchings, strict segregation, and enforced poverty. This "great migration" reshaped Detroit, Chicago, New York City, and many other northern and western cities. Most heartbreaking of all are the three personal stories woven through this Pulitzer Prize–winning book, illustrating why and how a plantation worker, a fruit picker, and a doctor had to leave their homes, exploring the racism they faced in their journeys and the triumphs and disappointments they found in the "promised land."

Zeitoun by Dave Eggers. This book exposes what our government did to a Muslim American New Orleans family after Hurricane Katrina. It is a chilling tale told in novel form by the brave Dave Eggers. Have we lost our minds in the name of homeland security?

Eating Animals by Jonathan Safran Foer. Foer is a novelist, but when his son was born, he wanted to know where his food came from. He offers a brave, creative investigation into the industry that cruelly confines, drugs, and slaughters billions of sentient creatures in our names.

Animal Liberation: A New Ethics for Our Treatment of Animals by

Peter Singer. This is a classic, now with a new updated introduction. It is a bold new way of thinking about our exploitation of animals.

The Lives of Animals by J. M. Coetzee. An aging professor decides to let loose her true feelings in a college lecture hall, embarrassing her family and colleagues. But doesn't she speak the truth? (This is fiction, but it's so fact intensive that I'm including it on the nonfiction list.)

Animal, Vegetable, Miracle: A Year of Food Life by Barbara Kingsolver. This is the story of one family's Appalachian year of only eating local, raising their own food, and getting to know their land and their neighbors. I've adored Kingsolver since her twin novels *Pigs in Heaven* and *The Bean Trees*.

Skinny Bitch: A No-Nonsense, Tough-Love Guide for Savvy Girls Who Want to Stop Eating Crap and Start Looking Fabulous! by Rory Freedman and Kim Barnouin. This in-your-face walk through the litany of horrors that meat and dairy products cause to your health is required reading for anyone who eats food. Somehow there's a laugh-out-loud line on every page too, with one of the best sassy narrative voices ever to get published.

The Life You Can Save: Acting Now to End World Poverty by Peter Singer. If you could save the life of your neighbor's child for a few dollars, wouldn't you? So why don't we give more to children overseas, where a small amount of money actually does save a life? What, exactly, is your moral obligation to help others? How much money, specifically, should you be giving to charity? This short, snappy, unnerving book gives you your ethical guidelines. And I couldn't think of a single flaw in his reasoning.

The 4-Hour Work Week: Escape the 9–5, Live Anywhere, and Join the New Rich by Timothy Ferriss. Not my usual genre, but this business guide offers great tips on saving time, especially for getting off the e-mail and the Blackberry. It is an inspiration on how to live an eccentric, travel-filled life while also making a living by taking advantage of technology and outsourcing, written by a justifiably cocky guy who's actually achieved it.

We've Got Issues: Children and Parents in the Age of Medication by

Judith Warner. Think children in America are overmedicated? I did too until I read this. Prepare to have your opinion upended by this writer, who thought kids and drugs didn't mix until she investigated kids with serious psychiatric disorders and the families that grapple with them.

Bright-Sided: How the Relentless Promotion of Positive Thinking Has Undermined America by Barbara Ehrenreich. This book challenges conventional American wisdom that looking on the bright side is always better for our health and our nation. Ehrenreich blows out our assumptions and proves that positive thinking can be positively moronic. Who knew?

The Rape of Nanking: The Forgotten Holocaust of World War II by Iris Chang. Here is another gigantic moment in world history that has been hiding in plain sight for too long. Chang tells the vivid true story of the Japanese slaughter of over three hundred thousand Chinese civilians in the run-up to World War II, the rape and brutal torture of many more, and the world's complicit silence during and after the massacre.

A Problem from Hell: America and the Age of Genocide by Samantha Power. We say "never again," but do we really mean it? Harvard University professor Samantha Power meticulously documents in this Pulitzer Prize–winning book how the U.S. government knew about genocide in the Ottoman Empire, Nazi Germany, Cambodia, Iraq, Bosnia, Kosovo, and Rwanda, yet we consistently turned away. The story of Raphael Lemkin's heroic one-man struggle to get the international community to recognize genocide is alone worth the read.

Everything by Jonathan Kozol, especially *Rachel and Her Children: Homeless Families in America* and *Savage Inequalities: Children in America's Schools*, as he tenderly documents the lives of poor children in our forgotten American ghettos.

A Long Way Gone: Memoirs of a Boy Soldier by Ishmael Beah. A twelve-year-old boy becomes swept up in Sierra Leone's brutal civil war, and for three years is a drugged, sociopathic mass killer. Harrowing. Should we hate him or pity him—or both?

The Girls Who Went Away: The Hidden History of Women Who Surrendered Children for Adoption in the Decades before Roe v. Wade by Ann Fessler. I cried in several places in this book for the girls who, pre-1973, had no good choices when they faced unplanned pregnancies. Lord, how far we have come. I had no idea adoption was so wrenching for birth mothers and that there was so much coercion levied on teenaged moms of my mother's generation to give up babies they yearned to keep.

The Kosher Sutra: 8 Sacred Secrets for Reigniting Desire and Restoring Passion for Life by Rabbi Shmuley Boteach. Well, I'll be damned. Rabbi Shmuley has some unnerving insights into female sexuality. It feels like he's been rooting around inside my brain. This is the best book on human eroticism I've read.

Angela's Ashes by Frank McCourt. "The happy childhood is hardly worth your while. Worse than the ordinary miserable childhood is the miserable Irish childhood and, worse yet is the miserable Irish Catholic childhood." The drip, drip of Limerick, surely the wettest city on earth; McCourt's alcoholic, reckless charmer of a father; his ever-suffering mother; and the stumbling toward adulthood of Frank and his neglected brothers make this Pulitzer Prize–winning memoir simultaneously hilarious, tragic, and exasperating.

The Glass Castle by Jeannette Walls. You want a miserable childhood? I'll raise you one: parents who choose homelessness for its freedom, leaving their kids freezing, starving, and destitute, yet somehow still loving their reckless father and artsy mother. Also by Walls, the newer *Half-Broke Horses: A True-Life Novel*, a terrific novelized biography of the author's no-nonsense rancher grandmother, who often reminded me of my own, Fox.

Written by my mother, Gloria Allred, with a forward from me, *Fight Back and Win: My Thirty-Year Fight Against Injustice—And How You Can Win Your Own Battles* is a rabble-rousing call to action spanning Mom's career, with brave personal revelations as well. Go, Mom!

My gynecologist isn't the only one who insists that everyone read Jeffrey Toobin's *The Nine: Inside the Secret World of the Supreme*

Court. I do, too. Think presidential elections don't matter? Oh, but they do, if only for one reason: the president selects these lifetime jurists, who wield enormous power over women's lives, especially our reproductive rights.

Fiction

Freedom: A Novel by Jonathan Franzen. This is the most hyped book of 2010, and yet the brilliant prose and unnervingly real characters of this modern family drama exceed even the hype. My best friend and daughter kept e-mailing me stunning sentences from this book. I read this as slowly as I could in order to savor it, and even with its surprisingly satisfying ending, I was so sad to reach the final page. This book makes a great gift to anyone who speaks English.

Super Sad True Love Story: A Novel by Gary Schteyngart. Though this novel could use some editing, its powerful portrait of a scary near-future stayed with me months later. Imagine everything bad about America just one degree worse: our economy is on the verge of collapse, our uber militarism caused us to invade Venezuela, young girls are wearing transparent "Onion jeans," our personal privacy is so obliterated that upon first meeting, your personal digital device can show you videos of your new friend's childhood sexual abuse. You'll look at our degraded culture with fresh eyes.

Intensity by Dean Koontz. This is not my normal genre. A psychological thriller, but after three pages you will not be able to stop reading this crazy, sick, twisted thing.

Little Bee by Chris Cleave. "No one likes each other, but everyone likes U2" in a globalized world where a Nigerian war orphan makes her way to England to confront a vacationing couple she'd met in a chilling encounter on an African beach. *Little Bee*'s pitch-perfect narrative voice carries you along through an ever-tightening plot that crosses continents.

Every single word ever written by Amy Bloom, including *Where the God of Love Hangs Out, A Blind Man Can See How Much I Love You*, and *Come to Me*. She is ideal for readers who find most literary fiction too fusty. The pages bloom with sexually creepy characters who are somehow humanized in stories that feel narrated by your too-honest, super-smart best friend.

Every single word ever written by Jhumpa Lahiri. *The Namesake: A Novel*, for example, and *Interpreter of Maladies*, a Pulitzer Prize winner. I want to send her printer cartridges, a snazzy keyboard, a new hard drive, whatever it takes to keep Jhumpa writing that gorgeous prose—subtle, bittersweet, delicate stories of Indians and Indian Americans facing universal love and family conflicts.

The *Rabbit* series, including *Rabbit, Run*, *Rabbit Redux*, *Rabbit is Rich*, and *Rabbit at Rest*, by John Updike, who is, in my opinion, the greatest American novelist. He brings to life middle-class, middle-American angst and especially sexual anxiety, rendered unexpectedly beautiful via his rich, intelligent, subtle prose.

Cutting for Stone by Abraham Verghese. Written by a Stanford University Medical School professor, this ambitious, sprawling novel follows a colorful group of Indian nuns and doctors in Ethiopia as the country convulses with civil war. Packed with medical drama, violent insurrections and religious imagery, it is ultimately a bittersweet expat story.

Both Ways Is the Only Way I Want It by Maile Meloy. Loneliness, yearning, and infidelity vs. the comforts of a long marriage: it's all in these tightly packed short stories that lay bare the emotional complexities of love if we have the guts to be honest, which Meloy does. Ouch. Devastating.

Say You're One of Them by Uwem Akpan. The author is a Nigerian-born Jesuit priest, and these short stories of child selling, a twelve-year-old prostitute who is the only hope for feeding her family, and Muslim vs. Christian violence are a machete-sharp take on the reality for millions of African kids caught in war-torn Africa.

Olive Kitteridge by Elizabeth Strout. This is a book of linked short stories of sturdy Mainers pulling toward and away from intimate connection. Olive Kitteridge is one tough old coot, rendered deeply human and sympathetic by this masterful author. Spoiler alert: Olive's instincts are usually right.

The Help by Kathryn Stockett. The Deep South, 1962: young, white, country club women feel the need to build separate home bathrooms for the African American "help"—women like Aibileen and Minny, who are good enough to raise their children but who are considered diseased, threatening, and inferior. Jim Crow is the real villain here, twisting and attacking the human spirit. Aibileen's story, told in her warm, rich dialect, was my favorite, but so many of these female characters shine through.

Snow Flower and the Secret Fan: A Novel by Lisa See. This is historical fiction at its luminous best. I was engrossed by this world, the female side of nineteenth-century rural China, with its cruel footbinding, its nearly complete gender segregation, and even a separate female language. At its heart, this is a love story between two girls, friends paired for life, as each tries to navigate through rigid cultural rules for every aspect of their lives. Stunning.

Fall on Your Knees by Ann-Marie MacDonald. A sprawling generational novel set in Cape Breton Island, Nova Scotia, and New York City during the jazz age that, with a gorgeous sense of time and place, tells the stories of four sisters and a father with some sick secrets.

Holes by Louis Sachar. This is supposedly a kids' book. Hah! Sachar had me at Stanley Yelnats, the palindromic protagonist, who navigates through a bizarro world of a kids' labor camp in the middle of a Texas wasteland. Cheers for the underdog juvenile delinquents and vividly drawn jailers. Pay close attention because the plot picks up and spins you around until you applaud at how it all comes together in the end.

The Amazing Adventures of Kavalier and Clay by Michael Chabon. This book is the author's magnum opus. If you'd told me I'd love a long novel about two boys writing comic books in the 1930s and '40s, I'd have said you were sadly mistaken, my friend. Yet the shimmering, witty, dense prose, the political assaults on Hitler and anti-Semitism, the detailed rendering of New York City during the World War II era, the friendship, and the love story with Rosa Saks all add up to a masterful novel that well deserved the Pulitzer it won.

The Lovely Bones: A Novel by Alice Sebold. In all the years I covered missing children stories, I never imagined I'd savor a novel about a kidnapped and murdered girl. But then only Sebold could imagine telling that story in the first person, rendering it all the more poignant without a hint of sentimentality. Also terrific by Sebold: *Lucky*, the ironically named title of her rape memoir, which strips away all conventions and politically correct thinking about sexual assault in America. Intensely personal. Whew. You'll need to read something light next.

Lighter Stuff

Wishful Drinking by Carrie Fisher. What a life worth skewering this daughter of Hollywood legends has lived. Who knew that George Lucas wouldn't let her wear underwear as Princess Leia because "no one does in space," or that electroconvulsive therapy was a riot? Self-deprecating, insightful, and spit-out-your-cocktail funny.

Everything by David Sedaris, including *Me Talk Pretty One Day*, *When We Are Engulfed in Flames*, *Dress Your Family in Corduroy and Denim*, and *Naked*. You just don't know where these eccentric bits of storytelling are going to go. I'm so glad he has no filter, especially in telling tales about his boyfriend Hugh and his mother and sisters who surely cringe every time he publishes embarrassing family stories. "Hugh and I have been together for so long that in order to arouse extraordinary passion, we need to engage in physical combat. Once, he hit me on the back of the head with a broken wineglass, and I fell to the floor pretending to be unconscious. That was romantic, or would have been had he rushed to my side rather than stepping over my body to fetch the dustpan."

Running with Scissors: A Memoir by Augusten Burroughs. This is the tragi-comic, highly entertaining story of the author's wacky childhood, in which his alcoholic dad and unbalanced mom foist him off on her therapist, and then the craziness begins in earnest.

I'll Mature When I'm Dead by Dave Barry. Laughs, for real, on every page. Barry riffs on celebrities, marriage, parenthood, and vasectomies: "There is absolutely no reason to be afraid of a vasectomy, except that: THEY CUT A HOLE IN YOUR SCROTUM."

I Feel Bad About My Neck: And Other Thoughts on Being a Woman by Nora Ephron. Ephron's witty, sly, dead-on reflections on aging and womanhood have me still giggling six years later. Your disgusting, disorganized, out-of-style purse is, "in some absolutely horrible way, you." "Sometimes I think not having to worry about your hair anymore is the secret upside of death."

I discover brilliant new books all the time, so for updates and to add your own raves, please go to www.Think.tv.

un-recipes

Don't think of cooking as slaving away over a long, complicated recipe. Think of it as *assembling* items—ideally prewashed, prechopped items—into one warm bowl of deliciousness. The more you can get away from recipes, the faster your cooking time will be. Experiment a little. You'll make mistakes. So what? Laugh it off, eat it or feed it to the dog, and then try again.

I call these "un-recipes" because you don't have to follow them exactly, and you don't have to measure precise amounts of this and that. These are ideas for throwing things together and having a nice healthy dinner that people will savor, without you exhausting yourself night after night.

My guiding principle for cooking is: warm, moist, and tasty. Most food tastes better hot. Hustle everyone to the table while the food is still warm. Make sure there's enough moisture in the food by adding veggie stock, wine, salsa, or soy milk toward the end if it's become dry. And taste at the end for flavor, adding fresh herbs, lemon, wine, tamari, or a splash of vinegar to zazz it up if necessary.

I'm vegan because it's better for my health and I get to boycott animal cruelty and do my bit to slow climate change. So these are all plant-based dinners. Let me know if you enjoyed them at www.think.tv!

Pasta with Veggies Everyone Will Eat

Keep ridiculous amounts of whole grain pasta in your cupboards. When you are down to your last five dozen boxes, restock. *Never ever* run out of pasta and you can always throw something together for a quick dinner that your family will drool over.

Worrying about carbs is so 2004. Whole grains are in. Just have a reasonable portion size with a lot of veggies.

Boil a giant vat of water (if you don't have a huge witches' cauldron–sized pot, buy one today) and dump in two boxes of pasta. I like fusilli or linguine. However, don't mix types, artistic though that may be, because of the different cooking times. Cook as long as the package says to boil it, and test it by asking a family member to taste. They will, every time, contemplate the issue carefully and then tell you it's not quite done.

While the pasta is cooking and you're stirring it occasionally, depending on your mood, you now have about twelve minutes to do the rest. Perfect! That's all you need.

Throw a couple tablespoons of olive oil in a sauté pan. I like to use the wok, personally.

Throw in a few cloves of prechopped garlic, depending on if your eaters are garlic maniacs or not. After a minute or two, when the garlic is cooked but not brown, throw in a large bag of washed and prechopped (do you sense a theme here?) veggies. I like broccoli, cauliflower, kale, string beans, carrots, spinach, corn—okay, I like all veggies.

Add oregano, basil, thyme, salt, fresh pepper, a splash of white wine if you're feeling it, and if not, a cup or two of veggie broth. Stir. Put the lid on. Yell for someone to set the table. Feed the dogs. Stir again. Read a poem. Stir one more time. Veggies should be done. Turn off heat.

Drain pasta. Toss pasta in with the veggies. Taste with your fingers if no one is looking and, if needed, adjust seasonings. Top with vegan cheese, like Daiya, or toasted pine nuts. Serve immediately.

This should feed a family of four with leftovers for an entire second night's dinner—as God intended.

You can also throw in canned kidney beans, leftover lentils, garbanzo beans, cannelloni beans, or canned diced tomatoes.

Beginner Burritos

The trick here is to buy two containers of *fresh* salsa at your market.

In a very large sauté pan or wok, warm a few tablespoons of canola oil. Throw in a few cloves' worth of prechopped garlic and one onion's worth of prechopped onion. Stir and cook for a few minutes until the onion is translucent. As this delicious smell lures people into the kitchen, ask them sweetly to set the table and how about taking out that recycling?

Throw in four cans of black beans and four cans of kidney or pinto beans. Stir. Dump in a small container of salsa (mild if kids are eating). Turn the heat down, stir for a few minutes. With a masher, my favorite kitchen implement, smash the heck out of about half the beans. Let the others remain intact. Stir.

Take a whole-wheat tortilla for each person and warm it for a few seconds on each side on a gas burner. (If you have electric, warm all the tortillas together on a baking sheet in the oven for a few minutes.) Top with a glop of the beany mixture, chopped red or green cabbage or lettuce, chopped tomatoes, homemade guacamole (recipe below), more salsa, fresh corn in the summer (yum), and vegan sour cream if you like. If you have leftover veggies, chop 'em small and toss 'em in.

If you have picky eaters, lay out all the ingredients and let them make their own.

Roll and eat. Those leftover beans will keep for a week in a good container, and you can have burritos again for breakfast, lunch, or dinner.

"Homemade" Guacamole

People go ape for my "homemade" guacamole. They think I am Martha Stewart. Ha! This is all there is to it.

Peel a few ripe avocados, dump in a bowl, mash. Add some fresh salsa (tomatillo salsa is my fave in this) and a little lime juice. Stir.

You are done. Pretend like it was a lot more work. Serve with precut celery, carrot sticks, and baked tortilla chips. Glop a little more salsa right in the middle for a fetching bull's-eye look.

Veggie Burgers

The trick here is toasting the buns and having good condiments on hand. Why not? Condiments last forever. My mother has some Dijon mustard in her refrigerator from the Eisenhower administration. (Not that my mother knows where her refrigerator is.)

Veggie burgers on their own aren't that exciting, let's be honest. Buy your favorite brand, but buy the top-quality whole-wheat buns. While you're frying up the burgers in a little canola oil, warm the buns, chop up some fresh lettuce, and thickly slice some tomatoes and red onion. Then slather vegan mayo (tastes better than the eggy kind, I swear) on your warm buns. Serve it up open-faced like they do in restaurants: hot on one side (the burger), cool on the other (lettuce, tomato, onion). Insist that people stop everything and eat immediately: The key is that warm/cool combo.

Put ketchup, Dijon mustard, chutney, and other nice condiments on the table. Encourage discussion about which is best on the burger.

On the side, serve steamed veggies, baked potato, baked sweet potatoes, or Two-Minute Kale (below).

Two-Minute Kale

It's a superfood, and none of us eats enough of it.

Wash and chop a few bunches of fresh kale. It seems like an unmanageable pile, but it does a Houdini-worthy disappearing act when cooked, trust me.

Warm just a little olive oil, throw in some prechopped garlic if you like. Throw in all the kale, and on medium-high heat, stir. Salt and pepper your greens. Keep stirring until it is all cooked but not wilted to oblivion; this should take about two or three minutes. Turn off heat and splash with good balsamic vinegar. Serve hot and salty.

Everyday Stir-Fry

Make a giant pot of brown rice about once a week and then top it with different stir-fry concoctions depending on what's in season.

Take a container of fresh firm tofu and cube it. Warm some canola oil in the pan, cook tofu until brown (maybe five minutes each side), turn over, and then brown some more. Take out with a spatula onto paper towels and drain. Throw a bunch of prechopped veggies into the warm oil, stir-fry on high for a few minutes, stirring of course. Throw the tofu in at the end, toss in a prepared sauce, like green curry or teriyaki. In a minute the whole thing will be warm and ready.

Serve over rice. Sesame seeds or gomasio (available in health food stores) are nice to add at the end, or consider bits of shredded coconut or sliced almonds. For extra credit, toast the coconut or almonds.

Easy as Pie

For dessert, people are blown away that you made a homemade pie. And it is super easy.

Chop up six or eight peeled apples, pears, or peaches or eight or ten plums or apricots. In a large bowl toss in agave (a delicious lighter-than-honey sweetener available in health food stores like Whole Foods), a little cinnamon, maybe some nutmeg, and a little brown sugar if the fruit isn't amazing to begin with.

Dump it all into a frozen whole-grain crust. Take a second whole-grain crust, put it on top, press sides together with your wetted little fingers, poke air holes in top crust with fork or sharp knife. Cook for forty-five minutes or so. If you like, five minutes before the end, brush on a little oil or agave for shine.

You just made a pie! Serve warm with ice cream.

Cooking is easy. Make the decision that it doesn't have to be perfect. In fact, those little imperfections are what make homemade food charming and appealing. That's what I tell my family and, so far, they're buying it.

For more quick and easy recipes/food assembling tips, check out www.Think.tv.

notes

Chapter 1.

1. The Black Panther Party was founded in 1966 to oppose police abuse against African Americans, especially young African American men. Conflicts with the police led to shootouts in New York, Los Angeles, and Chicago during the 1960s and 1970s. Although the Panthers were at times violent themselves, police and the FBI subjected the entire group to regular violence and harassment. For more information, see www.blackpanther.org.

Mother Jones magazine is still covering cases of white police officers shooting unarmed African Americans. For example, see Titania Kumeh, "When Police Shoot and Kill Unarmed Men," *Mother Jones*, July 14, 2010, http://motherjones.com/mojo/2010/07/when-police-shoot-unarmed-man-oscar-grant-verdict-Mehserle.

2. None of this, of course, justifies China's repeated acts of aggression against Tibetan Buddhists, aggression that the Dalai Lama has opposed bravely for decades. For instance, see Ashwini Bhatia, "Dalia Lama: China Want to Annihilate Buddhism," *USA Today*, March 10, 2010, www.usatoday.com/news/religion/2010-03-10-dalai-lama-buddhism_N.htm. Jeffersonian American values despise both state-sponsored religion and state attacks on religion. They advocate both no government-established religion *and* free exercise of religion. These values are both right there where they belong—in the First Amendment to our Constitution.

3. U.S. Department of Justice, Federal Bureau of Investigation, "Crime in the United States, 1996, FBI Uniform Crime Report," September 28, 1997, www.fbi.gov/about-us/cjis/ucr/crime-in-the-u.s/1996/toc96.pdf; Liz Kelly, Jo Lovett, and Linda Regan, "A Gap or a Chasm? Attrition in Reported Rape Cases," Home Office Research Study, 293, February 2005, http://rds.homeoffice.gov.uk/rds/pdfs05/hors293.pdf.

Chapter 2.

1. United Negro College Fund, "Who We Are," UNCF, www.uncf.org/aboutus/index.asp.

2. "Dan Quayle Quotes," ThinkExist, http://thinkexist.com/quotes/dan_quayle/. All of the following quotes from Dan Quayle can be found at this website.

3. "Ronald Reagan Quotes," ThinkExist, http://thinkexist.com/quotation/trees_cause_more_pollution_than_automobiles_do/337369.html; "Ronald Reagan Quotes," ThinkExist; "Ronald Reagan: 'If You've Seen One Tree . . .'," Snopes.com, www.snopes.com/quotes/reagan/redwoods.asp; "Ketchup as a Vegetable," Wikipedia, http://en.wikipedia.org/wiki/Ketchup_as_a_vegetable.

4. Steve Crabtree, "New Poll Gauges Americans' General Knowledge Levels," Gallup, July 6, 1999, www.gallup.com/poll/3742/new-poll-gauges-americans-general-knowledge-levels.aspx.

5. Frank Newport, "Majority of Republicans Doubt Theory of Evolution," Gallup, June 11, 2007, www.gallup.com/poll/27847/majority-republicans-doubt-theory-evolution.aspx.

6. "Growing Number of Americans Say Obama Is a Muslim," Pew Research Center Publications, August 19, 2010, http://pewresearch.org/pubs/1701/poll-obama-muslim-christian-church-out-of-politics-political-leaders-religious.

7. "Many Americans Mix Multiple Faiths," Pew Research Center, December 9, 2009, http://pewforum.org/Other-Beliefs-and-Practices/Many-Americans-Mix-Multiple-Faiths.aspx; Jesse McKinley, "Did Your Horoscope Predict This?" *New York Times*, January 15, 2011, www.nytimes.com/2011/01/15/us/15zodiac.html?_r=1&partner=rss&emc=rss.

8. "Stupid Americans," YouTube, posted December 16, 2007, www.youtube.com/watch?v=LVz4VweMqFE&feature=player_embedded#!.

9. "Americans Are NOT Stupid—WITH SUBTITLES," YouTube, posted January 25, 2007, www.youtube.com/watch?v=fJuNgBkloFE.

10. "Europe Is a Country and Everyone Speaks French There," YouTube, posted November 28, 2007, www.youtube.com/watch?v=ANTDkfkoBaI.

11. "Sarah Palin Doesn't Know What a Vice President (VP) Is," YouTube, posted October 21, 2008, www.youtube.com/watch?v=1KKyEM-BDJI.

12. "George W. Bush Quotes, ThinkExist, http://thinkexist.com/quotation/they_misunderestimated_me/339627.html.

13. Kate Linthicum, "Joe Biden's History Lesson Off by 4 Years and 1 Pres-

ident but Otherwise Pretty Accurate," *Los Angeles Times*, September 24, 2008, http://latimesblogs.latimes.com/washington/2008/09/biden-fdr.html; Xuan Thai and Ted Barrett, "Biden's Description of Obama Draws Scrutiny," CNNPolitics, January 31, 2007, http://articles.cnn.com/2007-01-31/politics/biden.obama_1_braun-and-al-sharpton-african-american-presidential-candidates-delaware-democrat?_s=PM:POLITICS.

14. "Americans Are NOT Stupid—WITH SUBTITLES." Twenty-five million people have viewed Morrow's "Stupid Americans" YouTube videos, though they are not well known in the United States. They have, however, obviously struck a nerve in the rest of the world.

15. Laurie Goodstein, "Basic Religion Test Stumps Many Americans," *New York Times*, September 28, 2010, www.nytimes.com/2010/09/28/us/28religion.html.

16. PIPA, "Americans on Foreign Aid and World Hunger: A Study of U.S. Public Attitudes," February 2, 2001, www.pipa.org/OnlineReports/ForeignAid/ForeignAid_Feb01/ForeignAid_Feb01_rpt.pdf.

17. YouGov and R. M., "This Week's Economist/YouGov Poll," *The Economist*, www.economist.com/blogs/democracyinamerica/2010/04/economist yougov_polling.

18. "United Nations Millennium Development Goals," United Nations, www.un.org/millenniumgoals/bkgd.shtml.

19. Mike Pflanz, "U.S. 'Failing to Keep Up with Britain' on Aid Promises," *The Telegraph*, September 20, 2010, www.telegraph.co.uk/news/worldnews/northamerica/usa/8013514/US-failing-to-keep-up-with-Britain-on-aid-promises.html.

20. "Daniel Patrick Moynihan" Wikiquote, http://en.wikiquote.org/wiki/Daniel_Patrick_Moynihan.

21. Ina May Gaskin, "Maternal Death in the United States: A Problem Solved or a Problem Ignored?" *The Journal of Perinatal Education* 17, no. 2, (Spring 2008): 9–13.

22. "USA Urged to Confront Shocking Maternal Mortality Rate," Amnesty International, March 12, 2010, www.amnesty.org/en/news-and-updates/usa-urged-confront-shocking-maternal-mortality-rate-2010-03-12.

23. "Few See U.S. Health Care as 'Best in the World'," Pew Research Center Publications, July 24, 2009, http://pewresearch.org/pubs/1293/health-care-public-gives-lukewarm-rating-to-american-system.

24. Author Robert Louis Stevenson.

25. John Stossel, "John Stossel's 'Stupid in America'," ABCNews, January 13, 2006, http://abcnews.go.com/2020/Stossel/story?id=1500338.

26. Ibid.

27. DeeDee Correll, "In Utah, a Plan to Cut 12th Grade," *Los Angeles Times*, February 15, 2010, http://articles.latimes.com/2010/feb/15/nation/la-na-utah-school15-2010feb15.

28. Russell Goldman, "Utah Lawmaker Seeks to Eliminate 12th Grade," ABCNews, February 16, 2010, http://abcnews.go.com/WN/utah-mulls-eliminating-12th-grade/story?id=9853553.

29. Farah Tamizuddin, "Eliminate Senior Year to Save Schools Money?" The State Journal Register, March 15, 2010, www.sj-r.com/carousel/x427970167/The-tough-measures-being-discussed-include-eliminating-senior-year.

30. Greg Toppo, "More High-Schoolers Reinvent or Skip Their Senior Year," *USA Today*, February 24, 2010, www.usatoday.com/news/education/2010-02-25-senioryear25foronline_st_N.htm.

31. Teens who are "often bored" are 50 percent more likely than not to smoke, drink, get drunk, and use illegal drugs. "CASA 2003 Teen Survey: High Streess, Frequent Boredom, Too Much Spending Money: Triple Threat That Hikes Risk of Teen Substance," The National Center on Addiction and Substance Abuse at Columbia University, Abuse, www.casacolumbia.org/templates/PressReleases.aspx?articleid=348&zoneid=46.

32. Toppo, "More High-Schoolers Reinvent or Skip Their Senior Year."

33. "The Underworked American," *The Economist*, June 11 2009, www.economist.com/node/13825184.

34. David von Drehle, "The Case Against Summer Vacation," *Time*, July 22, 2010, www.time.com/time/nation/article/0,8599,2005654-1,00.html.

35. Ibid.

36. National Endowment for the Arts, "To Read or Not to Read: A Question of National Consequence," November 2007, www.nea.gov/research/toread.pdf.

37. "Yahoo! (YHOO) Entertainment Site Hammers Competition, TMZ.com Should Pass," 24/7 Wall St, July 1, 2009, http://247wallst.com/2009/07/01/yahoo-yhoo-entertertainment-site-hammers-competition-tmz-com-should-pass/.

38. "Us Weekly Circulation," *Us Weekly*, www.srds.com/mediakits/us_weekly/circulation.html.

39. Drew Pinsky and S. Mark Young, *The Mirror Effect: How Celebrity Narcissism Is Seducing America* (New York: HarperCollins, 2009).

40. "Media Effect on Teenagers," Peers United, www.peersunited.com/media-influencing-teenagers/.

41. Nicholas D. Kristof, "The Boys Have Fallen Behind," *New York Times*, March 27, 2010, www.nytimes.com/2010/03/28/opinion/28kristof.html.

42. Ibid.

43. "Opening Up Education to Girls in Iran's Poorest Province," UNICEF, www.unicef.org/sowc/iran_30050.html.

44. Bram Van den Bergh, Siegfried Dewitte, Luk Warlop, "Bikinis Instigate Generalized Impatience in Intertemporal Choice," *Journal of Consumer Research* 35, no. 1 (June 2008): 85. I'd really like to use this to our advantage, if only I could figure out how. In classes graded on a curve, should college girls show up for exams in bikinis?

45. Claudia Goldin, Lawrence F. Katz, and Ilyana Kuziemko, "The Homecoming of American College Women; The Reversal of the College Gender Gap," *The Journal of Economic Perspectives* 20, no. 4 (Fall 2006): 133–56.

46. Ibid.

47. Myra Sadker and David Miller Sadker, *Failing at Fairness: How Our Schools Cheat Girls* (New York: Touchstone, 1994), 8.

48. Sharon Jayson, "Generation Y's Goal? Wealth and Fame," *USA Today*, January 10, 2007, www.usatoday.com/news/nation/2007-01-09-gen-y-cover_x.htm; Deborah L. Rhode, "The Injustice of Appearance," 61 Stanford Law Review 1033, 1040 (2009).

49. Deborah L. Rhode, "The Injustice of Appearance," *Stanford Law Review* 61, no. 5 (2009): 1033.

50. Geraldine Brooks, *Nine Parts of Desire: The Hidden World of Islamic Women* (New York: Anchor Books, 1995); Ayaan Hirsi Ali, *Infidel* (New York: Free Press, 2007); Irshad Manji, *The Trouble With Islam Today: A Muslim's Call for Reform in Her Faith* (New York: St. Martin's Griffin, 2003).

51. We have a few more female congresspeople—17.5 percent. Two Muslim countries have more elected female legislators than we do: Iraq (25.5 percent) and Pakistan (22.5 percent).

52. Nearly half the Moroccan population still believes that the practice of husbands beating their wives in some circumstances is acceptable. Furthermore, tradition limits Moroccan women's ability to own or inherit land

equally with men. "Gender Equality and Social Institutions in Morocco," Social Institution & Gender Index, http://genderindex.org/country/morocco.

53. Michael Luo, "Top Salary in McCain Camp? Palin's Makeup Stylist," *The New York Times*, The Caucus, October 24, 2008, http://thecaucus.blogs.nytimes.com/2008/10/24/pains-makeup-stylist-fetches-highest-salary-in-2-week-period/?hp.

54. Nora Ephron, *I Feel Bad About My Neck: And Other Thoughts on Being a Woman* (New York: Alfred A. Knopf, 2006).

55. Tad Safran, "American Beauty?" *The Times*, December 11, 2007, http://women.timesonline.co.uk/tol/life_and_style/women/beauty/article3029451.ece.

56. A good summary of these studies can be found in Robert Cialdini's book, *Influence: Science and Practice* (Boston: Allyn and Bacon, 2001). As Cialdini documents, good-looking political candidates are two-and-a-half times more likely to get elected. Good-looking criminal defendants are twice as likely to avoid jail than their plain counterparts. Attractive victims get double the damages that others get from civil juries. Both men and women unwittingly participate in the beauty bias, though most believe they don't.

57. "Feminist Bra Burning: Red Hot Mamas,"Snopes. com, www.snopes.com/history/american/burnbra.asp.

58. "American Beauty Industry, COSMETICS History, Post-World War II Decades," http://manager-info.com/?p=38645; Geoffrey Jones, "Globalizing the Beauty Business before 1980, Working Paper, http://docs.google.com/viewer?a=v&q=cache:81gP5g9lXoYJ:www.hbs.edu/research/pdf/06-056.pdf+1976+U.S.+cosmetics+sales&hl=en&gl=us&pid=bl&srcid=ADGEESgJD3wTC7ttT5J_IhUwQQk5v39LM_qy1CHzGaz1ue4aEboCHQKBCavM8qTwNM6cvl-sRllyo-Ultsz3fobX4DAgP9UsQx9b9hpDKD4hGobslpBhrSZyUMw8dBavg01Xt2A1RiBS&sig=AHIEtbSkmywitubOLFdDeDN4nYb1-I9O-Q; "Cosmetics: Kiss and Sell," *Time*, December 11, 1978, www.time.com/time/magazine/article/0,9171,919923-1,00.html.

59. "The Beauty Top Hundred," Scribd.com, www.scribd.com/doc/3027409/Top-100-Cosmetic-Manufacturers.

60. Dodai Stewart, "Black Women Love Makeup, but Does the Beauty Industry Love Them Back?" Jezebel, May 19, 2009, http://jezebel.com/5261089/black-women-love-makeup-but-does-the-beauty-industry-love-them-back.

61. Nadia Michel, "The Cost of Beauty and How to Spend Less," *The Examiner*, October 6, 2009, www.examiner.com/style-in-houston/the-cost-of

-beauty-and-how-to-spend-less; "Women and Retirement: Facing Unique Challenges," NAGDCA, The Contributor, Spring 2007, www.nagdca.org/content.cfm/id/contributor22007women_and_retirement_facing_unique_challenges; Deborah Rhode, *The Beauty Bias: The Injustice of Appearance in Life and Law* (New York: Oxford University Press, 2010).

62. Kirsten Dellinger and Christine Williams, "Makeup at Work," *Gender and Society*, 1997; Elaine Sciolino, "Sans Makeup, S'il Vous Plaît," *New York Times*, May 25, 2006, www.nytimes.com/2006/05/25/fashion/thursdaystyles/25skin.html; Douglas Quenqua, "Graduating from Lip Smackers," *New York Times*, April 28, 2010, www.nytimes.com/2010/04/29/fashion/29tween.html; "The Beauty Top Hundred."

63. Sciolino, "Sans Makeup, S'il Vous Plaît."

64. Michael Stetz, "Waitress Says Bare Face Let to Firing," Sign On San Diego, May 20, 2009, www.signonsandiego.com/news/2009/may/20/1m20stetz014224-waitress-says-bare-face-led-firing/.

65. Sara Rimer, "For Girls, It's Be Yourself, and Be Perfect, Too," *New York Times*, April 1, 2007, www.nytimes.com/2007/04/01/education/01girls.html.

66. Ephron, *I Feel Bad About My Neck*.

67. Courtney Hutchison, "'Bridalplasty': Plastic Surgery as a TV Prize?" *ABC Good Morning America*, September 20, 2010, http://abcnews.go.com/Health/Wellness/bridalplasty-compete-nose-jobs-implants-dream-wedding/story?id=11663378&page=1.

68. Rhode, *The Beauty Bias*.

69. Broward County Florida, "Investigative Report in the Death of Vicki Marshall (AKA) Anna Nicole Smith," February 8, 2007, BCME: 07-0223, http://www.broward.org/Medical/Documents/investigative_report.pdf.

70. Roxanna Sherwood, "Heidi Montag: 'I Wish I Could Go Back to the Original Heidi'," ABCNews, November 22, 2010, http://abcnews.go.com/Entertainment/heidi-montag-back-surgeries-back-original-heidi/story?id=12193864; "Heidi Montag Reveals Her Scars a Year after Surgery," *Life & Style*, December 21, 2010, http://dynamic.bauerpublishing.com/mt-search.fcgi?blog_id=2&tag=Heidi%20Montag&limit=20&IncludeBlogs=2.

71. "What Could Go Wrong?" *Glamour*, October 30, 2006, www.glamour.com/health-fitness/2006/10/breast-implants-complications.

72. Patricia Lieberman, "Breast Surgery Likely to Cause Breastfeeding Problems, breastimplantinfo.org, www.breastimplantinfo.org/augment/brstfdg122000.html.

73. D. L. Miglioretti, C. M. Rutter, B. M. Geller, et al. "Effects of Breast Augmentation on the Accuracy of Mammography and Cancer Characteristics." *Journal of the American Medical Association* 291 (2004): 442–50.

74. "Breast Implants: National Cancer Institute Breast Implant Study," Cancer News, May 4, 2006, www.cancernews.com/data/Article/332.asp.

75. "Former Miss Argentina Dies After Plastic Surgery," CNNWorld, December 1, 2009, http://articles.cnn.com/2009-12-01/world/argentina.model.death_1_plastic-surgery-telam-medical-tourism?_s=PM:WORLD.

76. Deborah Mitchell, "Heidi Montag and Obsession with Plastic Surgery," EmaxHealth, January 13, 2010, www.emaxhealth.com/1275/57/35106/heidi-montag-and-obsession-plastic-surgery.html.

77. Alice Park, Assessing the Risks of Tanning Beds," *Time*, July 31, 2009, www.time.com/time/health/article/0,8599,1914188,00.html.

78. Nina Rotz, "Side Effects of Skin Bleaching Creams," eHow, www.ehow.com/about_5106404_side-effects-skin-bleaching-creams.html; "Pink Cheeks Anal Bleaching," Pink Cheeks, www.pinkcheeks.com/analbleach.html; Tristan Taormino, "Britesmile for Bungholes," *The Village Voice*, July 5, 2005, www.villagevoice.com/2005-07-05/columns/britesmile-for-bungholes/.

79. Gardiner Harris, "If the Shoe Won't Fit, Fix the Foot? Popular Surgery Raises Concern," *New York Times*, December 7, 2003, www.nytimes.com/2003/12/07/health/07FOOT.html.

80. Ibid.

81. Rhode, *The Beauty Bias*.

Chapter 3.

1. Samantha Power, "A *Problem from Hell*": *America and the Age of Genocide* (New York: Harper Perennial, 2002), xv.

2. Ibid., xxi.

3. Nicholas Kristof, "The Secret Genocide Archive," *New York Times*, February 23, 2005, www.nytimes.com/2005/02/23/opinion/23kristof.html.

4. Clinton's foundation, the William J. Clinton Foundation, has devoted significant resources to Rwanda since he left office, assisting the government with the purchase of fertilizer, helping develop coffee companies, providing fifteen thousand children with latrines and water for hand washing, renovating a hospital, and supporting local businesses.

5. U.S. Environmental Protection Agency, "Climate Change Indicators in the United States: Introduction," 2010, www.epa.gov/climatechange/indicators/pdfs/CI-introduction.pdf.

6. National Aeronautics and Space Administration, "Climate Change: How Do We Know?" NASA, http://climate.nasa.gov/evidence/.

7. Ibid.

8. Stefan Lofgren, "Warming to Cause Catastrophic Rise in Sea Level?" *National Geographic News*, April 26, 2004, http://news.nationalgeographic.com/news/2004/04/0420_040420_earthday.html (my emphasis).

9. Ibid.

10. Ibid.

11. Anwen Roberts, "What Will Become of Tuvalu's Climate Refugees?" Spiegel Online International, September 14, 2007, www.spiegel.de/international/world/0,1518,505819,00.html; Ben Namakin, "Climate Witness: Ben Namakin, Kiribati, and Micronesia," World Wildlife Federation, May 7, 2007, http://wwf.panda.org/about_our_earth/aboutcc/problems/people_at_risk/personal_stories/witness_stories/?uNewsID=100800.

12. UNICEF, "Climate Change and Children," December 2007, http://www.unicef.org/publications/index_42166.html.

13. Save the Children, "Feeling the Heat: Child Survival in a Changing Climate," 2009, www.savethechildren.net/alliance/what_we_do/drr/publications/feelingtheheat.html.

14. Christopher Field, "To What Degree? What Science is Telling Us about Climate Change," National Science Foundation, www.nsf.gov/news/special_reports/degree/ipcc.jsp.

15. "U.S. Prepared to Cut Greenhouse Emissions, Bush Says, CNN, September 28, 2007, http://articles.cnn.com/2007-09-28/politics/bush.climate_1_emissions-greenhouse-biofuels?_s=PM:POLITICS; "The Candidates on Climate Change," Council on Foreign Relations, September 11, 2008, www.cfr.org/publication/14765/candidates_on_climate_change.html.

16. Joint Science Academies, "Joint Science Academies' Statement: Global Response to Climate Change," May 2005, http://docs.google.com/viewer?a=v&q=cache:x7ifEgWQkSIJ:www.nationalacademies.org/onpi/06072005.pdf+identify+cost-effective+steps+that+can+be+taken+now+to+contribute+to+substantial+and+long-term+reductions+in+net+global+greenhouse+gas+emissions&hl=en&gl=us&pid=bl&srcid=ADGEEShqfcfBGPmHZjvpk8ykE80dzQP3qdDfm8E8k3x3akp7l_C50CVteOak4JIKJyJl2XA7aBwZRf9DkJyl

XoNtuYhdrqoIevpzae1rOfm2lUX1kEmboNbEAKL4k9b77hp8ECxVJc9b&sig =AHIEtbQOBJkoKo33xsSGUeiOO2wBz9Squw.

17. The Pew Research Center for the People & the Press, "Public's Priorities for 2010: Economy, Jobs, Terrorism," January 25, 2010 http://people-press.org/report/584/policy-priorities-2010.

18. The Pew Global Attitudes Project, " No Global Warming Alarm in the U.S., China America's Image Slips, but Allies Share U.S. Concerns Over Iran, Hamas," Pew Research Center, June 13, 2006, p. 5, http://pewglobal.org/files/pdf/252.pdf.

19. Robert Goodland and Jeff Anhang, "Livestock and Climate Change," World Watch, November/December 2009, www.worldwatch.org/files/pdf/Livestock%20and%20Climate%20Change.pdf.

20. "Being a Celebrity Is the 'Best Thing in the World' Say Children," Mail Online, December 18, 2006, www.dailymail.co.uk/news/article-423273/Being-celebrity-best-thing-world-say-children.html. Luton First, sponsors of Britain's National Kids Day, conducted the survey.

21. "Britney Spears: Trust Our President in Every Decision," CNN Entertainment, September 3, 2003, http://articles.cnn.com/2003-09-03/entertainment/cnna.spears_1_tucker-carlson-open-mouth-kiss-britney-spears?_s=PM:SHOWBIZ.

22. David Von Drehle, "Criticizing Rush Limbaugh: Over the Line?" *Time*, March 4, 2009, www.time.com/time/politics/article/0,8599,1883032,00.html.

23. "Britney Spears: Trust Our President in Every Decision."

24. "Endless Wars," Journalism Today, http://journalism-today.com/?page_id=85.

25. Gary Kamiya, "Iraq: Why the Media Failed," Salon.com, April 10, 2007, www.salon.com/news/opinion/kamiya/2007/04/10/media_failure.

26. Dana Milbank and Claudia Deane, "Hussein Link to 9/11 Lingers in Many Minds," *Washington Post*, September 6, 2003, www.washingtonpost.com/ac2/wp-dyn/A32862-2003Sep5?language=printer; Brian Braiker, "Dunce Cap Nation," *Newsweek*, September 4, 2007, www.newsweek.com/2007/09/04/dunce-cap-nation.html.

27. See the Iraq Body Count at www.iraqbodycount.org for up-to-date figures; Tina Susman, "Civilian Deaths May Top One Million, Poll Data Indicate," Los Angeles Times, September 14, 2007, http://articles.latimes.com/2007/sep/14/world/fg-iraq14; Joseph E. Stiglitz and Linda J. Bilmes, "The True

Cost of the Iraq War: $3 Trillion and Beyond," *Washington Post*, September 3, 2010, www.washingtonpost.com/wp-dyn/content/article/2010/09/03/AR2010090302200.html.

28. "Iraq," Polling Report, www.pollingreport.com/iraq.htm.

29. Nicholas D. Kristof and Sheryl WuDunn, *Half the Sky: Turning Oppression into Opportunity for Women Worldwide* (New York: Alfred A. Knopf, 2009).

30. Ibid.

31. Ibid.

32. Ibid.

33. M. Cherif Bassiouni, "Investigating International Trafficking in Women and Children for Commercial Sexual Exploitation," The International Human Rights Institute, DePaul University College of Law, March 23, 2001, www.law.depaul.edu/centers_institutes/ihrli/downloads/Investigating.pdf.

34. Kristof and WuDunn, *Half the Sky*.

35. E-mail interview with Howard Kurtz, 2010.

36. Jeffrey D. Sachs, *The End of Poverty: Economic Possibilities for Our Time* (New York: Penguin Books, 2005), 1.

37. Alison Kamhi, "Private Funding for Public Justice: The Feasibility of Private Donations to the Cambodia Tribunal," Harvard International Law Journal 48, no. 2 (2007): 581–91.

38. In his book *All the News That's Fit to Sell: How the Market Transforms Information into News* (Princeton, NJ: Princeton University Press, 2004), economist James T. Hamilton observes the direct correlation between female viewership and the decline in hard news reporting on television news: "An increase in one percentage point in a program audience's female viewing percentage results in .23 fewer national hard news stories and .09 fewer state and local officials stories." Ibid., 145. Working backward from female viewership numbers, Hamilton can accurately predict the number of "soft" news stories—celebrity and lifestyle pieces—in a broadcast. Ibid., 143–45.

39. "Angelina Jolie Fact Sheet," UNHCR, February 11, 2009, www.unhcr.org/pages/49db77906.html.

40. "Angelina Jolie Named Goodwill Ambassador for Refugees," UNHCR, August 23, 2001, www.unhcr.org/cgi-bin/texis/vtx/news/opendoc.htm?tbl=NEWS&id=3b85044b10%20Angelina%20Jolie%20named%20UNHCR%20Goodwill%20Ambassador%20for%20refugees.

41. "Angelina Jolie Fact Sheet."

42. Chris Heath, "Blood Sugar Sex Magic," *Rolling Stone* 1, no. 872, July 5, 2001, 68–79, 196.

43. "Goodwill Ambassador Field Missions," UNCHR, April 2010, www.unhcr.org/4399624c2.html.

44. Ibid.

45. Ibid.

46. "UNHCR Goodwill Ambassador Angelina Jolie Launches Centre for Unaccompanied Children," UNHCR, March 9, 2005, www.unhcr.org/cgi-bin/texis/vtx/news/opendoc.htm?tbl=NEWS&id=422f33944.

47. "Liberian Women Stitch Together New Future after Angelina Jolie Skills Courts," UNHCR, February 23, 2006, www.unhcr.org/cgi-bin/texis/vtx/news/opendoc.htm?tbl=NEWS&id=43fdd3d44.

48. *Real Time with Bill Maher*, HBO, February 26, 2010.

49. "Biography for Angelina Jolie," IMDb, www.imdb.com/name/nm0001401/bio.

50. Refugees cross international borders; internally displaced persons (IDPs) are forced to flee their homes but remain within their own country. There are an estimated twenty-four million IDPs worldwide due to violence, human rights abuses, or natural disasters, and the number is expected to increase as climate change intensifies, causing droughts and desertification in countries that are already poor.

51. "Angelina Jolie Releases Personal Journal on Plight of Colombian Refugees," UNHCR, November 19, 2002, www.unhcr.org/3dda5c4ca.html.

52. Matthew Swibel, "Bad Girl Interrupted," *Forbes*, July 3, 2006, www.forbes.com/forbes/2006/0703/118.html.

53. Associated Press, "Source: Jolie-Pitt Baby Pics Fetch $14 Million," MSNBC, August 1, 2008, http://today.msnbc.msn.com/id/25967334/ns/today-entertainment/.

54. Donald G. McNeil Jr., "Dose of Tenacity Wears Down a Horrific Disease," *New York Times*, March 26, 2006, www.nytimes.com/2006/03/26/international/africa/26worm.html.

55. Ibid.

56. India.Arie, "Video," *Acoustic Soul*, Motown, 2001.

57. Ibid.

Chapter 4.

1. Alan Gathright, "Study: Men Slack Off More Than Women," December 7, 2009, ABC 7 News, www.thedenverchannel.com/news/21888019/detail.html.

2. Associated Press, "Working Women Do More Chores Than Men," MSNBC, September 15, 2004, www.msnbc.msn.com/id/6011245/ns/business-us_business/;"How Much Housework Does a Husband Create?" University of Michigan News Service, April 3, 2008, http://ns.umich.edu/htdocs/releases/story.php?id=6452.

3. Wendy Mogel, *The Blessing of a Skinned Knee: Using Jewish Teachings to Raise Self-Reliant Children* (New York: Scribner, 2001); *The Blessing of a B Minus: Using Jewish Teachings to Raise Resilient Teenagers* (New York: Scribner, 2010).

4. The National Sleep Foundation says that 60 percent of high school kids report extreme daytime sleepiness. University of Kentucky studies show that high school seniors average only 6.5 hours sleep a night. Only 5 percent get the eight hours they need. Half of adolescents are sleep deprived. My experience with teens is that when allowed to sleep in on nonschool days, they sleep much more than eight hours because they need more like ten hours sleep per night, which is impossible for nearly all teens on school nights because of their extracurricular activities, sports practices, homework, and early morning start times for schools."Why Sleep Is Important and What Happens When You Don't Get Enough," American Psychological Association, www.apa.org/topics/sleep/why.aspx#; Carol Josel, "Sleep Awareness Week: Are Your Kids Getting Enough Zzzz's?" Examiner.com, March 11, 2010, www.examiner.com/wise-parenting-in-philadelphia/sleep-awareness-week-are-your-kids-getting-enough-zzzz-s?render=print.

5. Sleep deprivation makes *you* stupid too. In studies surely funded by the Department of the Obvious, scientists discovered that tired people do poorly on tests, make lots of mistakes, and can't solve simple puzzles. Less obvious are neuroscientists' findings that lack of proper sleep physiologically alters your brain with a molecular anatomical signature that causes cognitive, attention, and emotional deficits. "Specific Changes in the Brain Associated with Sleep Deprivation Described in New Study," Science Daily, November 4, 2010, www.sciencedaily.com/releases/2010/11/101103111154.htm.

6. Adam Ostrow, "Social Media Dominates Our Time Spent Online," Mashable.com, August 2, 2010, http://mashable.com/2010/08/02/stats-time-spent-online/; Katie Hafner, "Texting May Be Taking a Toll," *New York Times*, May 26, 2009, www.nytimes.com/2009/05/26/health/26teen.html.

7. National Endowment for the Arts, *To Read or Not to Read: A Question of National Consequence*, November 2007, p. 5, www.nea.gov/research/toread.pdf.

8. "Many Teens Spend 30 Hours Per Week in Front of Screens During High School," Science Daily, March 14, 2008, www.sciencedaily.com/releases/2008/03/080312172614.htm.

9. National Endowment for the Arts, *To Read or Not to Read*.

10. Ibid.

11. Julie Bosman, "Struggling Borders to Meet with Publishers," *New York Times*, January 3, 2011, www.nytimes.com/2011/01/04/business/media/04borders.html?_r=1&scp=1&sq=borders%20bankruptcy&st=cse.

12. Gina Kolata, "Taking Early Retirement May Retire Memory, Too," *New York Times*, October 11, 2010, www.nytimes.com/2010/10/12/science/12retire.html.

13. Natalie Paris, "Americans Spend Most Time on the Internet," *The Telegraph*, May 9, 2008, www.telegraph.co.uk/news/1940196/Americans-spend-most-time-on-the-internet.html; Vera H-C Chan, "2010 Year in Review: Top 10 Searches," Yahoo! News, http://yearinreview.yahoo.com/2010/us_top_10_searches#Top 10 Searches.

14. Peter Applebome, "A Quest to Read a Book a Day for 365 Days," *New York Times*, October 11, 2009, www.nytimes.com/2009/10/12/nyregion/12towns.html.

15. Stephen King, *On Writing: A Memoir of the Craft* (New York: Pocketbooks, 2000), 147–48.

16. The Norman Lear Entertainment Center, "Sports & Weather, Crime, Fluff Dominate L.A. TV News," The Lear Center, March 11, 2010, www.learcenter.org/pdf/LocalNewsRelease.pdf.

17. Howard Kurtz, "Michael and Lindsay Lohan Lies Go Viral, and the Truth Is Hard to Corral," *Washington Post*, May 7, 2010, www.washingtonpost.com/wp-dyn/content/article/2010/05/06/AR2010050605861.htm.

18. "Louis CK: Everything Is Amazing Right Now and Nobody Is Happy," YouTube, posted April 11, 2010, www.youtube.com/watch?v=itn8TwFCO4M.

19. Ibid.

20. Ibid.

21. "Obesity Survey: The Disconnect Between Size and Weight," National Consumers League, 2007, www.nclnet.org/health/86-obesity/161-obesity-survey-the-disconnect-between-size-and-weight.

22. Valerie Ulene, "What the Doc Doesn't Say: You're Overweight," *Los Angeles Times*, October 12, 2009, http://articles.latimes.com/2009/oct/12/health/he-themd12.

23. General Social Survey, www.norc.org/GSS+Website/.

24. Betsey Stevenson and Justin Wolfers, "The Paradox of Declining Female Happiness," *American Economic Journal* 1, no. 2 (2009): 190–225, http://bpp.wharton.upenn.edu/betseys/papers/Paradox%20of%20declining%20female%20happiness.pdf.

25. Rochelle Schieck, e-mail interview, spring 2010.

26. Jean Lawrence, "Train Your Brain With Exercise," WebMD, June 26, 2007, www.webmd.com/fitness-exercise/guide/train-your-brain-with-exercise.

27. Kathleen Doheny, "Ten Surprising Health Benefits of Sex," WebMD, March 30, 2009, www.webmd.com/sex-relationships/features/10-surprising-health-benefits-of-sex.

28. Christie Aschwanden, "Five Vitamin Truths and Lies," *Reader's Digest Magazine*, March 15, 2010, http://shine.yahoo.com/channel/health/5-vitamin-truths-and-lies-1147230.

29. Janet Kornblum, "Study: 25% of Americans Have No One to Confide In," *USA Today*, June 22, 2006, www.usatoday.com/news/nation/2006-06-22-friendship_x.htm.

30. Jonathan Haidt, *The Happiness Hypothesis: Finding Modern Truth in Ancient Wisdom* (New York: Basic Books, 2006).

31. Nicholas D. Kristof and Sheryl WuDunn, *Half the Sky: Turning Oppression into Opportunity for Women Worldwide* (New York: Vintage 2010), 250.

32. Roni Caryn Rabin, "Talk Deeply, Be Happy?" *New York Times*, March 17, 2010, http://well.blogs.nytimes.com/2010/03/17/talk-deeply-be-happy/.

33. "'They Want Us to Be Stupid Things'," *New York Times*, January 17, 2009, www.nytimes.com/2009/01/17/opinion/17sat3.html.

34. "Taliban Blamed for Bombing Five Schools," *Washington Times*, www.washingtontimes.com/news/2009/jan/19/taliban-blamed-for-bombing-five

-schools/; "Swat Valley," *New York Times*, November 16, 2010, http://topics.nytimes.com/top/news/international/countriesandterritories/pakistan/northwest-pakistan/swat_valley/index.html.

35. Caitlin Bergen, "Once a Month Campaign Helps African Girls Stay in School," America.gov, December 19, 2008, www.america.gov/st/develop-english/2008/December/20081219123021DCnigreB0.225033.html.

36. "Girls' Education: Basic Education," UNICEF, www.unicef.org/ethiopia/education.html.

37. A good place to find worthy projects to support girls and women in the Third World is www.globalgiving.org.

38. "The Child Brides: Send Them to School Instead," Global Giving, www.globalgiving.org/projects/prevent-child-marriage-through-education/.

acknowledgments

Books have transfixed me since I gnawed on them in my crib. Once I could hold a pen, I yearned to cross over from reader to writer. But as a grownup, I found excuses—career, kids—to avoid writing anything more than the occasional article for nearly the first half-century of my life.

Then some writers and artists whose work I truly admire told me that really, seriously, I could and should do this, and that made a big impression on me. Joe Loya, Jeffrey Toobin, and Rabbi Shmuley Boteach, thank you for granting me permission to join your ranks. Moby, you told me dozens of times to turn my e-mail rants to you into a book—this book. (You promised that if I did, you'd set it to music. You're on!)

Dr. Phil McGraw, thank you for launching this book on your show, a promise you made to me based on your simple faith that I had a message for women worth broadcasting. I am humbled.

When Rory Freedman heard I was writing this book, she buttonholed me at a PETA party and demanded that I immediately, if not sooner, call her literary agent, Laura Dail. Thank you, Rory, my feisty vegan sister. Tough broads have yet to steer me wrong.

To anyone who has a book in her, I wish Laura Dail upon you. Laura cajoled and prodded and cheered me through months of drafts and revisions, somehow eviscerating what I'd thought were killer arguments while simultaneously making me feel loved.

Laura, in turn, brought me to Vanguard Press, where I learned the meaning of "author-centered." Ever-gracious Georgina Levitt and Roger Cooper had my back through every bit of the editing process.

And they bestowed the gifted editor Dan Smetanka upon me, who, on a short deadline, jumped in and challenged me to go deeper, page after page. I am forever indebted to Dan's fat brain and good humor.

My boisterous gang of Facebook friends and Twitter followers sounded off on my intentionally provocative posts, many on topics in this book. Thanks for being my unsuspecting focus group, for matching wits with me, and for keeping me on my toes.

I followed Stephen King's advice in *On Writing* and enlisted a merry little band of readers to give it to me straight on my first draft. Angie Rupert, thank you for dropping everything to give this an enthusiastic read. That you went right out and bought three new books after you finished mine gave me the assurance that I might really be onto something here. Rochelle Schieck, bless you for your inspired marginalia. Has it really been four years since you had us all jot down our true soul's dreams in your yoga class, when I sheepishly scrawled, "write my book"?

Julie Greer, my lifelong best friend, the Oprah to my Gayle, thank you for your unwavering unconditional support of this and every other project I've thrown myself into. Husbands and kids have moved in and moved out. Julie is forever.

To my radiant, brilliant daughter Sarah, who read the draft amidst college exams (which, naturally, she aced), thanks for giving me your unvarnished feedback—the good, the bad, and the ugly—laced with your trademark savagely hilarious wisecracks. I often thought of you and your friends while writing this book because you all deserve so much more than what our culture is feeding you.

To my intellectually alive, eternally kind son Sammy, bless you for encouraging me to persist, cheering for the completion of each new draft, each deadline met. Your artistic creativity and love of learning are exciting to behold. Mom loves you.

My spirited, brainy, fearless mother, Gloria Allred, surely reads this and thinks, "Please, haven't I *always* told you that you can do anything you set your mind to?" Yes, Ma. Yes, you have. Like, every day of my life. More persuasively, you've led by example. Thank you for insisting constantly that women should think for ourselves and take charge of our own lives, and for never giving a hoot about frivolity.

Finally, Virginia Woolf was right. A woman needs a room of her own, a place for her mind to be free to wander, to dream, to create. My man, Braden Pollock, knew this instinctively. Upon hearing that writing was my heart's desire, Braden snapped into action. He created for me an enormous, bright, sunny, and, best of all, *quiet* office upstairs in our home, installed a lightning-fast computer with a monitor the size of Milwaukee, lined up my beloved tomes on a wall of overstuffed bookshelves, and situated a comfy desk next to a picture window framing verdant hills and daily sunsets. My first and very own writer's studio! Next, to free up mental space and time, he insisted that I turn down television appearances and cases until the book was done, and he even handled all the boring business details of this project so they wouldn't slow me down. Then he ordered me each morning to get on up there and research and draft and revise, already. And though I stubbornly overrode most of his edits, he patiently read manuscript after manuscript. He secured the domain and created the website www.Think.tv to create the Think Community so that even after this book has been written and read, the conversation will continue.

What can you say to a man like this? This man to whom love is, daily, an action verb? Sweetheart, you'd have made Virginia proud. Thank you for this magnificent gift, more precious to me than diamonds. Is it any wonder you are the love of my life?

index